ROUTLEDGE LIBRARY EDITIONS: 18TH CENTURY PHILOSOPHY

Volume 16

ROUSSEAU

ROUSSEAU
The Child of Nature

JOHN CHARPENTIER

LONDON AND NEW YORK

First published in 1931 by Methuen & Co. Ltd.

This edition first published in 2019
by Routledge
2 Park Square, Milton Park, Abingdon, Oxon OX14 4RN

and by Routledge
52 Vanderbilt Avenue, New York, NY 10017

Routledge is an imprint of the Taylor & Francis Group, an informa business

© 1931 Methuen & Co. Ltd.

All rights reserved. No part of this book may be reprinted or reproduced or utilised in any form or by any electronic, mechanical, or other means, now known or hereafter invented, including photocopying and recording, or in any information storage or retrieval system, without permission in writing from the publishers.

Trademark notice: Product or corporate names may be trademarks or registered trademarks, and are used only for identification and explanation without intent to infringe.

British Library Cataloguing in Publication Data
A catalogue record for this book is available from the British Library

ISBN: 978-0-367-13518-8 (Set)
ISBN: 978-0-429-02691-1 (Set) (ebk)
ISBN: 978-0-367-13623-9 (Volume 16) (hbk)
ISBN: 978-0-367-13625-3 (Volume 16) (pbk)
ISBN: 978-0-429-02749-9 (Volume 16) (ebk)

Publisher's Note
The publisher has gone to great lengths to ensure the quality of this reprint but points out that some imperfections in the original copies may be apparent.

Disclaimer
The publisher has made every effort to trace copyright holders and would welcome correspondence from those they have been unable to trace.

ROUSSEAU
THE CHILD OF NATURE

BY
JOHN CHARPENTIER
Author of "Coleridge," Etc.

METHUEN & CO. LTD.
36 ESSEX STREET
LONDON, W.C.

First Published in Great Britain in 1931

PRINTED IN THE UNITED STATES
OF AMERICA

CONTENTS

Part One

CHAPTER		PAGE
I	Jean-Jacques's First Confession	3
II	Days of Unrest	19
III	"Mamma"	33
IV	Vagabondage	47
V	A Family of Three	63
VI	Madame de Larnage	82
VII	Les Charmettes	102
VIII	Paris Society	122
IX	Thérèse Levasseur	139

Part Two

I	The Peasant of the Danube	161
II	The Hermitage	179
III	The Keep of Glory	203
IV	The Refugee of Môtiers-Travers	223
V	England	240
VI	Apology for the *Confessions*	256
VII	The Copyist of Music	276
VIII	Ermenonville	289
IX	Le Banc des Mères	297

PART ONE

CHAPTER I

JEAN-JACQUES'S FIRST CONFESSION

IT was Sunday, March 14, 1728. Jean-Jacques had run out into the field immediately after the sermon to romp with other young ragamuffins like himself from the poorer quarters of Geneva, and at nightfall he got back to the gate of the Calvinist town just in time to see the soldiers pull up the outer drawbridge. Twice before, after lingering along the banks of the Rhone or the Leman, he had found the gates closed and had perforce slept out of doors, only to be well thrashed next morning by his master, the engraver Abel Ducommun. His back had smarted cruelly from the beating, but his pride had smarted still more, and to himself he had vowed that he would rather die than submit again to such punishment. Yet here he was caught by a cursed captain whose habit it was to close the entrance where he stood guard some time before the inner gates were shut. Jean-Jacques had heard retreat being sounded and the drum being rolled when he was still half a league outside the walls. The best speed he could get out of his sixteen-year-old legs had not got him back in time. Panting heavily, he threw himself at full length on the sloping outworks, groveled in despair, and fiercely resolved never to go back to his master.

The next morning, after his absence had been discovered, he tearfully said good-bye to his comrades as they were preparing to return to work, not forgetting to ask them to inform his cousin Bernard in secret of his decision and to tell him where he could meet him for a final farewell. Cousin Bernard, who had seen nothing of Jean-Jacques since the latter had begun his apprenticeship, and who lived in the aristocratic quarter of Geneva, met him, indeed, in answer to his plea, but made no attempt to persuade him to reconsider. The young blade's policy was modeled on that of his mother, who had been hoping for some time to alienate her own child from this impoverished orphan of questionable reputation. Bernard gave him a little money, and among other gifts a small sword with which the silly lad bedecked himself like a young noble. Then he turned on his heel and left Jean-Jacques to go adventuring. Jean-Jacques started off with a firm step but a catch in his throat. He was already under the domination of that pride which makes a man carry on, even if it costs him dear, the part he has elected in a rash moment to play. He thought with anguish of the uncertainty of his future, for he was timid, even weak, in spite of his vanity. Perhaps in his secret heart he had hoped Cousin Bernard would beg him to stay at home.

But before long a glorious sense of freedom, borne to him on the wind from the mountains, filled his soul. It is easy to imagine the boy's elation. His fears were no sooner dissipated than he gave free play to his eager imagination, enhancing his good opinion of himself. He was now his own master, and he felt capable of undertaking anything or everything. Needless to say, the picture of his future which he painted to himself was colored by his natural indolence and his self-indulgence. He looked forward to a long succession of banquets, for he was greedy; to handsome possessions, for he loved display; to devoted friends, for he craved affection; to mistresses striving to please him, for he was exceedingly susceptible to feminine attraction. No noble ambition and no desire to play an important rôle entered into his scheme of life. He was without religious or moral principles, aspired to no kind of greatness, and was importuned by no ideal. The quality in him which he himself euphemistically termed "moderation" confined him to a sphere of action limited in area "but deliciously choice." There he felt he could exercise his sway undisputed. "My ambition soared only to a single château, where I might be the favorite of both the lord and the lady, the lover of the daughter of the house, the friend of her brother, and the patron of the neighbors."

For a day or two he delighted in the countryside, still wrapped in winter chill but warmed between showers by the sun, and spent his time wandering about the outskirts of the town. He slept and ate in the homes of peasants whom he knew. But he quickly tired of their hospitality, simple folk that they were, and too familiar to him to be interesting. In quest of a change, he turned southward, outside the boundaries of French Geneva into the Savoy region, and curiosity led him to the house of Monsieur de Pontverre, the village priest of Confignon. This ecclesiastic carried on the tradition of the *Gentilhommes de la Cuiller*, the Catholic subjects of the duke of Savoy, who in the sixteenth century had waged fanatical war on the Huguenots. He never for a moment thought of sending Jean-Jacques back to his master nor of advising him to seek his father, Isaac Rousseau, who was living in exile in Nyon in the Vaux region. He saw in the wandering boy only a Huguenot whom Heaven had sent him to convert. He welcomed him cordially, discoursed to him about the Geneva heresy and the "authority of the holy Mother Church," and during the process of serving him an excellent dinner washed down with plenty of good local wine, he persuaded him to change his religion.

Jean-Jacques boasts that he was able to carry on a profound discussion with his host, and that of the two he showed himself to be the better grounded in theology, but under the influence of the white wine he gave free play to his fancy and to his craving for approbation, a craving which he compares to the instinctive coquetry of loyal wives who know how to stir hopes which they will never fulfill. He let himself be easily convinced that he should renounce his faith.

"God calls you," said Monsieur de Pontverre. "Go to Annecy. There you will find a kind and very charitable lady so situated, through the king's good will, that she can save others from the error which she has herself abjured."

"I felt deeply humiliated," Jean-Jacques assures us, "that I was in a position to need 'a kind and very charitable lady.'" He honestly believed that she must be an elderly individual completely absorbed in her religion, the very sight of whom would make him wish to sink into the earth. But one motive or another, indifference or a wish for some pretext to go on, perhaps faith in his lucky star, turned his steps over the highlands of Neydens, where the fresh green of the new grass tinged the last of the melting snows, towards the home of Monsieur de Pontverre's ally.

Between Confignon and Annecy there are only ten leagues, but Jean-Jacques took three days to cover the distance. His progress was like that of a schoolboy, or a minstrel, whose talent he believed he shared. Always hopeful of finding the happiness about which his imagination was playing, he passed no country estate without stopping, and when courage failed him to knock at the door, standing under the most likely window and singing. He kept on with his serenades until he was hoarse, amazed that no lady nor damsel was lured out by the charm of his voice or the piquancy of his songs. At last, at daybreak on March 21st, which happened to be Palm Sunday, he reached Annecy, the native town of Saint Francis of Sales. Instead of setting out at once for the home of Madame de Warens, he began to ponder on his chances of being welcomed or turned away by the noble lady. Confronted with a concrete situation, he felt overcome by shyness. He had never been out into the world, and distrusted the ways of society. Although he had, or thought he had, a pretty wit, he dreaded making an ass of himself in a thousand matters, knowing just enough to realize the depths of his ignorance. But he overlooked the main point, namely, that his physique was in his favor. I believe he is sincere when he assures us that he did not know he was well set up, bore himself with easy grace, had slender legs, an animated and attractive expression, a charming mouth (although his teeth were unsightly), fine eyebrows and hair—which was chestnut, not black—and eyes which, though small and deep-set, sparkled brilliantly with the inner fire which burned within him. If a boy of his age knows that he has a pretty face, it is because he has heard it talked about, and in the circle where he had grown up, no one had ever complimented him on his personal charms. Fearing that his appearance would not predispose the lady in his favor, he decided to try to make a good impression by other means, and he composed a fine letter "in oratorical style," in which, "stringing together sentences quoted from books with schoolboy phrases," he employed all his eloquence to captivate Madame de Warens.

He did not find her at home, for she had just left to go to mass. He was shown the way she had taken, raced after her, and caught up with her near the Church of the Cordeliers on a little square near a white stone fountain which still exists, at the end of a narrow street bordered by gardens from which one steps out over plank foot-bridges across the Canal de Chion. He accosted her, waving the letter from Monsieur de Pontverre, which he had folded in with his own epistle. She turned, and the sight of her filled him with such emotion that he felt faint.

Imagine his delight, for no such elderly lady as he had feared stood there before him! Madame de Warens was then a woman of twenty-nine, in the full bloom of her beauty, a little too short, it must be admitted, and already plump, if not roly-poly, but with a dazzlingly fresh complexion set off by ashen hair which she dressed in a simple coil to emphasize the piquancy of her face; with blue eyes full of sweetness, and an angelic smile, adding its gracious charm to that of her silvery voice. His first glance told him how wholly attractive she was, and his eyes missed none of her allurement. He admired "the curves of a delicious bosom," framed by her dress, and while she was looking over the papers which he handed her, he gazed greedily at her white, dimpled hand.

She did no more than run through Monsieur Pontverre's letter of introduction, but she spent some time on Jean-Jacques's own. His conceit led him to suppose that she would have reread it all through had not her lackey warned her that it was time to enter the church.

"Well, child," she said, "you are full young to be running about the country. It is really too bad. Go back to my house and wait for me. Tell them to give you something to eat, and I will come and talk to you when mass is over."

If we inquire into the facts about Madame de Warens, we find, first, that she was a missionary of a sort, her chief duty being to bring about conversions. Second, she was a kind of spy, or official diplomatic agent, of the king of Sardinia. As Lady Louise-Françoise-Éléonore de la Tour de Chailly, at that time a Protestant, she had been married at the age of fourteen to Baron de Warens, of the house of Loys, a man twenty years older than herself. At Vevey, where her husband filled a municipal office, she had established a silk-stocking factory in the hope of making a fortune, but had ended by running into bankruptcy. As a child, badly brought up by her aunts after the death of her mother, which occurred when she was only thirteen months old, she had been willful in the extreme. She had always looked forward to accumulating enormous wealth for herself by some means or other, not only from ambition, but from the desire to keep herself occupied as well. For she was a steady worker, as well as a thoroughly worldly woman, as fond of directing enterprises as of shining in society, of supervising numerous assistants as of being the center of a group of flatterers. She was not only a natural adept in intrigue, but was also capable of real sympathy with intellectual pursuits. Though she was unprincipled and impractical, if not a little unbalanced, she could conduct herself with dignity, and when circumstances dictated, she could assume an elegant manner. She had had several lovers, one of whom was a certain Colonel de Tavel, a man of position, of taste, and of wide acquaintance, though an incorrigible cynic. He had established a little court of literary people about her, and had directed her reading. The works of Bayle and of Saint-Evremond were to be found on her bedside table, together with La Bruyère, whom she liked better than La Rochefoucauld. On the other hand, she knew little or nothing of the Greek and Roman classics. Her name appears in the old quarrel between the Ancients and the Moderns, as having taken the side of the latter. Like most of her contemporaries, she was keenly interested in science, particularly in the occult branches, that is, in quack medicine and alchemy. She had a laboratory, furnaces, and alembics; she mixed and brewed herbs; distilled elixirs; manufactured dyes, balms, opiates, and other chemical compounds, and pretended to know secret formulæ. In short, she was typical of her age. However, having run into debt just at the time when the notorious François Magny was initiating her into Pietism, which, though a Protestant sect, was tinged with mysticism and was not in the least hostile to Catholicism, she heard the divine call at the height of her difficulties, when all her property was being confiscated. On July 14, 1726, on the pretext that she must take the waters of Amphion for her health, she deserted Vaux and her husband, crossed the lake to Evian, where Victor Amadeus and his entire suite were in residence, and cast herself on the mercy of the king. She first promised to abjure the Calvinist religion, then begged for his protection and for her daily bread. The monarch let himself be persuaded that she could be of practical use to him, and sent her in his own litter with an escort of four bodyguards to the Convent of the Visitation at Annecy. The supervision of her religious education was entrusted to the bishop of the town, Monsignor de Rossillon de Bernex, who was so well pleased with his proselyte that he was willing to add to the allowance of fifteen hundred livres granted her by the king a pension of five hundred livres to carry on the Catholic propaganda which she undertook and to which she promised to devote her best efforts. On September 8, after having solemnly disavowed her former faith, she settled in the Rue Saint-François in a house called "de la Monnaie," the smaller of two buildings owned by Monsieur de Boöge Conflans, very near the cathedral. She called herself a baroness, which was the least she could do under the circumstances, and from that time on she labored under the auspices of Monsieur de Bernex to recall strayed sheep into the fold of the Roman Church.

She was bound to do her duty by Jean-Jacques. He had been sent to her to convert; she was paid to work conversions. Thus she resisted her first impulse, which was to advise him to go back to Geneva. But it was not long before she had to struggle against the temptation to keep him by her side, for he appealed to her almost from the first. A woman of her worldly wisdom makes no mistake in regard to the impression she makes on other people, especially on a still inexperienced youth. Jean-Jacques, whether because she won his confidence or because he sensed, with the unerring instinct of his kind, that his best chance with her was in revealing his true self, made no effort to conceal his feelings. Neither then nor at any later time could this feeling be called love, nor yet passion in the full sense of either word. But it was enough that his affection for her was spiced with longing, enough for him as well as for Madame de Warens herself, who was not inclined to fine discrimination and never troubled to analyze the exact nature of her sentiments towards her protégé.

The surprising thing in the whole affair is the ease, one might almost say impudence, with which Jean-Jacques at once threw off all reserve with a lady whose position, as he must have felt, was so infinitely higher than his. Not only was he free from all shyness with her, but he even adopted in his speech the familiar tone which he afterwards always employed with her. She scarcely had to question him before he confided everything to her. A single word from her sufficed to start him on one train of thought or to throw him off onto another, delving into the depths of his soul to express his true self. He explored every corner of his past into which her voice or her smile encouraged him to penetrate, in order to reveal to her all the details which he felt she relished.

She was touched to hear that he, like herself, had been left in infancy without his mother, who had died of a puerperal fever in giving him birth. Women who seek to know us intimately learn, as a rule, what they can about our mothers, and seek to find out not only what they felt and thought, but also how they looked, or at least how they have impressed us. Jean-Jacques, although he could tell of his mother only what he knew of her from his father's memories, shared so ardently in the admiration of her by the latter, who had worshiped her and who had represented her to him as beautiful, vivacious, fond of approbation, and much sought after, that Madame de Warens felt something like jealousy of her, and had perhaps from the beginning an inclination to substitute herself for this idealized vision in the heart of the young man.

"My father," said Jean-Jacques, "never recovered from her loss. He felt that in me he saw her alive again, yet he could not forget that it was I who had deprived him of her. With every embrace he gave me, I felt from his sighs that his affection was tinged with regret. Whenever he said to me, 'We will talk about your mother,' I answered, 'Very well, Father, then we shall shed tears!' " His father had been a clockmaker and a dancing master, of unsteady and self-indulgent character, hot-tempered and quarrelsome, egotistical no doubt, and restless or fickle by nature. In spite of his ardent love for his wife, he had married again. Always ready to seek his fortune in some new field, and to pull up stakes, he had proved quite incompetent to give his children a proper training. The elder boy, François, ran wild and then disappeared, and his family heard no more of him; and when Jean-Jacques was nearing the age of ten, the father himself had fled from the Helvetic Republic after quarreling with a captain of the guard attached to the king of Poland.

The parentless boy, who had had little education and up to that time had done nothing more useful than play about his father's shop, was taken in charge by an uncle. He had read voraciously, for his mother had left a number of seventeenth-century books, and he had first learned to read in the novels of La Calprenède and of Mademoiselle de Scudéry, rather than from the works of Bossuet, La Bruyère, and Fontenelle, which were mixed in with them, because the former appealed to him as more entertaining. He had spent whole evenings and even nights reading, his father as deeply engrossed as he in the same occupation. Occasionally they had been recalled to earth only by the morning twitter of the swallows. Then, shamefacedly, the irresponsible parent would say to Jean-Jacques: "We must get to bed, my boy. I am even more of a child than you." Doubtless he had felt less ashamed when they had been devouring Plutarch, Tacitus, or Grotius, considering that they had been nourishing their souls on "the noblest and highest truths." Jean-Jacques wrote later: "I felt before I thought. When I had still no idea of realities, I was familiar with every shade of emotion." Discounting his obvious exaggeration, we are still struck by the truth that he mingled emotion with everything in his life, particularly with the republicanism which fired him with enthusiasm when he read the "Lives of Famous Men," even though the book drew from him "buckets of tears." Perhaps he did not, as he says, prefer Agesilaus, Brutus, and Aristides to Onondatus, Artamène, and Juba, but the heroes of antiquity were jostled in his mind by imaginary characters from heroic novels, or were confused with them. Cyrus, whose character was founded on that of the Grand Condé, seemed to him to be as great a hero as Mucius Scævola, whose courage so excited him that he could not tell the story without acting it out, and one day actually held his hand on a hot stove to illustrate Scævola's exploit.

To return to Jean-Jacques's recital: "My uncle sent me away with my cousin Bernard to live in the house of Dr. Lambercier, the pastor at Bossey, below Mont Salève. There the country was such a revelation to me that I never grew tired of my delight in it. I loved the simple rural life; and the pastor, who was unmarried and who lived in sage fashion with his sister, treated me very kindly. He could be severe with me when it was necessary, but as he was just, I never felt ill used. Besides, it was Mademoiselle Lambercier who undertook to punish me when I had done wrong. As long as she merely threatened to whip me, I feared the punishment. Once it was done, I considered it less terrible in actuality than the expectation of it had been."

"Did she take a stick to you?"

"She spanked me, and I know very well that the same kind of beating from her brother would have hurt far less."

Madame de Warens forced a laugh. "That was an amusing point of superiority." But her blue eyes glowed and she added, as she drew the youth close to her: "But a whipping is always a whipping, isn't it?"

"No, for I actually took pleasure in the pain, even in the shame, of the whippings Mademoiselle Lambercier gave me. I grew more fond of her because of them. Her punishments left me rather eager than afraid to try what she would do another time. But the second time she beat me was the last. After that I was given another room to sleep in."

"Were you sorry for the change?"

"More than I can tell you."

Madame de Warens stifled a sigh. "I see. Since then you have been in love with some girl more nearly your own age?"

"The truth is that I fell in love at the same time with two young ladies whom I met at my father's during a short visit I made him when I was about eleven. The first was twenty-two, but the second was a little younger, and the feelings I had for the two, though very strong in both cases, were entirely different. Mademoiselle de Vulson made a pet of me when others were about, and Mademoiselle Goton played with me on the sly. Openly and to everyone's knowledge I was the devoted slave of Mademoiselle de Vulson, and in secret I was the pupil of Mademoiselle Goton, who behaved to me almost like a schoolmistress. I never took the part I played with Mademoiselle de Vulson at all seriously, and never was more affectionate to her in private than I was in public. But, on the other hand, I never fell in with the playful whims of Mademoiselle Goton except when we were alone together. She took the greatest liberties with me but never allowed me to take any at all with her, and the only way I could reëstablish myself in my own self-respect after having been deliciously humiliated by her was by making scenes in public with Mademoiselle de Vulson. I would gladly have spent a lifetime at the feet of Mademoiselle Goton, and I think my jealousy would have led me to commit a crime if I had had any suspicion that she might reduce another member of my sex to the same state of mind. I was proud of the interest Mademoiselle de Vulson showed in me, but the intimacy with Mademoiselle Goton meant so much to me that I cannot put it into words. . . ."

"So now you remember her with more affection?"

"More? Yes, perhaps. Certainly the memory of her touches me more, and returns with less provocation. It always seems to me that in my love-affair with Mademoiselle Goton something was lacking which I am still waiting for. But my love-affair with Mademoiselle de Vulson has left neither bitterness nor longing in my heart. I like to think about it, and never have the kind of worried feeling with which I look back to the times I sat in the lap of Mademoiselle Goton.

"But I had to earn my living. I was severely punished by Uncle Bernard for an offense I had not committed, something which it would have killed me to think I could be guilty of, though Monsieur Lambercier and his sister persisted obstinately in trying to make me confess I had done it. This turned me against Bossey and my family. They entered me in a law-clerk's office in the hope that he would make a *Grapignan* of me, but I loathed the very name and made such stupid mistakes, due to paying no attention whatever to my work, that I was soon dismissed as useless.

The family thought I could master no profession and decided to teach me some manual trade, so I became an engraver's apprentice. I had quite a fine talent for drawing and had no objection to playing with a burin, so I might soon have done my work perfectly if I had not been turned against it by the harshness of my master. Whatever vices I have fallen into, Madame, are his fault, for I am not naturally a bad boy. In order to escape his violence, I learned to tell lies; and I learned to idle away my time so I could steal from him the hours of recreation he never gave me. I became greedy and light-handed from envy of his excellent fare, because I was always sent out from his table after the first course or two."

As Jean-Jacques went on with his story, he warmed up to telling it, and Madame de Warens, who had decided not to deprive herself of his friendship irrevocably by sending him back to his father, felt less and less courageous about letting him leave her at all. While he was describing for her the way in which he, accustomed as he had been to live on equal terms with his betters, had learned to tell lies by working under a cruel master, she laid plans for his whole future. As it was of first importance to induce him to change his religion, she based the entire fabric of the scheme she was elaborating on the supposition that he would be converted. She said nothing of this first step, however, until dinner, when it chanced that she had as guest a middle-aged person known as Monsieur Sabran. It was apparently from him that she received the opportune suggestion that Jean-Jacques might be sent to Turin, the capital of the Sardinian kingdom, where a hospice had been founded especially for the teaching of converts. Jean-Jacques looked on the man who thus settled his fate as a "roughneck," doubtless because of his bad manners and the hearty appetite which he indulged, while Jean-Jacques himself, excited by his conversation with Madame de Warens and

JEAN-JACQUES'S FIRST CONFESSION

enchanted by everything she said, forgot to eat anything at all. Monsieur Sabran was one of those sorry rogues who, like stray cats, rub up against the cassocks of the clergy and live by them and their flocks. He pretended to assure Madame de Warens, who needed no information whatever on the subject, that Jean-Jacques would be cared for physically and spiritually at Turin until he could enter the Church, and there, with the protection of those kind souls, find some position to suit him.

"So far as the expenses of the journey are concerned," said Monsieur Sabran, "his Lordship will certainly provide funds for it if you speak to him of your holy purpose; and," he added, bowing over his plate, "you, Madame, full of good works as you are, will no doubt be glad to contribute something also."

Thanks to his good offices, or rather to the efficient working of the diocesan administration, everything turned out as he had prophesied, for in three days the matter was settled. Monsieur Sabran represented so well the case of Jean-Jacques, who seems to have been completely taken in by all their play-acting, that when Madame de Warens went to see Monsignor de Bernex, the latter handed over to her at once the money intended for her young friend's trip. Madame de Warens requested Monsieur Sabran and his wife, who had come to meet him, to take good care of Jean-Jacques. Then she turned to him with a compassionate look: "Poor boy, you must go where God calls you, but when you grow up, you will remember me."

To tell the truth, he felt less grieved than she at the separation. As soon as his eloquence had failed of the immediate effect which he hoped to produce by it, that is, as soon as he knew he could not induce Madame de Warens to keep him with her, his imagination began to wander off into other fields. Later, it was to recall him to that spot where he had felt he might be happy and the memories of which were flattering to his good opinion of himself. But at the time he was intent on nothing but his own future, uncertain as that future was. He was soon in a mood even to enjoy the company of Monsieur Sabran, whom he had at first so heartily disliked, and of his vivacious lady.

He was under the confused spell of all the flattering things Madame de Warens had said to him, and of the many light caresses she had bestowed on him, treating him like a friend, almost like a lover, though postponing until later the pleasure of tasting the sweets of his devotion. And so he departed cheerfully and without hesitation, casting no backward glances. He wrote of this period: "Youthful desires, delusive hopes, and ambitious schemes filled my whole mind. Everything I saw seemed to me to promise me happiness in the near future. The houses we passed made me think of country festivals, the meadows of exciting games, the banks of lakes and streams and the edges of the woods suggested walks and fishing excursions, the trees put me in mind of luscious fruit, and the shade beneath them of pleasant hours of philandering. When I saw the mountains, I thought of tubs of milk and cream, of delightful leisure, of peace and simplicity, and the joys of aimless wandering."

CHAPTER II

DAYS OF UNREST

JEAN-JACQUES left Annecy on March 24, 1728. Nineteen days later the heavy iron-barred gate of the Hospice of the Holy Spirit at Turin was double-locked behind him. He could hardly have done otherwise than submit to virtual imprisonment, left to his own resources as he was, or rather thrown on the mercy of the catechists by Monsieur and Madame Sabran. They had taken pains not only to relieve him of the small sum of money he possessed, but even to tear from him, in default of his cousin Bernard's sword, to which he persistently clung, a bit of silver tinsel which Madame de Warens had given him for the handle.

He was first shown into a very large hall containing only a few chairs and a wooden altar surmounted by a crucifix. There he found gathered four or five ragged knaves who looked more like a gang of convicts than "aspirants to the state of children of God." The women whom he later encountered, "certainly the most brazen slatterns and the most hideous harlots who ever defiled the fold of the Lord," intensified his evil impression. This was further colored by the aversion, so strong that it may be called a repulsion, rather physical than spiritual in its nature, which Catholicism inspires in Protestants. We must admit that the surroundings in which his contact with Romanism was made, to a sensitive being like him, were little calculated to overcome his previous prejudices against it. He learned nothing good at the hospice. Quite the contrary, if it is true that his companions, long-standing "repeaters," that is to say, incorrigible scoundrels, confided to him that, being Slavs and being able to pass themselves off as Jews and Moors, they spent their time traveling in Spain and Italy and being baptized wherever there was enough in it to make it worth their while; if a saintly missionary who was instructing the only halfway pretty girl in the hospice really worked for her conversion with more enthusiasm than attention to business and was never ready to pronounce it accomplished; and, lastly, if one of the authorities to whom Jean-Jacques went, complaining of a slut who was soliciting him to join her sensual pleasures, actually gave him the shameless answer that there was nothing to make such a fuss about, for that kind of thing was constantly done. However, we can discount as mere rhetoric what he later wrote in his maturity denouncing the abjuration of his faith to which he reluctantly consented, and we can attribute to brag all that he says of the trouble he caused his instructors when he tried to convince them to turn Protestant as they labored over him. To sell his religion would have been a difficult matter, since he did not, strictly speaking, have any, and, however ignorant may have been the priest whose duty it was to discourse to him, he could certainly not have been so baffled by Jean-Jacques's objections as the latter would have us believe. The fact remains that, four months after he entered the hospice, he was judged by his teachers to be sufficiently well grounded, or well enough disposed, and was taken to the Metropolitan Church of Saint John, there to go through with the formal ceremony of abjuration and to be baptized under the given name of Joseph-François, in memory of Madame de Warens. He was clad in a gray robe with white frogs, while two men, one in front of him and the other behind, tapped on brass basins into which the congregation dropped alms.

He collected altogether a little over twenty francs in small change, and he was then dismissed with good wishes and exhortations to live the life of a good Christian. On

August 23, 1728, he found himself stranded in the streets of Turin, but, far from quailing, he accepted the situation light-heartedly and had no thought but of how to enjoy his liberty. He explored the city, went to see guardmount, followed processions, and visited the palace of the king of Sardinia, haunting the palace chapel less from admiration of its splendor than from pleasure in the music. He was also anxious to see whether some princess might not put in an appearance who should be "worthy of his homage and with whom he could have a romance." When the day was over, he retired to sleep on a pallet in the house of a soldier's wife, who kept a lodging house for down-and-outers. He paid a penny a night and was huddled in with all the other tramps, as well as with the woman and her half dozen children.

He lived parsimoniously, subsisting chiefly on brown bread, milk, cheese, and eggs, but his purse lightened rapidly and he soon felt the pressing necessity of finding some work by which to earn the little money he needed to keep alive. His first thought was to ply his former trade, but he was not well enough trained to be an engraver's assistant, so, for the time being, he asked from shop to shop for jobs engraving monograms or coats of arms on tableware. He "hoped people would employ him because his labor was cheap, to be had for whatever they felt like paying him." He was turned away from nearly every door, and the little he found to do earned him only a few meals.

However, a young woman named Madame Basile, the proprietor of a little shop, was attracted by his sweet face and his sad story, for he played on her sympathy by the same tactics which had worked so well with Madame de Warens. Sure of himself and talkative as soon as he felt himself the object of interest, particularly of feminine interest, Jean-Jacques expatiated on the extraordinary nature of his adventures and once again dreamed of being able to settle down at leisure with an affectionate companion. The kind little woman, whose husband was away on business and who was amorously inclined, was amused to see that she attracted the youth, and as she judged him harmless, she let him see that he attracted her as well. She even played at making a pet of him in the presence of the surly clerk in whose charge her husband had left her, not only speaking to him affectionately, but caressing him. However, when they were alone together and Jean-Jacques naturally would have preferred to have expressions of feeling from her, she stood on her dignity. Perhaps he was too bashful for her, perhaps she herself was too shy to make the first advances, perhaps she really intended to remain faithful to her husband. The reserve of her manner baffled her swain completely. At those times he stood about awkward and trembling with embarrassment, not daring to look at her, though he felt none of the same fond respect for her as for Madame de Warens.

But one day when the spying of the clerk had exasperated her, she went up to her room, and Jean-Jacques sped after her, slipping in before she saw him. She was seated at her embroidery beside a window, with her back to the door. Her pose was graceful; her head, bent over her work, revealed the whiteness of her neck; her hair, becomingly dressed, was adorned with flowers. She was altogether so lovely that Jean-Jacques utterly forgot himself. He fell on his knees and stretched out his arms towards her with a passionate gesture of supplication, believing that she could not see him. But over the mantelpiece hung a mirror which betrayed him. Faint with apprehension, he waited for the expected rebuke, but his courage rose when he saw that she was looking at him gently and that she was pointing out to him a mat on the floor beside her. He made his way to it without rising to his feet, and there he remained, in the most pleasurable situation, also the most cramped, which he had ever experienced. He did not speak, he even held his breath, merely touching her knee occasionally with so light a caress that he thought she did not notice.

Madame Basile appeared to be both as moved and as shy as her young lover. She was in a quandary of conflicting impulses, and in order not to have to drive him off after she had summoned him so close to her, she kept her eyes fixed on her work without once raising them. Her bosom rose and fell rapidly under her lace kerchief, and no one could have told whether love or embarrassment stained her cheeks so bright a red. But the little scene could have come to only one conclusion if the actors had not heard the opening of the door of the kitchen next the room they were in, and if Madame Basile had not exclaimed in alarm: "Get up, there is Rosina!"

Jean-Jacques obeyed, but, before doing so, he seized her extended hand and pressed upon it two brief but scorching kisses. At the second, he felt a gentle touch of caress upon his lips. He was led to expect the fulfillment of all his hopes. But his happiness was of short duration. Monsieur Basile came home and was told by the clerk of what had been going on in his absence. He at once turned, or, more properly speaking, threw, out of doors the fellow who had had the temerity to make up to his wife.

Jean-Jacques was considerably annoyed by the ignominious end of his adventure. He even felt so resentful of his rough treatment by Monsieur Basile that he developed a hatred for scarlet, the color of the coat worn by the inhospitable shopkeeper when he returned. But at least his afflictions were not complicated by constancy. For a few days he skulked about the shop in which he had imagined he had known happiness, and then he forgot Madame Basile as he had forgotten or relegated to the background his memory of Madame de Warens. He forgot her the more speedily because, shortly after his humiliation, his landlady told him that she thought she had found work for him and that a great lady wanted to see him. He interpreted this piece of news as a certain summons to a high destiny, for, as he confesses, he still labored under the same old delusion. But the truth was simply that an aged woman named Madame de Vercellis wanted a second man, and soon after he entered her service, she died. While he wore her livery, his principal duty was to write letters dictated by her to him in French, and nothing special happened to him. Her age was such that even if she pitied Jean-Jacques, she certainly never entertained for him the warm feeling of Madame de Warens or Madame Basile. She asked him no questions except to find out what she had to know, without any of the sympathetic curiosity of those other ladies, and her manner, unlike theirs, was curt and imperious, not calculated to stimulate his flow of talk.

With no one to whom to confide his soul thoughts, Jean-Jacques decided to remind his first friend and patron of his existence. He sent several messages to Annecy, and, having let Madame de Vercellis know, he was not at all displeased when she asked him for information about them. He was eaten up with desire to be singled out and pronounced superior, to be spoken of as "a young man with a good outlook," that is, quite a different kind of person from the run of servants with whom he was forced to associate and who, no doubt, were jealous of him.

It may well have been to avenge himself on the group about Madame de Vercellis for their unfriendliness to him, and to retaliate for having his name left out of her will, that he took advantage of the confusion caused by her demise to steal from a lady among her heirs, not a silver service, as has been said, but simply a piece of ribbon. The trinket was old and of very little value. He accused one of the maids of having given it to him, a girl named Marion, the very same, in fact, whom he had in mind when he committed the theft. Marion, who was pretty, kind, simplehearted, and strictly upright, appealed to him very much, and he intended to show her, by this present, that he liked her. In spite of the good will he felt for her, he spoke her name when he was found to have the ribbon in his possession and was pressed to tell how he got it. He assures us, and I believe him, that he never felt less inclined to do harm to anyone than at the moment when he made his accusation against the poor girl. He was thinking about her when he was being questioned, lost his head at being caught redhanded, and involuntarily threw the blame "on the very first person whose name came to his tongue." The statement is perfectly plausible and entirely consistent with the workings of human minds. Nothing but false shame deterred him from confessing the truth when he was confronted with the girl he had slandered, and forced him to persist in a lie of which the consequences might well be extremely serious, for thefts by domestic servants were treated as no laughing matter in those days. I believe his statement that he was later consumed with remorse, and am almost tempted to take his word, keeping in mind his tendency to exaggerate, when he declares that he wrote his *Confessions* partly to relieve his conscience of the burden of a secret sin which he had never dared to acknowledge to anyone.

Although Jean-Jacques had not been long enough in the service of Madame de Vercellis to cut a figure among the members of her household, her nephew, Monsieur de la Roque, felt it his duty to give him a thirty-franc tip. He also promised to look out for a position for him, and gave him permission to call on him; he even let him wear off the new suit of livery in which Madame de Vercellis had dressed him and which the lady's steward had intended to take back. Thus he was decently clad and provided for, at least so that he could live a few weeks without having to settle down to work. He returned to lodge with the woman who had formerly taken him in, at the beginning of the year 1729, and spent the last part of the winter at Turin, idling and dreaming.

He was entering on his seventeenth year, and, as he himself remarks, his lack of occupation combined with his physical condition and his youth to upset his emotional balance. He was restless, dreamy, and absent-minded; he shed tears and sighed for the happiness of which he had perhaps known more than he claims, but which was certainly not within his reach at the time. His hot blood filled his brain with visions, which sometimes took the form of poor Marion, the kind little servant whose reputation he had ruined, sometimes of Madame Basile or of Madame de Warens, oftenest of Mademoiselle Goton, the vivacious girl who had amused herself with him on the sly and of whose high-handed familiarities with him he could never think without remembering the severity of Mademoiselle Lambercier. He was cast in such a mold that thoughts of the sweets of love were always associated in his mind with the idea of some suffering, at least of some humiliation. No doubt the ill-advised punishments inflicted on him by the pastor's sister had operated on his sensitive nature at a peculiarly critical period and had tended to deprave his taste if not actually to pervert him to the point of insanity, exciting him to wish that every pretty woman in whom he took an interest might do as Mademoiselle Lambercier did, illtreat him. But the spinster must have merely aggravated by her beatings his natural proclivity to seek pleasure in pain, a proclivity inherent in his shyness and in his pride, so fierce but kept somewhat under repression by his timidity.

At this time he came under the wholesome influence of a priest whom he had met while he was in the hospice, not the questionable ecclesiastic romantically described in the

Émile, who had to flee his country because of a scandal, but a faithful servant of the Church, high in the esteem of the bishop. This was the Abbé Gaime, of whom we may find a more detailed description, touched up in a few details only from another priest, in the *Vicaire savoyard*. This man won the affection of Jean-Jacques, but although he was tutor to the children of the Count de Mellarède, he had not sufficient influence to secure our vagrant a position, and the friendship helped him only morally. The Abbé Gaime must have understood that he was dealing with a youth without religion, to be sure, but not essentially irreligious, and he contented himself very wisely with awakening his conscience or imbuing him with a few healthy articles of conduct which might later develop into principles. "In the successive stages of my tastes and my ideas," wrote Jean-Jacques, "I was always on too high or too low a plane. I was by turns Achilles and Thersites, a hero and a wretched cur. Monsieur Gaime took the trouble to set me right and to show me myself as I was, neither sparing my feelings nor discouraging me. He spoke very highly of my character and my talents, but added that he saw developing in me qualities which would prevent my using these to advantage, so that instead of helping me to raise my fortunes, they would, in his opinion, simply enable me to live along without rising."

In spite of the good that was in him, Jean-Jacques had to be humble. The Abbé Gaime attempted to make him realize the merits of this virtue. But he came up against a pupil who was the less able to profit by his teaching on the subject because a strange mental quirk made him feel he had fulfilled all the demands of humility when he, with a sincerity which bordered on cynicism, had confessed his vices or his sins, and felt superior, in consequence, to those who were free from faults and whose slate was clear of errors.

In any case, it was probably the insistence of the Abbé Gaime that decided Jean-Jacques to accept, against his inclination, the position procured for him by the Count de la Roque, who had not forgotten him. Again he was to be a servant, but at least the hope was held out that his service with his new master might be only a short probation period. He made up his mind to it. His kind reception by the Count de Gouvon, who was Master of the Horse to the queen of Sardinia and head of the illustrious house of Solar, and the interest which was shown in him encouraged him at once. He knew enough about the world to realize that a lackey is not welcomed with such politeness. The consideration with which he was treated as time went on confirmed his favorable first impressions. He was exempted from wearing the insignia of service, that is, he was not forced to put on livery, even though he had household duties and waited at table. He was not expressly assigned to any one member of the count's family, and his time was his own except for a few letters which were dictated to him and a few pictures which were given to him to cut out. Not only did he not abuse his freedom, but he scarcely took advantage of it. His punctuality and attention to his duties were exemplary. His motive was not so much that he designed to win the favor of Monsieur de Gouvon as that he had become infatuated with his granddaughter, Mademoiselle de Breil, a dark-haired girl with the gentle manner usually characteristic of blondes, which he declares he always found irresistible. His close attention to his work was inspired by no other desire than to be in the vicinity of so charming a person. He watched for an occasion to attract her notice, though nothing to favor his plan seemed to offer itself while he was passing her the dishes and gazing at her shoulders or her bosom.

"My ambition was merely to have the pleasure of serving her, and soared no higher than I had a right to let it," he wrote. But if Mademoiselle de Breil's lackey ever for a moment left his post beside her chair, Jean-Jacques instantly slipped into it. With this exception, his behavior to Monsieur de Gouvon's granddaughter was always respectful, if overassiduous. Trying to divine her wishes and to anticipate her most trifling wants, he would have consigned himself to perdition to induce her to say a word to him. But, alas! she appeared not to realize that he existed. He was deeply mortified, and as an offense to his pride pained him more than any other kind of injury, his proximity to her stirred him to such a pitch of nervous excitement, sharpening and loosening his wits, that he lost his shyness. One day the young lady's brother spoke to him rudely, and he flashed back a rejoinder as apt as could have been made by the most accomplished man of the world, so neatly turned that it brought him a quick glance, transporting him into the highest heaven. The next day he had even better fortune. There was a great dinner, and the conversation turned on the motto of the house of Solar: *Tel fiert qui ne tue pas.* Someone ventured the opinion that it contained a mistake in spelling, and said that there should be no *t* in *fiert*. Jean-Jacques chose the moment to smile with a knowing air, so broadly that the count noticed his expression and bade him speak out. Jean-Jacques then explained that he thought the *t* was correct, *fiert* being an old French word, derived not from the adjective *ferus*, meaning *fierce* or *violent*, but from the verb *ferit*, *he strikes* or *wounds*, and that to his mind the motto meant not *He who threatens does not kill*, but *He who strikes.*

Imagine the effect produced by this display of learning on the part of a servant! But the thing which enraptured Jean-Jacques was the sight of Mademoiselle de Breil, who gave him a second glance more expressive of interest than the one of the preceding day, and then turned to Monsieur de Gouvon as if to request him to bestow the praise which his servitor had earned by the exploit. It was not stinted, and the whole table joined in. But unhappily Mademoiselle de Breil, intending to signify still further her approval of Jean-Jacques, asked him to fill her glass, and the poor lad, reacting from his triumphant emotions, trembled so violently that he poured some of the water into her plate and some even on her.

His awkwardness undid the favorable impression he had made, and he did not again obtain a single sign of favor from Mademoiselle de Breil. In vain he haunted her mother's antechamber, and planted himself along her way as she passed in or out. She came and went without appearing to be aware of his presence. I have already spoken of his fickle emotional nature. In this case he was more speedily consoled for his humiliation than he might have been in other circumstances, partly because the count's youngest son, the Abbé de Gouvon, had become attached to him and had undertaken to complete his education, "begun along so many lines and carried through on none," and partly because he had made acquaintance with a highly amusing person, a native of Geneva, named Bâcle. He took more pleasure in the jokes of his fellow-townsman than in lessons from the Abbé de Gouvon, who was teaching him to translate Virgil, and he left the residence of his employers so frequently to spend hours, even days at a time, with this jolly companion, that he brought down well-deserved reprimands on his head. He paid no attention whatever to these, and a threat of dismissal followed. This decided his fate, either because it opened his eyes to the possibility of following Bâcle, who was on the point of returning to Geneva, or because he had only been waiting for some such excuse to indulge again his passion for a hobo's life. The hinted intimation that a brilliant career in diplomacy might be opened for him did not deter him. Love-affairs were the only means of rising to fortune which his wild ambition suggested to him, and from the moment that no woman figured in his plans, he preferred to roam at large over the mountains, meadows, and valleys. This last disappointment in love, moreover, had taught him to value at its full worth the interest shown in him by Madame de Warens. It will be remembered that he had already felt the need of writing to her some time before, after his failure with Madame de Basile. The wish to see her again certainly influenced him in his decision.

All happened as he expected. He was thanked with less ceremony than he anticipated, perhaps, but he had only his own arrogance to blame. He departed with Bâcle.

The Abbé de Gouvon had given him a little model of a fountain by Hiéron, not a "heron-fountain," as he describes it, making the common mistake in spelling by which the man's name is confused with the bird's, and he deluded himself into thinking that he could exhibit it and so collect enough money to pay his own and his comrade's expenses. No only did it bring them in nothing, but it got broken on its second appearance. Instead of being grieved by the accident, Jean-Jacques accepted it cheerfully. As a matter of fact, he was not sorry to use it as a pretext for a break with his traveling companion, for he seemed to be reaping no benefit from the association, nor, more particularly, was he getting any nearer Annecy. For as soon as he left Turin, his plans had crystallized and he had fixed on a definite goal for his journey. The idea of returning to knock at Madame de Warens's gate, which had taken shape in his mind during his service under the Count de Gouvon, developed and expanded as he tramped at Bâcle's side. For a short time he considered seeking out his patroness in company with his friend, but he prudently reflected that his chances of a warm welcome were twice as good if he arrived alone as if yoked with a second recruit as destitute as himself. Besides, that friend might, one never could tell, become a rival. He put the case to Bâcle that as they had no money at all and had lost the thing which might have brought them a little, they had better face bravely the necessity of separating. Bâcle, though wild and irresponsible, was no fool. He understood perfectly the reasons Jean-Jacques advanced, and also those of which he said nothing.

"Here you are at home!" he said, as they set foot in the town where Madame de Warens lived. Kissing Jean-Jacques merrily on both cheeks, he pirouetted about, and then disappeared.

CHAPTER III

"MAMMA"

HAD Jean-Jacques really written to Madame de Warens as often as he says he had, and did she expect to see him back? In any case, he had certainly informed her of the course of events since he went to Turin, and she knew what positions he had had. Far from heaping reproaches on him when he appeared, as he had been afraid she might, she let him see at once that she was glad to have him at her side again, pressing his lips to her hand and giving free vent to transports of emotion which her instinct advised her not to repress.

"Poor child!" she said in a soft voice. "So you are back again! I was sure you were too young for such a journey, and I am glad indeed that it ended no worse than it did." And she questioned him, her heart full of a gnawing anxiety which we can easily imagine. But no! her first impression was not at fault—he was the same as he had been and just as innocent. No designing woman had made him her prey, and as for him, the mad folly of his ambitions had kept him out of evil. All that he told her with simple boastfulness, "without hiding anything or making any excuses," reassured her further. She smiled and gave him a light tap.

"What room shall we give this big fellow?" He hardly dared draw his breath while she consulted with her maid on this important subject, and he was overjoyed to hear that he was to sleep in the house. The maid carried off his bundle. He could not resist the temptation to slip after her, and he heard Madame de Warens, who went out with her to give her her instructions, say in a low tone: "I don't care what they say. Heaven has given him back to me, and I am determined not to desert him."

So he was installed, and we may agree with Michelet that he was Madame de Warens's own child. Women were his whole existence, and it was a woman who made him what he became. At once the confidential relations which had been theirs were reëstablished, and they became as intimate as it is possible to be. "Little One" was Jean-Jacques's pet name, and he called Madame de Warens "Mamma." Her feeling for the boy under her protection was deliciously complicated, and in order to prolong even her enjoyment of the concern it caused her, she made no effort to explain it to herself. On his part, he did not love her, though he has written that he did, like a young and pretty mother whom he enjoyed caressing—she never made any objection to his demonstrative ways and his kisses—nor yet like an elder sister, but like a being of another race and of a different sex, expecting and desiring nothing of her.

With her, Jean-Jacques was free from the shyness which kept him tongue-tied among people in general and made small talk a torture to him. He was garrulous, gay and humorous, whimsical, moody, sometimes violent and tyrannical. He was, in other words, his natural self, and he opened his whole self to her. His genius, turbulent, disorderly, and wholly lyrical, began to bud and to flower. His teeming brain gave birth to no abstract ideas, unfolding in logical sequence; but thoughts bubbled to its surface and overflowed with the pressure of the emotions which inspired them. He must have been utterly charming, and the relationship must have been precious indeed to the woman who knew herself the sole object of the demonstrative lad's constant devotion, the center of all his hopes and all his dreams. If sometimes his pursuits irked and wearied her, she nevertheless shared them all, encouraged him in everything, and made fun of him until he broke off what he was doing with peals of laughter or effusions of affection, after he had given way to fits of anger or vexation. In her passion for sorting out herbs, grinding them to powder, and making them up into various preparations or elixirs, she associated him with her in her work, which he detested, and mischievously made him taste the most unpalatable drugs. He might draw back and make faces, but when she waved before his lips her dainty fingers, smeared with some one of her concoctions, he invariably ended by opening his mouth wide to suck them.

He played up to her as artfully as she to him, though she, for all her plumpness, was nimble and quick and never at rest. He was extremely jealous of her visitors, and acted in their presence as if he were beside himself, because he saw that it amused her to prod his impatience by delaying their departure. The caller might be a soldier, an apothecary, a canon, or a lay brother; once in a great while a lady or even an out-and-out beggar, all of them schemers who wished only to get what they could out of her and who more often than not made fun of her credulity behind her back after having received assistance from her.

But then the joy of being left alone with her once more! And the special joy of sitting down to meals! They ate alone together, and at first she took no pleasure in food, finding even the first whiff of soup and meat difficult to endure, betraying a sort of nervous repugnance at the very sight of anything to eat. But she recovered from it little by little as she saw Jean-Jacques feeding greedily with the hearty appetite natural to his youth. However, she never touched a dish until Jean-Jacques had entirely finished; he would then begin all over again to keep her company, and they would make the occasion the pretext for all sorts of nonsense as if they had been lovers, the most ardent of lovers.

Though he showered expressions of his affection on her,

he was never so dominated by his feeling as when he was away from her. In her absence he suffered from a kind of nostalgia which reduced him to tearful melancholy and to a distress from which he suffered intolerably. He might wander off into the fields to kill time when she left him, to attend to business in the town or to her devotions in the church, and there the notes of the bells, which always affected him strongly, the songs of the birds, the beauty of the sunshine, the charm of the landscape, the scattered cottages in which he dreamed of life with his beloved patroness, all these things combined to excite him until he fell into ecstasies. He built castles in the air and lost all sense of reality in illusions. His happiness should be to live out his life with "Mamma," never leaving her for a day; and in the far-distant future, rather than have it fall to his lot to close her eyes, he should enter his last sleep at the same moment with her, in order never to have to feel the anguish of living without her.

The surrounding country, which Eugène Sue has called a "promised land," lends itself well to the kind of idyl which Jean-Jacques was spinning there. It is free from swampy fevers in spite of the fact that the lake water percolates for some distance under the meadows, and the region is crossed by a network of greenish little canals, making of Annecy, as Michelet has said, a "little Venice." But it is misty and swept by light fogs on which the sunbeams break up into rainbows, and the climate is nearly always mild. There the lushly watered flowers bloom early and vie in number and brilliance with those of the most luxuriant regions of the South. The windows of the room in which Jean-Jacques lived opened on the fields beyond the brook and some gardens, and, as he says, he always had "greenery" to gaze at, a sight he could not bear to be without. For he could never be happy unless he felt that he had space about him. But he actually liked the town with its arcaded houses, relics of the sixteenth century, little altered since the time of Francis of Sales, and the narrow street where the singing school was, within twenty paces of his lodging. For after a short term at the seminary, where Madame de Warens had entered him on a scholarship from the bishop, he had taken it into his head to study music, under a teacher from Paris named Nicoloz, invariably known as "The Master." This man was "a composer of merit, cheerful, bright, and still young"; he was, to boot, a drunkard and an epileptic. His office was that of choirmaster to the cathedral.

Had Madame de Warens actually thought that Jean-Jacques was of the stuff that priests are made of? We may doubt it if, as he says, she had studied him carefully and at length before coming to any decision concerning him. Certainly she did not share the opinion entertained of him by Monsieur d'Aubonne, one of her relatives who stopped at Annecy, and who told her that he considered the boy, in spite of his alert expression, if not a perfect incompetent, at least something of a fool, "with no ideas, and almost no attainments—in short, exceedingly limited." She had had him read the books of which her first lover, Monsieur de Tavel, had composed her library, and as she discussed his reading with him, she had very soon perceived that he had more than average intelligence, but that if he had any special talent, it would develop only in the arts or in literature, unless possibly in medicine. Most of what she attempted to teach him concerned the ways of the world and its conventions, or else good manners, of which he was entirely ignorant. She also taught him how to write French correctly, for when he first knew her, he made almost illiterate mistakes.

Thus she had not been greatly surprised when he was dismissed from the seminary, two months after he entered it, on the pretext that he had no vocation. He had found the society of churchmen insufferably dull, and he particularly disliked one of his teachers, whose name he was unable to remember. "This filthy fellow had greasy black hair, combed flat back, a gingerbread face, a voice like a bull, an eye like an owl, and something like a boar's mane instead of a beard. He wore a forced smile, and moved his arms and legs like a puppet's, as if he were pulling strings." Many years after his deliverance from this oily pedant, Jean-Jacques shivered at the memory of his awful, insipid face. He could still visualize him holding his greasy cap in his extended hand, bowing his pupil with hypocritical courtesy into his room, which to Jean-Jacques was more dreadful than any dungeon.

The head of the college, on the other hand, whose name was Monsieur Gros, had treated Jean-Jacques kindly. This man was thin and growing gray, half blind in one eye, but alert in mind and not at all inclined to pedantry. He delivered Jean-Jacques from the clutch of his enemy and entrusted him to the most sympathetic fellow imaginable, a young abbé from Faucigny named Monsieur Gâtier, who was finishing out his religious education and who, as much from desire to oblige Monsieur Gros as from compassion, was willing to take the time from his studies to supervise those of the comrade entrusted to his care. The attraction which this seminarist had for Jean-Jacques can easily be understood, for he bore on his melancholy countenance the air of being marked by fate which later characterized the heroes of the romantic period. He became a deacon of the Church, but then, after his return to his native country, seduced a young girl and was put in prison. The best he was able to do was to impart some rudiments of Latin in addition to what Jean-Jacques had learned from his father and Dr. Lambercier, and the most lasting impression made by him on his pupil was that of his own personality. Jean-Jacques used him as model for the Vicar of Savoy, attributing to him, besides, a number of traits drawn from the character of Monsieur Gaime.

After his expulsion from the seminary, Jean-Jacques took up the study of music, already begun with Madame de Warens, who sang and played fairly well on the harpsichord. He had set to work to learn to sing the scale and to read music under the Master. He made rapid progress, and the six months that he spent between "Mamma's" house and the singing school were perhaps the best and happiest of his life.

Though he had his freedom, he lived a well-regulated existence. He loved the easy informality of it and the way in which work was done as if it were play. He never forgot any details of that blessed time, remembering vividly not only the people and the scenes, but even the most insignificant of the objects associated with them—"the dignified and handsome robes of the canons, the vestments of the priests, the conical caps worn by the choir, the faces of the musicians, an old lame carpenter who played the double-bass, a light-haired little priest who played the violin"—and finally all the music they performed. He even remembered, when he was growing old, the pride with which he went up on the platform to take his place in the orchestra, grasping his small, old-fashioned flute, in order to play a little composition written expressly for him by the Master.

On his return from the singing school, he was accustomed to sing either a cantata alone or a duet with Mademoiselle Merceret, one of the maids in the house of Madame de Warens. She was a native of Fribourg, who took more and more interest in him and whom he liked, not because she was particularly pretty, but because she was a born rebel, and, no doubt, clever as well. He was in everyone's good graces, and he was fond of everyone. Even the bishop, Monsignor de Bernex, though he recognized that Jean-Jacques was not fitted to take orders, summed him up as a pretty sound young man and not a bad sort—erring in this respect, and mistaken in at least half of his estimate. But he need not have been troubled at having been overindulgent, since, as soon as he was dead, Jean-Jacques testified in his behalf and was of assistance in the effort to make a saint of him. It happened on this wise: One Sunday one of the buildings connected with the establishment of the Gray Friars, next to the house of Madame de Warens, took fire, and Jean-Jacques saw the flames which were threatening the whole building, and were already licking around the windows, turn aside at the precise moment when the bishop, who had called out into the garden Madame de Warens herself and all who happened to be that day in the house, kneeled down to pray. Two years later, the soul of Monsignor de Bernex having taken its flight to heaven, the Antonines, members of his former order, set to work to collect all the instances which might be useful in getting him beatified. At the request of Father Bourdet, Jean-Jacques contributed a written account of the event he had witnessed, unequivocally stating that he interpreted it as a miracle. Later still, Fréron unearthed this document and confronted its signatory with it to his confusion. Though he claimed in his own justification that he had composed it in a fit of enthusiasm under the spell of a sincere belief in the truth of the Catholic faith and full of veneration for the memory of the good prelate, the best we can say of it, knowing as we do that at the bottom of his heart he was always hostile to the spirit of the Roman Church, is that he was influenced not only by the desire to be agreeable to influential people, who might be useful to him at the time, but also by a sort of myth-making frenzy. He delighted in the supernatural, and, moreover, his pride would certainly lead him to enjoy being connected with any affair in which he played an important or an illustrious part. And, chiefly, he was then, even more than later, a creature of impulses. His impetuous decisions might make any amount of mischief.

Madame de Warens had occasion to realize this truth when he became infatuated, just as he had previously been infatuated with Bâcle, with a rascally fellow who knocked at her door one winter evening, giving his name as Ventura de Villanova and claiming to be a musician from Paris, reduced by poverty to earn his way by performances of church music. The scoundrel was presentable in spite of his evident destitution, and his frankness made him appear like a man of some previous education able to make use of his talents, though in very wretched circumstances. Moreover, he sang divinely. Jean-Jacques was enraptured with him. Our Genevan tyro gaped in amazement at a young man so sure of himself and his methods that he made no effort to show off his actual accomplishments but, on the other hand, could boast with extraordinary cleverness of abilities he did not possess. "Sprightly and merry, of inexhaustible gaiety, charming in conversation, always smiling but never laughing aloud, he made in a most distinguished manner remarks in the crudest possible taste, so that no one took exception to them. Even the most delicate women were surprised at what they would let him say and do. It was all very well for them to feel that they ought to be angry with him; they were simply unable to be."

Naturally enough, Madame de Warens was alarmed at the thought that the "little one" might follow such an example. She tried every art to disillusion him about the Sieur Ventura de Villanova, and was all the more eager to attain her end with speed because she was on the point of leaving Annecy on secret business. A quarrel broke out between the Master and the choir director, Monsieur de Vidonne, as a result of which the former resolved that he would make a sudden departure immediately before the

Easter services, and thus throw the chapter into confusion. This gave her the pretext she needed to get her protégé out of harm's way. After having tried for the sake of appearances to dissuade the Master from carrying out his intention, she helped the plot along and ordered Jean-Jacques to leave with him and accompany him at least as far as Lyons. The most serious difficulty involved was that of transporting the chest in which the Master had stowed his instruments. A faithful servant of Madame de Warens, her superintendent and gardener, named Claude Anet, was consulted on this point, and gave as his opinion that the best course would be not to hire a pack-animal at Annecy and so arouse suspicion, but to lug the chest along with them by night seven leagues to Seyssel, where it would be in French territory and where they would be in no further danger. His advice was accepted, and Jean-Jacques, after kissing "Mamma" good-bye and slipping into his pocket the well-filled purse with which she had taken pains to provide him, set off with the Master.

As I have remarked before, Jean-Jacques had a tendency, if not to tell lies, at least to spin yarns. In the course of this adventure, he showed his love of romancing by representing himself in a false light to Monsieur Reydelet, the parish priest of Seyssel, who was a canon of Saint Peter's and was well acquainted with the head of the singing school at Annecy. Our hero succeeded in persuading the Master to go to Monsieur Reydelet and to tell him shamelessly that he was on his way to Belley, at the bishop's request, to take charge of the music for the Easter services. The priest at Seyssel received the travelers with open arms, and in support of the Master's story Jean-Jacques embroidered on it countless other perfectly unnecessary lies, taking delight the while in his own cunning. He was in the best of form and was all the more charming to his host because he was delighted with the thought of taking him in and astonishing the Master with his ingenuity and proficiency. Monsieur Reydelet thought him a "delightful lad," liked him, and showered him with marks of favor. He made much of the two gay deceivers and gave them of his best, while they held on to themselves to keep from laughing in his face. They said good-bye the next morning, promising to return and see him again, and then burst out in uncontrollable mirth as soon as they were out of sight.

The enterprise ended less merrily than it began. After they had spent four or five days at Belley, staying with the musical director, who entertained them royally, Jean-Jacques and the Master reached Lyons and soon received the chest, which they had succeeded by further misrepresentations in getting the priest at Seyssel to forward by water along the Rhone. But the Master, excited by his adventure, had been drinking even more heavily than usual and had got entirely out of hand. Suddenly his old malady became acute, and he was struck down repeatedly by seizures which recurred at shorter and shorter intervals. These attacks terrified Jean-Jacques, who loved miraculous occurrences but abhorred melodrama. When he saw the Master fall at full length on the road, foam at the mouth, and go into convulsions, he could hardly refrain from taking to his heels. So, when it happened in the middle of the city of Lyons, he could stand it no longer, and after shouting for help, he took advantage of the confusion caused by the gathering crowd to decamp, waiting just long enough to tell someone the name of the hotel at which the musician was stopping. To be sure, the Master had acquaintances in Lyons, and before his accident he had called on Father Caton and the Abbé Dortan. Even his chest was checked in his name and was not lost. All the same, it is not surprising that Jean-Jacques should beat his breast with shame when he told in his *Confessions* of the panic fear in which he abandoned his teacher in the street. However, we must accept the excuse he tenders and repeat his own statement that his brain, tuned up to accord with an unfamiliar instrument, was entirely out of key.

Having broken faith with the Master in this abrupt fashion, Jean-Jacques went no further on his way and decided to return at once to Annecy. But to his great surprise and greater disappointment, Madame de Warens was not at home. She had mysteriously left a short time before, to embark at Seyssel for Paris by boat. She was wearing a mask and had two male escorts, one of whom was her servitor, Claude Anet, and the other the Monsieur d'Aubonne who had visited her a few months earlier.

The object of the trip taken by Madame de Warens was not known for a long time. Rousseau knew less than anyone what she had gone to do in the capital, or at least knew only what she chose to tell him about it. She gave him to understand that she had been alarmed lest she lose support at Turin in consequence of the revolution which followed the abdication of the king of Sardinia, and had wished to curry favor to compensate herself at the court of France. But Victor Amadeus did not abdicate until September, 1730, that is, four or five months after her departure. Nor yet did she go on any church errand, as has been stated as recently as 1914. Thanks to the researches of Monsieur L. F. Benedetto, we now know that she was acting as a spy in the intelligence service of the Sardinian monarchy, for she was a member of the "flying force" attached to the Sardinian embassy. European diplomacy was at the time in a state of high suspense, the various governments being concerned to know whether war would break out between the emperor of Austria and the Allies, signatories of the Treaty of Seville. Victor Amadeus, who was, as usual, prudently playing a vacillating game between the two enemy camps, was endeavoring to find out everything he could about the negotiations which were taking place, in order not to have to make a leap in the dark. He was using every means which came to his hand, and employed a multitude of widely scattered agents. The mission of Madame de Warens should have ended on July 21, 1730, the day when the government at Turin became convinced that peace would not be broken during the summer. A letter from the Count Maffei to the Count de Saint-Georges, the first president of the Savoy senate convened at Chambéry, speaks of the fact that the indiscreet observer was subjected to special supervision at Seyssel on her return journey, but this was because she had quarreled in Paris with Monsieur d'Aubonne, and the latter, who was scheming for the conquest of the Vaud region by the king of Sardinia, was afraid she might avenge herself on him by going over into Switzerland and betraying his plans. He gave orders that she should be arrested in case she started toward Berne. But Madame de Warens had no intention whatever of crossing the Swiss frontier and was all the less unwilling to answer the summons which she received to Chambéry, because she did not at all relish the prospect of returning to Annecy and being called on to explain her actions to Monsignor de Bernex.

What had she expected Jean-Jacques to be doing during her absence? She supposed, no doubt, that he would first spend a few weeks with the Master and then come back to Annecy to wait for her. But her journey was prolonged beyond her expectations, and circumstances necessitated a change in her plans when she returned to Savoy. She was grieved when she learned, later on, how the "little one" had deserted his traveling companion on the road at Lyons. She was still more grieved when she knew that instead of taking advantage of the bed and board she had ordered her household to provide for him while she was away, he had chosen to run off to Fribourg with her maid, Mademoiselle Merceret, and, if not to seduce the girl, at least to let himself be seduced by her.

CHAPTER IV

VAGABONDAGE

JEAN-JACQUES'S first impulse, when he found his patroness away from home and learned that she had gone to Paris, was to speed after her. But he reflected that in the course of the six days which were then required for the journey between Annecy and Paris he ran a great risk of crossing her on the way. She might very well have remained only a few days in the capital, and in that case he might better wait for her, or at least wait for some news of her plans. The friendly Mademoiselle Merceret, who had received the orders already indicated in regard to the upkeep of the establishment, succeeded in calming his impatience, and he was somewhat influenced by the further consideration that he had in his purse no money except what remained of the sum presented to him before his expedition with the Master. He took care not to go to Monsignor de Bernex for consolation or advice, for his conscience troubled him in that quarter, and neither did he go to the seminary, for the head, Monsieur Gros, had retired. But he did find Ventura de Villanova, who had settled down permanently at Annecy and had become the darling of all the ladies. He attached himself to the roving warbler and begged to be allowed to share his lodging in order to learn more from him.

This lodging, which was nothing but a cobbler's den, could not be called sumptuous, but Jean-Jacques preferred it to the residence of Madame de Warens, intolerably dull to him in the absence of its presiding genius. He was not at heart plebeian, for he had sensitive tastes and nice instincts which attracted him to people of breeding, not fine ladies only, but men of parts and fastidious ways. But he had, all the same, a decided weakness for the rabble. Ventura de Villanova, with his natural charm, his sophisticated ease of manner, and his talents, which shone from under his disreputable appearance, represented the type of man he himself would have liked to be. Though he felt no restraint when soothed by such affectionate intimacy as "Mamma" accorded him, he was in general ill at ease among the aristocracy, whose arrogance and haughty insolence aroused his resentment as long as he could not meet them on terms of equality. On the other hand, he took no pleasure whatever in the society of middle-class people or peasants.

Between Mademoiselle Merceret, who was overjoyed at having him all to herself, and an acquaintance of hers, named Mademoiselle Giraud, who had taken it into her head to fall in love with him and constantly urged her friend to bring him to her house, he was troubled by embarrassment, or rather by indifference, which is even worse in the case of a young man of his type, and was so affected by a sense of uneasiness that it depressed his emotions and left him passive and uninspired. I believe him when he says that he would have spit in the wizened, dark little phiz, sprinkled with snuff, that Mademoiselle Giraud occasionally put too near his own, if he had not restrained himself from motives of policy, explicable enough in view of his destitute condition. The actual pleasure he received from her circle of friends, dressmakers, domestic servants, and shop-girls was not enough to make him respect her feelings, for they had no appeal for him; but he was able to sponge on them to a certain extent. It never occurred to him to pay court to any one of them. He had to have young ladies for that, and he felt that these common jades, with unpowdered faces and hair, rough hands, and home-made toggery over coarse underwear that smelled of soap, were entirely un-

VAGABONDAGE

worthy of him. Though they made much of him, and he was far from insensible to their flattery, he took no pleasure in their simple conversation. Much more entertaining to him than their silly jokes and worn-out compliments were the pretensions to gallantry of Monsieur Simon, an absurd little justice with a long gray beard, highly learned but thoroughly ridiculous, to whom Ventura had introduced him; or the bad language addressed to his wife by Ventura's landlord, whose stock of oaths was supplemented by phrases in Provençal dialect savoring strongly of garlic.

Once in a while he found relief from the general monotony of his existence in some intercourse with a better sort of people, occasioning a pleasant interlude like the one he describes at length, so exquisitely, in his *Confessions*. Through Madame de Warens he had been introduced into the rather heterogeneous circle of recent converts at Annecy, and had made the acquaintance of a delightful young girl, a native of Berne, named Mademoiselle de Graffenried, and with one of her friends, Mademoiselle Galley. One summer morning, when he had gone out to roam in the fields, as he frequently did, to see the sunrise, he came upon the two young ladies on horseback, halted at a brook which they could not induce their mounts to cross. He rescued them from their difficulty at the cost of wading into the water up to his knees, and would then have departed sheepishly if they had not been so gracious as to invite him to go with them back to Thônes and spend the day with them.

He liked Mademoiselle de Graffenried well enough and was greatly attracted to Mademoiselle Galley, a blooming maiden of sixteen whose given name was Claudine. He obeyed the instructions which she gaily gave him to mount behind her friend and ride on the crupper; and thus he returned with them, without having dared to make the least advance, although he might no doubt have presumed without giving any great offense, since his arms were wound about a waist which he had been advised to clasp very tightly indeed. With a rapidly thumping heart, he arrived at the country-house of the Galleys, where a dinner had to be improvised. What a dinner, and what preparations for it! What a feast they made on the cherries which Jean-Jacques had to climb the tree to get, throwing down handfuls of them even into the open bosom of his lady's dress! But there was nothing out of taste nor even anything immodest in the behavior of those three young people, as they romped freely together. The girls gleefully led him on and then rebelled when he responded; he sighed and composed timid songs; he went so far as to kiss the back of one of their hands, no further. "There is voluptuous joy in innocent play," he wrote when he sat down that very evening to compose his first poems, under the spell of his delightful expedition. I have no doubt that when he got back to the sordid hole where Ventura lived, he was less glad than usual to see his dissolute friend. But our amorous youth was not one to grasp the realities of love and hold them fast. His tendency was rather to put them from him, to push them beyond his reach; and as soon as his real feelings were involved, his passions cooled.

The Merceret girl, after a time, grew tired of waiting in vain for news of her mistress and decided to leave the place and to go back to her father in Fribourg. She liked Madame de Warens's protégé, and cherished under her narrow little forehead the project of making him her husband. Without great difficulty she persuaded him to go with her. The thought of taking a journey at the best time of year, having his expenses paid for him, was all the more attractive to Jean-Jacques because of the fact that they were to do it on foot, by easy stages, sending his bundle on ahead.

So they left, and as they trudged along, they chatted

VAGABONDAGE 51

freely. It appears that Mademoiselle Merceret, less impudent than little Mademoiselle Giraud, who had no objection to trying to kiss Jean-Jacques on the mouth, went no further than to tease him, "imitating his tone of voice, his enunciation, repeating what he said, paying him the little attentions he should have been paying her." They had to pass through Nyon, where his father was living in exile. Since the day when the latter had fled from Geneva in Jean-Jacques's tenth year, he and his son had seen each other only once, in 1724 or 1725, when Jean-Jacques was about thirteen. The irresponsible parent had remarried since that time, but nevertheless, when the prodigal to whom he had paid no attention for so long felt under obligation to leave Mademoiselle Merceret at the inn and pay his respects, he was received with open arms. They shed many tears over each other, but Madame Rousseau, with a honeyed tongue, merely pretended to try to detain Jean-Jacques, and Isaac Rousseau on his part put little conviction into his efforts to alter his son's plans, assuming that the son had any plans; in short, he made no attempt to set him on the right road, much less to take him in. To be sure, Jean-Jacques, who always found promises easy to make, vowed to give a little more time to his family on his return trip, and left in their care his little bundle, which had been forwarded thus far by boat and which would have encumbered him considerably. Perhaps he took this means of cheating his father, whose behavior annoyed him, and who shortly afterwards was to cast him off entirely, after having summarily ordered him to return to Calvinism. In any case, Jean-Jacques left, and he and Mademoiselle Merceret arrived in Fribourg together, though the relations between them had become somewhat strained.

The young lady was vexed that Jean-Jacques had betrayed no amorous inclinations during the journey, and her parent, "who was none too well off," showed no enthusiasm for the traveling companion she had picked out. They arrived unexpectedly, and Jean-Jacques, who had perhaps counted on a share of the fatted calf, was forced to content himself with a meal in an eating house. In compensation he was invited to dinner the next day, but simply out of conventional politeness, and he thought best after the simple meal, which was served to him with no warmth, to set out again on his travels without knowing where he was going—proof enough that the "plans" which he had imparted to his father were not particularly definite.

Chance, or a wish to see Lake Leman from a point unfamiliar to him, led his steps to Lausanne. He arrived not only without a red cent in his pocket, but in debt for seven *batz* to the manager of the last village inn where he had eaten and slept. Like his friend Ventura de Villanova, he conceived the bold idea of solving his difficulties by teaching singing, though he could not read even the simplest air. As there was no singing school in Lausanne, his first step towards carrying out his clever inspiration was to make inquiries at an unpretentious inn, and there he had the luck to meet a certain Monsieur Perrotet, who kept boarders. This man was persuaded by his prevarications to give him a room and board on credit, and promised to turn himself inside out to find pupils for him. Jean-Jacques then wrote to his father to ask him to send on the bundle of old clothes which he had left on his way through Nyon. Isaac Rousseau did as he was requested. But it is not true, as his son claims, that he sent with it an affectionate letter full of "excellent sayings"; else Jean-Jacques would not have written him six months later: "Please see fit to oblige me with an answer from you. It will be the first letter I have received from you since I left Geneva."

Thus Jean-Jacques set himself up as a music-master, transposing the letters of his patronymic to spell "Vaussore," and calling himself "Vaussore de Villanova." In a moment of madness he went to even greater lengths, and, not content with trying to teach an art of which he knew little or nothing, he professed to be a composer. Taking unworthy advantage of the confidence of the unbalanced music-lover who had received him into his house and who vouched for him, he was so audacious as to arrange a concert for the performance of a composition of his own, which, except for a popular minuet of the day incorporated in it, was such a collection of dissonances as has never before or since been inflicted on human ears. His action must be interpreted as a piece of moral irresponsibility highly characteristic of him. For, far from improvising his astounding composition, Jean-Jacques worked it out with care and labored two weeks over his piece, or rather, his puzzle, of which he lost the clue as soon as he had written it. He arranged it and determined the different parts to be given out to the performers with such assurance that we may almost believe he ended by deceiving himself. The concert came to an end amid hoots and shouts of laughter, and the rash musician describes his humiliation in detail in the *Confessions,* not omitting to point out the contrast between that occasion and the success he later achieved with *Le devin du village.* But at the time he was terribly mortified by the ridicule to which he was subjected. Moreover, as can be imagined, the consequences of such a *début* were not such as to make Lausanne a pleasant abiding-place for him. He had great difficulty in securing a small handful of pupils, fat, stupid "Chermans," and a "girl, a snake in the grass," who delighted in showing him scores he was unable to make head or tail of, and then in reading them with ease under his very nose.

He learned something about music, however, by teaching it. When winter came on, after a short stay at Vevey, which enraptured him and which he later made the scene of the action of *La nouvelle Héloïse,* he left for Neuchâtel.

There he hoped to find new fields to conquer, and to succeed better than in Lausanne, where his reputation was irrevocably ruined. But, alas! Fortune again failed to smile on him in his new home. He ran into debt and soon was reduced to desperate straits. He then confided his troubles to Mademoiselle de Graffenried, with whom he had continued to correspond, and the kind young lady undertook to bring about a reconciliation between him and Madame de Warens. The latter had concluded her mission, and, after a period of resentment against her "little one" for his flight, was once more feeling kindly towards him and was ready to forgive him. There had certainly been many times when Jean-Jacques, however fickle at heart, had thought of Madame de Warens and sighed not only for the comforts of her hospitable house, but for the sweetness of her affection. He felt a deep tenderness for her, in spite of all his philanderings. Accordingly, he was preparing to return to his patroness, after having received assurances from Mademoiselle Graffenried that if he would make his excuses they would be favorably heard, when a chance meeting in a tavern at Boudry reawakened his adventurous mood and changed the course of his plans.

The encounter was with an extraordinary person muffled in a huge beard. He wore a purple tunic and a fur cap, and gabbled a jargon remotely resembling Italian. Jean-Jacques, who noticed that he was having difficulty in making himself understood, offered to act as his interpreter, whereupon the man rose, embraced him fervently, and obliged him to share his dinner. When the meal was over, the wine having done its share, the two were fast friends. The man of mystery informed Jean-Jacques that he was a Greek prelate and the superior of a monastery and that he was begging alms all across Europe for the reëstablishment of the Holy Sepulcher and the ransoming of Christian slaves. He exhibited resplendent letters-patent from the

VAGABONDAGE

Czarina and the Emperor, and had in his possession others from sovereigns of lesser importance. He asserted that he was fairly well pleased with the results of his collections up to that time, but that he had encountered almost insuperable difficulties in Germany and the same kind of thing in the country where he then was, because he knew no German, Latin, nor French. Doubtless Jean-Jacques's poverty-stricken appearance led him to think that the suggestion of joining forces would give no offense, for he baldly proposed that Jean-Jacques should come along with him as secretary and dragoman. Jean-Jacques demanded nothing, the archimandrite offered much. The bargain was struck immediately and they at once set out.

They began their campaign in the canton of Fribourg but collected very little. Then they went on to Berne and put up at the "Falcon," one of the inns most renowned for its excellent fare. Jean-Jacques had not eaten his fill for many days, and made the best of the heaven-sent opportunity. Consequently he was in a festal mood when, after receiving permission from the senate for the archimandrite to present his case, he did the talking before the Right Honorables. His ambition was aroused, and in spite of his shyness he improvised a speech, the only successful one he made in his whole existence, which brought him many compliments and elicited funds for his companion.

This success ended an association which, if it had continued, might have involved Jean-Jacques in an Odyssey across all Hungary and Poland. For at Soleure the Marquis de Bonac, who represented France in the Swiss Confederation and who had been ambassador to the Porte, unmasked the archimandrite. The Reverend Father Athanasius Paul, of the Order of Saint Peter and Saint Paul of Jerusalem, was discovered to be nothing but an impostor and a sharper, and Jean-Jacques, pressed to reveal his true colors, had to admit that he was no Parisian, as he had claimed to be.

However, the irresistible impulse to unbosom himself in full, which constantly took possession of him and which drove him to tell his whole story in minute detail, helped instead of harming him. He fell at the feet of Monsieur de Bonac and unburdened his soul, giving vent, in the process, as he endeavored to arouse the sympathy of that nobleman, to expressions of exquisite shades of feeling such as still touch his readers in these modern days, and which must have been all the more moving at a time when nothing to resemble them had been heard before. No matter if his logic is unsound and his interpretation not only of his actions, but of his motives too, has a specious ring; he convinces us of his sincerity for the moment and disarms our criticism by his candor. In short, he was sympathetic; or, even better, he had charm, a faculty for making an appeal which was liable to eclipses but which, as we have had occasion to remark, operated more and more powerfully as people betrayed susceptibility to it. The fact is that Jean-Jacques was at once aware of the fact that Monsieur de Bonac felt kindly disposed to him, and by a kind of subconscious art was led to express in his effusion more than his natural simple-heartedness and innocence.

He was comforted and petted, and appeared so entirely in his best light that the secretary of the embassy to whose care he was entrusted remarked, when he showed him to the room assigned to his use: "A famous man who bore the same name as you once slept in this room [the poet Jean-Baptiste Rousseau]. It depends only on yourself whether you rise in every way higher than he did, and whether some day people speak of the two of you as 'Rousseau the Greater' and 'Rousseau the Lesser.'"

Jean-Jacques failed to form any high opinion of people unless they addressed him in such manner as this. He felt a desire to read the works of his namesake, and, in order to see at once whether he could equal him, composed some poems. The first he had written, some months earlier, were of courtly inspiration. These, in cantata form, which he wrote out of conceit, he thought fit to dedicate to the Marquise de Bonac. At least he had the grace not to fall in love with the lady, and as he was assured that he would be assisted in working his way, and realized that he "could not advance very far" in the embassy offices, he expressed a desire to go to Paris. Perhaps he finally became something of a nuisance and they were not sorry to be rid of him. Anyway, he was given a hundred francs and some letters of introduction, especially one to a Colonel Godard, who was looking for a tutor for his nephew.

He set out with a heart full of high hopes, and a light step. As he traveled on, having decided to go from Soleure to Paris on foot, he built all sorts of castles in the air. The journey took him two weeks. His pace was hastened by the dreams of martial glory with which he regaled himself, imagining himself in the service of a military man, becoming a soldier also, and thinking how handsome he would be in a splendid officer's uniform. His illusions were soon shattered. To begin with, he was shocked by his first sight of the French capital, which he had pictured to himself in the image of Babylon. He entered the city south of the Seine, through the suburb of Saint-Marceau, which was at the time a mere labyrinth of malodorous streets and alleys hedged in by tumble-down houses set all awry. It swarmed with "beggars, push-carts, second-hand-clothes dealers, and women hawking dried herbs and old hats." No doubt there was much to be seen that was interesting and picturesque, but Jean-Jacques was too thoroughly a country boy to appreciate it. When he could not have the mountains, woods, meadows, lakes, and streams which delighted him, he could admire nothing less than palaces. As he had not the luck to see any of these when he first reached Paris, he formed and retained so disagreeable an impression of the city that he thought of nothing else during all the rest of his stay than "how to amass sufficient resources to be able to live away from it." And finally, though the people to whom he took his letters welcomed him cordially enough, he was rather badly treated by Colonel Godard, who turned out to be a skinflint. The old miser had money to burn, but when he saw the destitute condition of Jean-Jacques, he made an attempt to get him for nothing, that is, he proposed to give him a position as a sort of valet without pay to his nephew rather than as a tutor. Jean-Jacques confided the terms of the colonel's offer to a lady named de Merveilleux, who had shown a disposition to befriend him, and the intelligent woman, to whom he had as a matter of course related his story, advised him not to accept it. He waited for some other position to open, but nothing else was found. He began to grow impatient, and besides, in spite of a remittance which came from the Marquis de Bonac, his funds were getting very low. So, with homesickness to egg him on, he turned his face in the direction of Savoy, where he had been intending to go when he met the archimandrite.

In the *Confessions* he tells us that he had spoken of Madame de Warens to Madame de Merveilleux, who knew her, and that she had told him of Madame de Warens's departure from Paris, two months before, for Savoy or for Turin. We know from his correspondence with Mademoiselle de Graffenried, however, that he had no need of this information concerning his patroness' movements, though he did not know where she had finally settled. He set out to rejoin her, but before he left he shot his Parthian arrow at niggardly old Godard in the shape of a rimed epistle whose satirical wit greatly amused Madame de Merveilleux. Throughout these early wanderings, he was constantly writing and trying out his talents; the fact is worth noting once for all, because Rousseau is frequently cited

VAGABONDAGE

as a representative of the class of authors who begin to write late in life, and he himself encouraged the rise of the legend concerning the extraordinary flowering of his genius by repeatedly stating that he aspired to no literary glory in his youth, and began to write only when he was nearing the age of forty, or, as he says in one passage, "in his declining years." The actual fact is that he had long been feeling his way, desultorily, to be sure, like La Fontaine; and, again like La Fontaine, he found it definitely only in his ripe age. But early in life he had the bee in his bonnet, and it stung him to action by fits and starts, setting him to scribble verses or compose music, or, as we shall see, to construct plays.

So we find him once more on the road, traveling on foot as usual, but this time in no haste, drinking in deep breaths of country air, imbibing strength and spirit with it. He was never so happy nor so well as when he felt that he was "lording it over Nature" and attributing to himself the mastery over her countless denizens. He felt at those times no restraint, no curb on the fantasies of his imagination, and nothing obliged him to watch his manners and hold on to himself in fear of doing something to be scolded for. He even ceased to be troubled by the chronic ailment *— dysuria consequent on nervous spasms—from which he suffered all his life and which grew worse after he was thirty. He traveled as he liked, free to stop, to be alone

---

* This disorder, fairly common among women but much less frequent among men, is occasioned by the unfortunate habit sometimes contracted by shy individuals of holding back their urine for long periods. The doctors who were ordered to make the autopsy on Rousseau found his genito-urinary organs "in perfect condition." Dr. Jules Janet, who is quoted by Dr. Cabanès in *The Secret Findings of History*, Series 3, explains the matter perfectly. Rousseau was a psycho-asthenic who, in consequence of having been scolded by his Aunt Susan for wetting his bed, was obsessed all his life by the fear of being seized with a pressing need of urinating. Thus he often suffered from attacks of uræmia, not because of renal lithiasis, but because of paresis of the bladder, with headaches, fits of dizziness, and vomiting. See in this connection the article of Dr. Elosu, the most explicit on the subject which I know of, dealing with "The Ailment of Jean-Jacques Rousseau."

when he felt like it, enjoying to the full the sights he saw and the feelings they aroused in him. So intense was his rapture that it exhausted him, and if he felt like giving expression to his thoughts in writing so that he could pass them on to others, the pen, even if he felt no compunction at profaning his communion with divinity, would fall from his fingers as if it were too heavy for them to hold. Anyway, how could he ever explain the multitudinous shades of emotion which crowded into his mind and exalted him in his hours of inspiration? Volumes would not contain them.

One day he lost his way in the fields on the outskirts of Lyons and, weary and ravenous, entered a peasant cottage. Instead of the open hospitality he expected, which he was accustomed to encounter among the Swiss, the boor offered him nothing but skimmed milk and a hunk of barley bread, assuring him that he had nothing else in his larder. Jean-Jacques drank the tasteless milk and ate the coarse bread, which was not fit to offer to pigs, so eagerly that his host perceived he was in reality what he claimed to be, an actual traveler who had lost his way. No longer suspecting him of double-dealing, the man "opened a little hatch beside his kitchen, went down into it, and shortly returned with a good brown loaf of pure wheat flour, a delicious-looking ham, some of which had been cut off, and a bottle of wine." An omelet was added to the bill of fare, and Jean-Jacques, casting aside the remnants of the poor food, sat down to a meal which he greatly relished. When he tried to pay for it, the fellow pushed back his money with surprising agitation. He insisted, however, and finally learned that the tax-collector was the cause of all this suspicion and fear. The story which then fell from the lips of the trembling wretch, a story of tithes, "aids," and persecution from which a peasant could escape only by appearing to be at the point of starvation, made an indelible impression on Jean-Jacques. "That," he says, "was the origin of the inextinguishable hatred I cherish for the tyranny from which the unhappy lower classes are suffering, and for their oppressors."

He is not exaggerating. On the other hand, if his subsequent existence had not been what it was, the spectacle of that peasant, forced to conceal what he had stored up in order to reap any benefit from it, would have affected him only sentimentally. The cast of mind which he later developed, after many minor personal disappointments, led him to meditate bitterly over this experience and cite the wrongs of other men to support his condemnation of society—a condemnation based on his own petty causes of dissatisfaction.

He felt a desire to visit the scene of *Astrée*, which he had formerly read with delight, and he almost postponed going on to Lyons. But an old woman of whom he asked the way to Forez told him, mistaking him probably for a workman, that the happy land through which flowed the Lignon was a region of foundries, so he renounced the idea of turning aside and marched straight on to the ancient Gallo-Roman city. The first thing he did on his arrival was to call on a Mademoiselle du Châtelet who, he knew, was there, and who was one of Madame de Warens's friends. She gave him news of his patroness but was unable to tell him whether she was in Savoy or in Piedmont, and advised him to wait for further information. He waited. But as he was being received on an equal footing, he was ashamed to confess that he had no money; and he was reduced to the bare necessities of existence, often sleeping out of doors, stretched out on the ground or on a bench, "as peacefully as on a bed of roses."

A number of mishaps befell him during the few weeks he spent at Lyons, but nothing worth relating in detail. The long-awaited news from Madame de Warens finally arrived, and with it a sum of money as joyously welcomed as her letter. "Mamma" was at Chambéry and ready to receive her "little one" with open arms. Jean-Jacques said good-bye to Mademoiselle du Châtelet. She had introduced him to the works of Le Sage, notably to *Gil Blas,* whose picaresque adventures bore some resemblances to his own. She had also introduced him to a sweet little girl who was being educated at the convent where she lived. The child's name was Mademoiselle Serre. She interested him already, and eight or nine years later she was to inspire in him, if we take his word on the subject, the only disinterested love he ever felt.

CHAPTER V

A FAMILY OF THREE

MADEMOISELLE du Châtelet had advised Jean-Jacques to make the trip from Lyons to Chambéry either by stagecoach or on horseback, but he foresaw that, for some time at least after he rejoined Madame de Warens, he would have to behave himself with circumspection and be on his guard against attacks of his passion for playing the vagabond. So he determined to take his fill, while he might, of what to him was the greatest joy in life. The landscape which unrolls south of the Rhone, between the river valley and the elevation on which stands the Grande Chartreuse, is one of those of which Jean-Jacques speaks particularly as full of inexhaustible delight for him. "I must have," he said, outlining in a few words the characteristic features of romantic scenery, "torrents, boulders, fir-trees, dark woods, and mountains, rough roads to climb up and down, with precipices alongside steep enough to fill me with convincing terror." All these things he had in the tangle of narrow valleys hedged in by cliffs which constitute the landscape around the old capital of the duchy of Savoy. The gorges of Chailles, especially, pierced by a road cut in the living rock, while a small stream tears below through chasms as "terrible as mythical monsters," gave him the chance to enjoy in safety, leaning over a parapet, the delicious sensation of dizzy height, while crows and birds of prey screamed overhead.

When he reached the house in which Madame de Warens was living, he did not find her alone. Don Antoine Petiti, commissary-general of Savoy, was calling on her. She immediately took Jean-Jacques by the hand and introduced him to the important personage: "Here is that unfortunate young man, Monsieur. If you will be so kind as to help him as long as he deserves your assistance, I shall not worry about him again as long as he lives." She then turned to Jean-Jacques, whose eyes were starting out of his head with terror, and without giving him time to think or to make any kind of objection, she said to him: "My child, you belong to the King. Thank this gentleman, the Commissioner, who is providing you with your daily bread."

The bread was not cake, as Jean-Jacques's excitable imagination had at first inspired him to hope. He was given an unimportant position in the land office. But at least he had for the first time a chance to earn an honest living and with it an excuse for staying, as in the past, in "Mamma's" house. Now that he was no longer a child, nor even an adolescent youth, it was necessary to have some plausible pretext for taking up his abode with an unattached and still eligible woman, lest malicious tongues take to wagging. As long as he could pass for a boarder who paid his way instead of for a pensioner on her bounty, appearances were preserved. He was, to be sure, given a room which seemed to him the dreariest in the whole house, and the house was far from as attractive as the one in Annecy. Madame de Warens, in order to excite no envious attention and to give her enemies time to forget their hostility, had taken an old and badly constructed building which had long been without a tenant. Rash schemer that she was, her mission to Paris and the Revolution which had just shaken the throne at Turin, together with the loss of the support of Monsignor de Bernex, had nearly wrecked her. However, she had lain low, at the same time taking pains not to let herself be entirely forgotten in high circles, and she had succeeded in making friends with a number of personages who might counterbalance the influence of her detractors at court.

Uncomfortable as he was in the damp den assigned to his use, in which he had little space, little air, and little light, all being cut off by a wall just outside his window, Jean-Jacques expressed himself as content with his lot as long as he was in "Mamma's" house, at her side, and in her own room when he was not in the office. He had resumed his former relations with his patroness as if he had left her only the day before, and accepted without question, just as he would have done earlier, the understanding which existed between her and Claude Anet, nephew of her head-gardener, the superintendent who had accompanied her to Paris. It never occurred to him that this peasant fellow, a former Calvinist, six years his own senior, "slow, self-controlled, deliberate, circumspect, and cold," could be the lover of a lady like the Baroness de Warens. Not, on second thoughts, that he was any longer an innocent-minded child. But the importance of Anet's position and his value to "Mamma" were apparently enough to explain the interest she showed in him. In Jean-Jacques's scheme of life, only one person in the world had Madame de Warens's affection, and that person was himself. No one could possibly have a warmer place in her heart or live with her in closer intimacy than he. Moreover, she never spoke to Anet as she did to him, nor called Anet her "little one," nor took any liberties with him, much less indulge with him in playful familiarities. One may surmise, too, that after Jean-Jacques came back, Madame de Warens insisted that the silent Claude keep strictly on his guard. We can almost hear her replying to the reproaches of her jealous lover, whose expressionless countenance hid a passionate disposition: "But you can see for yourself that he is all innocence. How can you be so silly as to object to his kissing me?"

The pangs from which Claude suffered were all the more intense because she unconsciously began to treat him more coldly, feeling that she was being watched, and vexed at being obliged herself to restrain expressions of feeling. She was an easy-going, kind-hearted, and adaptable creature, but she began to find herself quivering with impatience at her superintendent's terse manner of speech. His rustic impassivity got on her nerves to such an extent that she began to resent even his eagerness to please her. It came to a point where she scolded him; discussions which sometimes arose between them concerning household matters began to run into sharp quarrels; and finally one day Madame de Warens, in a fit of anger, insulted him in the presence of Jean-Jacques. He turned pale and left the room with the air of a desperate man. His strange demeanor struck Madame de Warens, and the fact that he went straight to his room increased her anxiety. A presentiment took her to the pharmacy, or laboratory, cluttered with all sorts of drugs and chemical compounds which she used in her studies of quack medicine and alchemy. On the floor she found an empty phial of laudanum, and jumped instantly to the conclusion that the wretched man had drunk its contents. She rushed to his assistance and shrieked so loudly that Jean-Jacques ran after her. He found her at Claude's bedside, weeping, praying, and begging forgiveness, for Claude actually had drunk the poison and was quietly waiting for it to take effect.

"Wretch that I am, I have killed him! I have killed my lover! To think that I should be so cruelly punished for being too kind—not for being wicked. Surely I had a right to do as I liked with myself. But a good man cannot bear injustice. Come back to life, for I love you better than anyone on earth! And you, my little one, you see that I have no more shame before you. Help me to save your comrade from death. Henceforth I will do everything to make you both happy and I will devote myself to you both, with no favoritism."

Jean-Jacques thus learned the truth, and it gave him a considerable shock. We cannot say that he had entertained any definite idea of enjoying "Mamma's" favors, though his imagination had certainly played around it. But he was vexed, even grieved, that someone else should be where he had vaguely, dreamily, from time to time, longed to be. He was exacting in love and extremely punctilious in fulfilling the obligations imposed by the devotion of others. But he had no exclusive sense of monopoly, and he tells the truth when he assures us that instead of hating Claude Anet, who, by the way, was successfully treated with antidotes, he began to feel his attachment to Madame de Warens extending to him after he learned the truth concerning their relations. He did not feel toward Claude as toward a rival, but rather enjoyed the sense of intimacy with an additional member of what took on for him the aspect of a little family. But though he gained something, he also felt that he lost something. A sort of glamour which had hovered about his affection for "Mamma" faded out of it as soon as Claude began to seem like half a father to him—and, at that, Claude's age put him rather in the light of an elder brother.

He became restless and sought distraction in study and in independent occupations. After he became accustomed to it, his office work fell into a sort of routine, and he used his spare time reading, after drawing for a while with the excited intensity he always displayed in pursuing any pleasant interest. "I would have spent months on end," he wrote, "with my crayons and paint-brushes without ever putting them down." Before long, however, his love of music took possession of him in full force. He took up practising with all the more enthusiasm because he had several times been on the point of starting on botanical expeditions with Claude and he wanted, perhaps without realizing that he did, to beware of his natural interest in plants, later so strong. If he had encouraged it at that time, it would have drawn him close to Madame de Warens's superintendent rather than to Madame de Warens herself. Consciously or unconsciously, he sought to stand apart from Claude and to have a common interest with her peculiar to the two of them, in order to bring up subjects of conversation in which the honest fellow was unable to join. Feeling that he was not likely in botanical knowledge to go ahead of Claude, who had known about plants from his earliest youth, he adopted an attitude of dislike and of scorn for the science. He pretended to consider it "an apothecary's subject," and he never alluded to it except sarcastically, for which he got an occasional light slap or box on the ear, half in vexation, half in amusement, from his patroness.

But music, a closed book to Claude, gave him and Madame de Warens a meeting ground to which he, not in all innocence, delighted to lead her. When he saw her busy about one of her fires, he would say:

"Mamma, here is a lovely duet, which makes me think your old drugs smell as if they were scorched."

"See here!" she would answer. "If you make me burn them, I will make you taste them."

And as they had it back and forth, Jean-Jacques would get her to sit down at the harpsichord. And there they would forget everything else. "The extract of juniper or of absinthe would be a handful of ashes." His "Mamma" would smear his face with them. "And all that was great fun."

It was all the more fun because it seemed to Jean-Jacques that he was trespassing on Claude's preserves when he could get Madame de Warens to scold and to tousle him.

For, as I have said, a woman's rough treatment of him, even when it was all in play, was to him the height of voluptuous bliss. He wrote: "To be at the feet of a haughty mistress, to obey her commands, to have to ask forgiveness of her, was to me the greatest of joys." The bright and vivid memory which he retained of Mademoiselle Goton was due to the fact that the impudent minx had made a slave of him. Mademoiselle de Breil appealed to him as she did only because she disdained him, and the Merceret girl had failed to seduce him only because she would have been too easily won.

But he had, besides, an old score to pay. His pride had been so bitterly hurt by the failure of his concert at Lausanne that he was bound to retrieve himself by becoming a real musician. He had, too, a real love for the art which makes the strongest appeal to human sensibilities. He continually returned to it in the midst of all his passing fads, and was truly carried away by its intangible charm. To his chaotic soul, music was only another form of dreaming, and to the end of his life, in spite of constant practice, he continued to be indifferent to or rebellious of musical technique. "Mamma" had rented a small wine-shop with a little garden on the outskirts of Chambéry, in order to have a breathing place and to find relief from the close atmosphere of the house she lived in. Thither Jean-Jacques retired to lose himself in his music and to yield himself up to melody as to feminine caresses.

This retreat, to which the three escaped fairly often for dinner together, was hallowed for Jean-Jacques. In it a bed was set up for him, and after a time he took to sleeping there, letting "Mamma" and Claude go back without him though it cost him a pang to say "good night" to them. The imaginative young man had plenty to fill his thoughts as he lay on his solitary couch after the departure of the pair whose secret he knew. He had books and prints in his room, and spent part of his time decorating it and preparing pleasant little surprises for his patroness on her next visit. There he loved most to think of her, and there he thought of her most happily. Not that he felt the need, when he was with her, to go off alone in order to love her better. But she was so frequently with other people, many of whom he detested, that annoyance and tedium were apt to drive him to his shelter, where he could have her all to himself. At those times he took her even from the too fortunate Claude, recapturing his former mood of delicious uncertainty as to whether any man possessed her and whether he himself might not, even after having felt a son's tenderness for her, eventually adore her as her lover.

The operas of Rameau began at this time to excite discussion, and Jean-Jacques, having heard of Rameau's treatise on harmony, developed a strong desire to have it. Once this was gratified, he felt entirely at sea in the work, which seemed to him "long, diffuse, and badly constructed," and he plowed through it only with great difficulty. He consoled himself by working very hard at the cantatas of Bernier, of which he memorized four or five, and at those of Clérambault. His absorption in these pursuits, with the languor induced by an illness of an inflammatory nature to which he succumbed and which was followed by a long convalescence, combined to make him loathe his office, whither he ceased to go except under compulsion. By this time he firmly believed himself to be an accomplished musician, and confidently expected some day to be recognized as such. He had arranged monthly concerts in "Mamma's" rooms, at which he had conducted, and their success had completely turned his head. He felt altogether relieved of his old sense of shame, and began to consider giving up his post in order to devote himself solely to music and to earn his living by teaching it.

Madame de Warens endeavored, by every means she could contrive, to demonstrate to him what she termed his folly in planning to desert an honest position and a regular income in order to run after hypothetical pupils. She had, moreover, come to entertain a very high opinion of his intellect, and she thought it unworthy of him, and of the ambitions she felt he ought to be developing, that he spent all his time exercising a talent which in her opinion amounted to very little. But it was of no use whatever to reason with him. Perhaps he finally "extorted" from her the consent he desired before he handed his resignation to Monsieur Cocelli, director-general of the land office, or perhaps, as is more likely, he handed it in in a fit of exasperation and went off to Besançon without a word to her, to show his independence. In any case, when the autumn of 1733 came round, he was liberated from the "dreary office, stinking of bad breath and sweat," and from fellow-clerks who were mere "dirty ignoramuses," and was teaching singing to a bevy of prettily dressed young ladies in a festive atmosphere scented with roses and orange-blossoms. His day over, he returned to "Mamma's" for the night.

No longer was he forced to toil at tasks he hated among vulgar companions. He was on the outskirts of high society, among the "best people," as he says. He chatted with them, laughed with them, had a good time, and the lesson-hour passed like a dream. He went from mansion to mansion, and was everywhere received with cordiality. His dearest wish had come true. Far from feeling any regret at having given up his position in order to practise his profession, he considered that even if his earnings had been approximately the same, he would be better off teaching music. As it was, he had more than enough pupils to make what he had been paid in the office, and his pupils were all so charming and so pretty that he could not make up his mind between them. At least he thought they were, which comes to the same thing; and he was in love with all of them and with some of their mammas as well. Life at Chambéry must have been idyllic, to be sure, for it is the exception to see a handsome young man of twenty-one engaged without any thought of the consequences to teach young ladies.

Some, like Mademoiselle de Mellarède, whose lesson was early in the day, received him in their morning-gowns, "with no coiffure but their natural hair dressed simply and adorned with flowers"; others, like Mademoiselle de Menthon, dressed elaborately in his honor. And though he was strongly affected by the sight of a pretty woman in a *négligé*, he was also very susceptible to feminine charms set off by a blue mull scarf. Certainly there were individuals to suit every taste among his pupils and their mammas, young girls and married women. There were slender, youthful, feminine types, and plump, filled-out matrons, shy women and hardy ones, blondes and brunettes, even red-heads, alas! for he did not much like their sort. And though he preferred young ladies of good birth and breeding, the most trifling little middle-class person, though less flattering to his pride with her friendship, made with her free and easy ways perhaps an even stronger appeal to him physically.

Among his pupils there was in particular a Mademoiselle Lard, the daughter of a grocer, who might have served "as a model for a Greek statue," but whose manner was appallingly chilly and indolent. This girl, with whom he became infatuated, had a mother who, by contrast to herself, was particularly up-and-coming. She may have made at first a sincere effort to look after her daughter, whose name, curiously enough, was Péronne, and who was so dull that in spite of her cold nature she might well have been seduced by the first gallant to come

A FAMILY OF THREE

her way who lost his head over her beauty. But the sight of Jean-Jacques sighing for a Galatea who remained marble, finally stirred Madame Lard and gave her a desire to have all that youthful ardor expended on herself. She was not pretty, but her face had a bright and saucy expression, though disfigured by smallpox, like most faces of the period, and her eyes, though a bit bleary, betrayed an intense and passionate nature. But her chief advantage was that she had no conscientious scruples and knew how to go about the business. The first sign of affection she gave Jean-Jacques was to greet him, when he crossed the threshold with all her usual cordiality and a hearty kiss full on the lips besides.

He defended himself weakly, if at all, against her advances. He assures us that he attributed them only to exuberant kindliness, and it is true that the grocer's wife treated him in many respects like a child, for we know that she took care to serve him with a cup of excellent coffee and hot milk as soon as he arrived at the house. Her attentions, together with the chaotic state of emotion in which his pupils kept him, set his head to whirling. He went about thinking he owed to one or another what he was really getting from someone else, his vision colored all the while by the excited condition in which Madame Lard kept him. He lived in a magical world, and when he went home each evening and related to Madame de Warens all the events of the day, his animated expression and feverish chatter would have warned a less astute woman than Monsieur de Tavel's former mistress of the danger that threatened him. I use the word "danger" not because I personally see any dire consequences which would have followed had he succumbed to Madame Lard, but because "Mamma" viewed such a possibility as the worst misfortune that could befall her dear "little one." She rebelled at the thought that another woman might be the object of Jean-

Jacques's first deep passion. She had allowed the youth who had appeared to her one morning in the bloom of his sixteen summers to preserve his innocence, though beset with many perils, beyond its normal hour. As long as he had remained, thanks to her, a child, we must do her the justice to note that she deliberately treated him like a child. But since he was about to emerge from his chrysalis into man's estate, she was unwilling to have him complete the metamorphosis without her having a part in the process and without herself savoring the sweet emotion of it. She may have been a sensual woman, but, seen through the eyes of Rousseau at least, she does not appear to have brought much passion into love. In any case, she seems to have kept a perfectly clear head through her love-affairs and to have noted the madness which overtakes the male in such circumstances and the kind of abject gratitude which he feels. Consequently, she had come to the conclusion that there can be no complete understanding between two people of opposite sex without possession. She knew Jean-Jacques thoroughly and knew his changeable moods. She believed that he would be lost to her if he should come into the knowledge of his manhood through another woman, and she aimed to bind him to her by the strongest, that is, by the tenderest, ties. From the time she decided on the initiation of her protégé by herself, she behaved more seriously with him and—let us not smile at her—talked to him on a higher moral plane. She gave up entirely the teasing play which she had been accustomed to carry on with him. "All at once the exuberant gaiety with which she was accustomed to give her instructions," wrote Jean-Jacques, "was superseded by a sustained manner, neither familiar nor formal, but suggestive of some serious talk to follow. After having wondered in vain by myself what could be the reason of the change in her, I asked her about it. That was what she had been waiting for." We can see her game. The subtle creature, who knew that she had her "little one" wound around her finger, was preparing a situation most likely to impress an imagination like his. Even after she had made up her mind to the final step, the woman in her was doing her best to appear to be yielding to him. She took her part seriously, however, and would have indignantly denied the charge of scheming, because she was acting at the dictates of her heart and in the interests of a person indispensable to her happiness.

As soon as Jean-Jacques had requested that she enlighten him concerning her mysterious attitude, she suggested that they make an expedition next day to the little garden of the wine-shop. They arrived early in the morning. Madame de Warens had seen to it that they should be alone there all day, and she employed the hours in preparing him for the favors she meant to bestow on him. Jean-Jacques does not give the date of this memorable scene, but there is every indication that it must have been near the end of the year 1733 or at the very beginning of 1734. Madame de Warens used no coquetry on him, as they walked together countless times back and forth over the sanded paths of the garden, between the heaps of snow which covered the flower-beds, but she talked to him with great "feeling and logic." So he actually expresses it— "feeling and logic"! How many sophistries afterwards originated in the coupling of those two incompatible principles! Jean-Jacques, to whom "Mamma's" talk seemed more instructive than entertaining, admits with simple frankness that his senses were not at all stirred by it. The consequence was that, unfortunately for us, it made no impression on his memory. It would have been interesting to know the words Madame de Warens used to convince him that his own interests, his future success, his whole fate indeed, would be favorably affected by his obtaining from her the revelation of sensuous pleasure. Doubtless her tone is reproduced in *La nouvelle Héloïse*, and probably some of her reasoning is preserved in the precepts of the *Émile*. Logic may properly draw on feeling to supplement its appeal, and may use its processes to justify the most violent outbursts of passion, but logic is out of place in the complete abandonment of self to ecstasy. Anyhow, there was, or appeared to be, too much compassion or kindness behind the idea which dictated the behavior of Madame de Warens for Jean-Jacques to be stimulated by it. He felt a kind of embarrassment when he heard the thirty-four-year-old woman talking about giving herself to him in somewhat the tone she might have used to speak of making some household plan, or at best of coming to some decision of a moral character, out of foresight or propriety. If only he had been more touched by a phrase, even a word, betraying her own heart's inclination! Of course he was too conceited and too oversexed, as well as too completely obsessed by the mystery of love's fulfillment, not to have his uneasiness and the strange timidity he felt routed by his curiosity and his desire to appear as a full-fledged man. In spite of his secret hesitation, he hastened to agree to all the conditions imposed by his patroness in consideration of the crowning benefit she was prepared to bestow on him. She gave him a week to think it over. He protested that a week was a long time, too long. But she had no sooner left him to himself than he felt that it was not long enough.

The truth was that he no longer craved to be the lover of Madame de Warens. The sort of sacrificial ceremony which was to take place, arranged with such solemnity, was nothing like the ecstatic experience his imagination pictured when he thought of the fulfillment of love. And her action in thus preparing his mind gave to this autoerotic hours of nothing less than torture. Moreover, the intimacy with which he had lived in her house had stripped her of much of her glamour. She had been too familiar with him, and he no longer looked up to her as sufficiently superior to himself. "Mamma" was never so much "Mamma" to him as after he knew that he could enter into the relationship with her of which he had formerly dreamed with rapture. He also felt that such a relationship might have something blasphemous about it, and feared to meet the situation. In short, behind all the ins and outs of his tortuous doubts and terrors, the truth was that he longed to be the lover of Madame de Warens only if he could be sure that his longing was in vain. In this miserable uncertainty he spent the greater part of his knightly vigil. Sometimes he actually tried to think up "some honorable way of getting out of the blessedness which would be his." We might reasonably suppose that the vision of Claude would obtrude itself on him, and the form which jealousy took in this hypersensitive soul might be unwillingness to become his partner in Madame de Warens's favors. But this was not so. Jean-Jacques takes pains to tell us that it would be a mistake to believe that "Mamma" was lowering herself in his eyes by accepting both of them. The most he could think was that such a division of herself was unworthy of her and of him. He takes his oath that, from thinking less well of her, he thought more affectionately of her for her proposal.

The dreaded but, in spite of everything, eagerly awaited hour struck. Jean-Jacques meekly repeated his promise that he would keep all the conditions Madame de Warens had imposed, and retracted nothing. In his weakness, he could not have done otherwise. To her, the new relationship was a source of emotions which Nature had not before vouchsafed to awaken in her, and from that moment she definitely adopted her "little one" and recognized him as her son. For the strange woman found herself overwhelmed with tenderness instead of being exalted, as she had hoped, and her deepest maternal instincts were stirred. She lost whatever scruples she may have entertained concerning the possibility of living as the mistress of two men at once, both lodged under her roof, and perceived so much difference in her feelings for the one and the other that she considered the situation from that time perfectly simple, if not normal.

All the indications are that she told Claude of the intimacy of her relations with Jean-Jacques. She must have assured him with the best faith in the world that, all appearances to the contrary notwithstanding, her love for the boy was as pure as love can be. She insisted on the difference which she had always felt existed between her relationship with her major-domo and her relationship with her protégé; and she ended by making such a distinction between them that it seemed as if they could not regard each other as rivals. She adopted for Claude a more attentive manner than before, and made an effort to inspire in Jean-Jacques a respect for him commensurate with her attentiveness. She tried to make Jean-Jacques consult him about all his affairs and treat him with the affectionate esteem accorded by us to the wise and kind among our elders. Claude was either a monument of discretion or else he was ashamed to complain before Jean-Jacques, so he let nothing of his pain appear to the latter, and probably attempted to conceal it from Madame de Warens, in order not to show himself a rough boor incapable of appreciating the point of view which was represented to him as the enlightened one. He concealed the jealousy of which he would have been made to feel ashamed, but suffered all the more for the restraint he put on himself. In grief and despair, he consented to act the part Madame de Warens assigned to him, and was frequently compelled to throw his arms about the neck of Jean-Jacques, who in the meantime was weeping fond tears, while Madame de Warens called Heaven to be her witness that they were both indispensable to her happiness.

But he was far from grateful to his mistress for the distinction she made by her behavior between himself and Jean-Jacques; on the contrary, he felt that every mark of favor she bestowed on the latter was stolen from him, and naturally was left untouched by what she reserved especially for him. She was indeed more confidential with Jean-Jacques, though she appeared to trust and rely on him less; and the wretched Claude understood that, while he was treated in a manner flattering to his manly pride, he was losing all the sweet communion of heart to heart which is the best gift of love. Madame de Warens never held with Claude the conversations she enjoyed with Jean-Jacques, whom she no longer regarded as a child but to whom she talked as some still young mothers talk with their grown-up sons, seeking to impart to him her own experience of life and to imbue him with the fastidious discrimination in details which is the acme of truth to women. This is the significance of Michelet's statement: "Rousseau was the child of Madame de Warens." For "Mamma's" chat did more to make him what he became than all the books he read, and more than what he calls the "sermonizing of a pedagogue" could ever have done. No lessons teach a mind like his as much as the lessons it learns from intimate relations with a woman and from her inexhaustible sympathy.

"Mamma" succeeded in discovering the true nature of her dear "little one," and tried to adapt it to the canons of society so that it would there be accepted at its proper valuation. The refined delicacy of his sensibilities should have vested him with aristocratic quality of a kind. But he was clumsy, and it is on record that he was the despair of both the fencing master and the dancing master who were told to exercise him until he lost weight. His common clay was not to be concealed. Not that he was awkwardly built or unresponsive; we already know that he was neither. But he simply could not acquire an easy manner, nor make up for the lack of it by natural grace of movement, noticeable in persons of fine physical endowment who have well-trained muscles. Any kind of discipline was intolerable to him, and he was untidy both in his person and in his dress. The habit of wandering had accustomed him to dirt. He had corns which forced him to "walk on his heels." He had dangling arms, and was so heavy on his feet that he could not jump over a gutter. The effort to teach him fine manners was eventually abandoned in utter weariness. He was entirely indifferent to his failure at the time, wrapped up as he was in the pleasure of knowing he could interest "Mamma" and of having a witness to her fondness for him, someone who could not keep up with him mentally. There is no doubt that in their circle, "perhaps unique in the world," his was the most brilliant part. And in spite of the delight of being alone with Madame de Warens, he really preferred to have all three together, because unconsciously he so loved to shine. When they were gathered, especially at meals, over which they lingered for the pleasure of conversation when they did not have to put up with the presence of an unwelcome outsider, Claude, though he was so useful in other ways, served as a mere figurehead. And it is not hard to imagine that he was annoyed when he had to hear his rival read to "Mamma" after dinner one of the virelays he had composed in her honor. Jean-Jacques was still too undiscerning or too artlessly egotistical to perceive the humiliation of Claude and the sorrow he concealed under his stern expression. He can at most have dimly suspected the sentiments to which that honest, straightforward fellow had recourse for comfort in a situation which to him was revolting. Jean-Jacques wrote: "Though Claude was not even as old as Madame de Warens, he considered us almost like children whom he might as well indulge." But none of us at twenty ever thinks that other people, in situations which we are enjoying and which give us confidence, may be suffering vexation or actual pain. With childish simplicity Jean-Jacques imagined that Claude was sharing in his own gratification. He went so far as to say: "All our hopes, our cares, our sympathies, were ours in common." Moreover, he certainly confused in his mind memories of his impressions of the time when Madame de Warens was Claude's mistress only, and those of the time when he and Jean-Jacques shared her favors.

This period lasted only three months. On March 13, 1734, Claude died, after an agonizing illness of five days. Jean-Jacques tells us that the trouble was pleurisy contracted on a walk which he took to gather artemisia on the very tops of the mountains. But the snow which shrouds the Alps at the end of winter is too heavy to allow of picking aromatic herbs. If Claude took cold, he did so in some other fashion, and on purpose; and it may be that as he had already drunk laudanum once, he simply took some poison which he knew would kill him.

CHAPTER VI

MADAME DE LARNAGE

THE death of Claude Anet upset the household arrangements of Madame de Warens at a time when that impractical woman, who always had numbers of irons in the fire, was planning to establish at Chambéry a "royal botanical garden," of which her major-domo would have been the official demonstrator, with a college of pharmacy in connection with it, where Jean-Jacques would have filled an important place. The latter was not only less competent than his rival, but he also lacked Claude's energy and his strength of purpose, qualities necessary to the head of an establishment. He was violently impatient, as well, of all domestic responsibilities. He had no head for business, and, being entirely helpless to cope with the financial difficulties of his patroness, could see nothing for it but to cut down on expenses. He was to terrified by the way money slipped through their fingers that he assumed the attitude of an overzealous watchdog, not only over her income, but also over his own, and thus he contracted (at least so he assures us) a miserly habit of mind which he could never afterwards shake off.

He was worried, no doubt, lest Madame de Warens's creditors deprive her even of the roof over her head, but if he really turned "mean," as he says he did, he certainly had other motives than "the high and noble purpose" of which he speaks—to save something for "Mamma" out of the ruin he foresaw. He was actuated by something more like an instinct for self-preservation. For instance, Claude was hardly in his grave before Jean-Jacques began to think about stepping into his fine clothes, particularly into a handsome black coat "which had dazzled him." So intense was his longing for the coat that he could not resist speaking about it to Madame de Warens, who shed copious tears. Since he confesses to such an exhibition of vulgar greed, I am not disposed to believe that when he began to conceal a few coins at a time here and there in odd corners, he was acting entirely from disinterested motives. However, it is no matter, for "Mamma" invariably discovered his hoard, and abstracted the gold, changing the coins for larger amounts in small change, and in the end the sum was always spent on him.

For some time "Mamma" went on petting him. She gave him his clothes, made him a present of a watch, and insisted on his accepting a sword with a silver handle so that he might wear the insignia of a gentleman as distinguished from one of the common herd. But their financial troubles grew more and more pressing and it came to the point where they lived simply from hand to mouth. Jean-Jacques, whose laziness did not prevent him from feeling ambitious and who now considered his position in Madame de Warens's house only a stepping stone, began to take thought for his future.

Our knowledge of his nature would play us false and we should be wronging him if we supposed that he disregarded his mistress in his plans. His pride must have been mortified by the thought that he was responsible for this woman twelve years his senior, but he must have suffered many hours of keen remorse and must have burned with the desire to repay magnanimously the debt he owed her. Thus, while there were times when he longed to be free of her, he anxiously considered how he could manage to provide for "Mamma" when she should be left without bread to eat. Sincerely, with his whole heart, he wished to avert her financial ruin, but all the same he looked forward to making his fortune only apart from her. He could see nothing but poverty ahead for them both as long as he stayed with her, and he cites his dread of poverty as his excuse when he caught himself, under the sway of his emotions and his senses, wishing fervently for his liberation. However, he was quickly disheartened by failure, for all his fertility in thinking up expedients, and readiness to evolve new plans out of the ruins of the old. So he had despondent moments when he reflected that the safer way for him would be to remain attached to his patroness. Then he conceived the idea of marrying her in order to bind his destiny to hers as closely as possible. In 1836 he wrote to his father that he was ready to regularize his situation in regard to his benefactress by bestowing his name on her. "So my plan is to implore Madame de Warens to let me spend the rest of my days in her company. We have already settled down together, and our establishment is certainly based on the most solid foundations and is the happiest in the world; for besides the advantages it offers me, it rests on kind-heartedness and character in both of us." But his proposal was unfortunately not received as he had hoped it would be. In spite of the fact that he told her he would soon be receiving a legacy from his mother, Suzanne Bernard, due to him on his majority, which, according to the laws of Geneva, was at the age of twenty-five, Madame de Warens did not appear overpleased by the honor he had done her, and went so far as to refuse him.

I think she was already beginning to grow tired either of him or of looking after him. She had seen him so long "flitting incessantly from one thing to another," restless, unstable, never able to decide what to try next in order to get out of his difficulties, that she finally began to think him a nuisance and to repent of having believed in his future. At his request, she gave him a couple of years more to complete his education before choosing a definite career.

Her relations with him, questionable as they were, had by this time been accepted and aroused no comment among her social acquaintances, even among the churchmen who came to her house. But when that period expired, she had some bitter arguments, running into disputes, with him, which invariably ended in a violent rupture. In anger or spite, he would flee from Chambéry, "for short trips to Nyon, Geneva, or Lyons, which helped him to forget his secret sorrow," but which, incidentally, aggravated its cause by involving him in further expense. After such outbreaks, his sermons to Madame de Warens on the subject of economy, and his rebukes because she could never refuse alms to those who came begging, were ill-advised. His discourses and his protestations of affection began to fail of their effect on her, and particularly to hold her for shorter periods. He might cast himself at her feet, cling to her, shedding tears while he covered her hand with kisses, but when she succumbed, it was not for long. She learned to recognize without difficulty the element of more or less conscious play-acting in these demonstrations, for which he drew emotional inspiration less from any devotion to her than from pity for himself. Little by little, as their relationship grew stale, she grew clearer-sighted. She saw perfectly that the spell of love was no longer the force which brought Jean-Jacques to his knees before her.

It must be kept in mind that her "little one" had become her lover without a spark of passion and that he had never adapted himself to the ways of this woman who took affairs of the kind so tranquilly. The *Confessions* leave no room for doubt in our minds that Jean-Jacques felt disappointed and hungry for an affinity, and they tell us in detail of the extent of his disappointment and of its effects. His indifference to his mistress increased, encouraged by her tendency to grow rapidly stouter, so that, from being plump, she became actually fat. "I was consumed by the need of love even in the lap of pleasure," he wrote. "I had a tender mother, a beloved friend, but what I wanted was a mistress."

His first attacks of uræmic poisoning helped to bring on disturbances, faintness, palpitations, dizzy fits, general exhaustion, and weakness of his limbs, which worried him greatly, and finally turned him into a hypochondriac. In vain he tried to seek outside distraction, resuming his former habit of taking long tramps, making acquaintances and forming friendships; his discomfort only increased, and with it his eccentricity. At the time he cannot have been so peculiar as to get himself disliked, for we know of a number of people who became deeply attached to him: Monsieur Gauffecourt, the son of a clock-maker of Geneva, himself a clock-maker for a while, who later made a great deal of money selling the Le Valais salts; Monsieur de Conzié, a gentleman of Savoy, of wide reading and general culture, who inspired Jean-Jacques with the ambition to imitate "Voltaire's highly colored style"; and Monsieur de la Closure, a Frenchman living in Geneva, who had known his mother and spoke feelingly of her to him two decades after her death.

He had, I repeat, the knack or the talent for enlisting the sympathetic interest of his auditors when he told them all his most intimate thoughts and feelings. Even his sensitive pride, which embittered him as he grew older but which at this time got the upper hand of him only on the occasions when Madame de Warens took him to task for his indolence, seemed to be mere shyness and charmed those who met him by the contrast between his usual manner and his outbursts of enthusiasm. He was not without justification, moreover, when he complained of the harshness of his fate and pictured it in moving terms. He had no fortune which would have enabled him, with his studious nature, to prepare himself either for the church or for the bar. He could hardly have gone even into trade without means to pay for his apprenticeship and to procure "a suitable amount of capital to set himself up properly." His father continued to neglect him and even tried to discourage Madame de Warens from helping him. He made a number of efforts to find for himself a way out of the deadlock, but each in turn came to nothing. After his plans for matrimony went awry, he wrote to his former patron, Monsieur de Bonac, to ask for a position, but he received no answer. Though he went on practising his music and believed he had a talent for it, he saw no future in it; and he did not feel that he was fitted for the practice of medicine to which "Mamma" would have liked him to devote himself, one of her great-grandfathers having been a doctor in Montpellier. What he really wanted was to become the secretary of some great lord or the tutor of a young nobleman, but he could not secure such a position without good fortune and time to spare.

He was making headway, as he puts it," in the good opinion of people of quality," but this was of no practical advantage to him. The fact was that though he thought he could do anything, he was fitted to do nothing. Incidentally, he had shown that he was incompetent to conduct a public concert, having been given the direction of one at Chambéry. He was trying to write, under the influence of Monsieur de Conzié, but was producing nothing very good; and though he was studying mathematics, he was combining with it the study of physics—needless to say, in a haphazard fashion.

His uncle Bernard died and Jean-Jacques went to Geneva to look over his papers. There he had a brief moment of believing that his luck had turned. He came upon a collection of documents whose possession flattered his self-importance and which he thought might be of practical use as well. There actually was a set of unedited memoirs disclosing state secrets, bequeathed by Micheli Ducret, a famous personage in Genevan history, to his grandfather, Pastor Bernard. In the enthusiasm of his find, he was so imprudent as to deposit it for safe-keeping with Monsieur Cocelli, director of the land office, who hastened to submit it to the Sardinian government for his own profit and glory. Jean-Jacques had never stopped to consider that he laid himself open to the charge of being a traitor to his country, any more than he had thought of the possibility that the man in whom he confided might betray him. He was fated to see no more of his documents. This last blow completely demoralized him, and it seems to have fallen at almost the very time when he proposed marriage to Madame de Warens and was humiliated by her rejection of him.

It is probable, in fact certain, in spite of the confusion of dates and events in the *Confessions* concerning this period, that he already suspected "Mamma" of having given him a rival, if not a substitute. Among the strangers who continually flocked from all quarters to see his patroness, he had noted in particular a tall, washed-out blond fellow with a good figure, "a flat face, and just as flat a mind," whose social status was that of a hairdresser and wigmaker, but who was cutting a figure as a gentleman and was calling himself Monsieur de Courtilles, after his native Swiss village. Before long the stupid ass, whose real name was Rudolph Wintzenried, settled all Jean-Jacques's doubts in regard to his degree of intimacy with Madame de Warens by treating him with insufferable insolence. Jean-Jacques no longer felt secure enough with "Mamma" to act the jealous lover and to require that she break with the usurper, who was, moreover, four years younger than he and remarkably powerful. So he only whined, acted abused, and asked her how far he was expected to carry his self-abnegation. According to him, it was not until later that

MADAME DE LARNAGE

Madame de Warens suggested that he share her favors with Wintzenried. But if, as he tells us, she actually declared that "he and she should remain on the same intimate footing" in spite of the addition of a third member to the group, and that he "would have the same rights as before," it must have been at the time we are considering. For though she was no longer in love with him, and though she was disappointed in him, she still at this period had a tender affection for him, and, above all, compassion. Moreover, she must have been touched by a recent impulse of his to make his will. He had been hurt, while he was attempting to manufacture "synthetic ink," by the explosion in his face of a bottle into which he had put an effervescent mixture. He thought he was going to die, and dictated his last testament, leaving almost everything he had to Madame de Warens. He bequeathed to her two thousand pounds in the coin of Savoy out of his share in his mother's inheritance—which turned out to be only sixty-five hundred florins.

However, he soon recovered and came into his legacy. But his health, instead of improving, grew worse and worse. He "fell a victim to a slow fever, and even had fits of coughing up blood." His illness was certainly a fact. His manner of life may have brought it on, and his bad habits may have aggravated it. But, such as it was, he played it up with a skill in which morbid enjoyment played some part, and when he found out that the hateful Wintzenried had stepped into his shoes, he had recourse to it. Nothing betrays the feminine side of his nature so entirely as all the unmanliness and trickery with which he cultivated his ailments for the sake of the effect he saw they produced on Madame de Warens. Her change of heart certainly caused him real grief, for even when a man has no further use for his mistress, he cannot without a pang see her in the arms of another; moreover, he trembled lest he lose together with "Mamma's" affection, which he still held dear, her support, which he still needed. His hysterical outbursts moved her. He wept and dragged himself at her feet, he sobbed until he lost his breath; he swore, between hiccoughs, that he loved her too much to disgrace her and that his love for her meant so much to him that he could not possibly share her with another.

"I shall always adore you; be worthy of my adoration. It is even more necessary to me to honor you than to have you for my own. For the sake of our hearts' union, I sacrifice all my delight. I would rather die a thousand deaths than have any joy which disgraces the thing I love."

How could she possibly turn out of her house an abject wretch who spoke with such eloquence and who raised her on so high a pedestal? Persuasion was the only method open to her for getting rid of him. But no man is so deaf as the one who will not listen.

Jean-Jacques was perfectly aware that "Mamma," however indifferent or even antagonistic she might be to his arguments, must weaken when he wept, and that she lost her head completely if he went into convulsions. So I feel quite certain that he was seized with the serious illness of which he speaks at the end of Book V of his *Confessions* immediately after he learned of the misfortune which had befallen him. Madame de Warens nursed him to the end of it with care such as "no mother ever gave to any child." The fright he had received when he awoke to the danger that hung over him was so severe that he would have been a fool not to take measures to strengthen his position. He seized on the shock he had had as a pretext for appearing stricken, with one foot in the grave. Instead of taking to flight, as he had formerly done, he now never set foot out of the gloomy Chambéry house, and whenever he was not confined to his own room, he flitted like a ghost, wan and unkempt, from chamber to chamber, heaving deep sighs.

He does not say what medicines "Mamma" administered to him, but spares us no details of the course of mental and emotional treatment through which she put him, or which he contrived to have her give him. He writes in all seriousness: "I have little confidence in the remedies prescribed by physicians, but I have a great deal in those of one's good friends." We cannot suppress some amusement, in spite of the compassion we must feel for his misery, when we learn the whole truth about the treatment which, according to him, saved his life. It consisted of lamentations on his part, uttered not only through the daylight hours, but prolonged far into the night. He often rose from his couch, on which he had been tossing in anxious wakefulness, and tottered in the darkness to Madame de Warens. He would wake her up, sit down on her bed, and take her hands in his, holding them sometimes till dawn to comfort himself and quiet the gnawing care which his affairs were causing him. Meanwhile he poured advice into her ears,—advice, he assures us, full of practical wisdom and common sense—as to her behavior when he should be no more, for he never got away from the thought of his untimely death. He found in it material which he could elaborate so that no woman could remain unmoved, and which drew from him the tears with which he "flooded" the breast of Madame de Warens, as a substitute for his caresses. His health improved only after he had received definite assurance that she had no mind to be rid of him and was resolved to let him take his own time in choosing how he should earn his living.

Once he had recovered his peace of mind, his bladder began again to function properly. For his condition was not entirely mean pretense, and I have misled the reader if I have so implied. It is no simple matter to pass judgment on a man of his temperament, in whom imagination works to raise mountains out of molehills and to distort his vision, deceiving him first and foremost and making him suffer tortures whenever he has to say he has a pain. He became the mere shadow of his former self, poisoned as he was by uræmia and exhausted by the insomnia which he had at first, to be sure, induced by artificial means but on which his anxieties and his horror of the dark soon began to work in earnest.

His constitution was naturally sound but had never been robust. The strain he put on his nerves in acting out his heart-rending scenes ended by breaking him down. His ill health, originating with his nerves, then reacted on his nerves again, in a vicious circle. To make matters worse, he undertook at this time to please "Mamma," who again conceived the idea of making a physician of him, by plunging into the study of anatomy and by reading all sorts of books on physiology. He thus discovered that he had every known ailment and detected with despair the symptoms of each one. He got to the point, only a short time after he had boasted that he disregarded all medical prescriptions, of dieting, of taking the milk cure, and finally the water cure. He drank a large glass of water the first thing every morning, and during his walk he took the equivalent of two bottles. The water was from a mountain stream, "somewhat hard and difficult to assimilate." It upset his stomach, which had hitherto been strong; at least he thought it did, and that sufficed to set up gastric troubles. Doubtless he had a slight inherited tendency to gout; but he fell a victim not to it, but to acute neurasthenia, which followed in the wake of the chronic poisoning of his system. Of this disease he developed all the symptoms, even to the throbbing arteries which one morning deafened him and threw him into a panic. He grew melancholy, preoccupied, and apprehensive. Some distraction was necessary for him. Before he obtained it, he came to the conclusion that he certainly had a tumor of the heart; and from that moment he thought of nothing else except the possibility of discovering some method of cure. No peace of mind could he find until he should embark on this marvelous cure.

Up to this point I have said nothing of Les Charmettes, though Jean-Jacques says that his health broke down at the end of his first visit to that delightful spot, to which disciples of Rousseau have made many a pilgrimage. I have traced his history thus far through the summer of 1737, and the move to Les Charmettes was not made until July 6, 1738, two years after the date given for it in the *Confessions*. Madame de Warens, at the time we have been describing, was carrying on negotiations for the lease of the Anne Révil farm, acting on the advice of Wintzenried, who was now helping her to manage her affairs, and she was about to sign the contract before a notary. Possibly Jean-Jacques had already suggested that country air might be good for his health, but another plan was proposed for him. "Mamma" remembered that Claude Anet, during a trip to Montpellier, had once been told that Monsieur Fizes had cured a tumor. Wintzenried kept urging her to seize the opportunity to rid herself of her encumbrance, so she pressed Jean-Jacques to betake himself thither, the town being at that time a perfect hive of famous doctors. He himself rashly states—and his statement proves that the events of which I speak did not take place until 1738, even if we were not sure of the fact from his correspondence— that he still had a few crowns left of his mother's inheritance after having paid his debts. He was divided in his mind whether or no to make way for his fortunate rival and to go in search of health. Eventually his dread of his malady overcame his spite and his anger; and he was desirous, too, impelled by his secret instinct, to go a-roving again, to taste the pleasures of freedom, change of scene, and adventures. Madame de Warens promised not to forget him and to send him more money when his funds should be exhausted. He could take his own time and stay as long as he thought necessary.

So he left on September 2nd, riding a horse in order to demonstrate to that great oaf of a Wintzenried that he was good as anybody else. But he could not ride long without exhaustion, so, in spite of his keen enjoyment of the landscape where the valley of the Isère turns about the foot of the Rock of the Grande Chartreuse, he took the post chaise from Grenoble on. When he reached the Dauphiné capital, on the 13th, Monsieur de Voltaire's *Alzire* was being played. Monsieur de Conzié had opened his eyes to the grand style of that author, and he succumbed to the desire to see the tragedy. It threw him into ecstasies and was very bad for his heart. He wrote to "Mamma" about it, and "Mamma" must have felt that he was being very extravagant. But he asked about her health, begging her to take good care of herself, and he got in a thrust at Wintzenried: "Madame, why are some souls so sensitive to grandeur and sublimity while others seem fit only to wallow in their own base emotions?"

He did not, however, reach Montpellier on the evening of September 18th, as he had notified his patroness that he would. Far from it. At Moirans, just outside the gates of Grenoble, only five leagues away, he fell in with the party of a young married woman, Madame du Colombier, and dazzled the eyes of one of her friends, Madame de Larnage. The incident, trivial as it appeared at the time, delayed him considerably. To take his own statement at its face value, the young bride herself was deterred from making up to him only because she already had too many curs after her and, particularly, because she was not going much further. In any case, she handed him over to Madame de Larnage, a lady who could have been neither young nor beautiful, since she was born in 1693, and must consequently have been close to the ripe of age of forty-four; hence she was less "besieged" by suitors than her friend.

Jean-Jacques wrote: "My natural shyness interfered with my scraping acquaintance with women of fashion and their escorts, but, traveling along the same road, stopping at the same inns, and necessarily, unless I wanted to be taken for a surly boor, appearing at the same table, I eventually had to make their acquaintance." No doubt he did his part, that is to say, he made himself look interesting, even if he left to Madame de Larnage the delicate task of making the first advances. To that robust woman he could have made no stronger appeal than by appearing as an invalid. When he spoke to her of his health, his eyes burned with the consciousness of his secret suffering. He expressed gratification that she liked him as he was, enfeebled, feverish, and hysterical—he had a tumor! She realized perfectly, however, that he was far from being as ill as he claimed to be. As soon as she began to pay some attention to him, he felt better, and let her see that he did. All his troubles vanished in her company "except some palpitations of the heart," of which she declined to undertake the cure.

One morning when they stopped to change horses, Madame du Colombier continuing to travel with her friend as far as Romans on the Valence slope, the ladies sent to ask how he was and invited him to take a cup of chocolate with them. They inquired how he had spent the night, and it happened that he answered in a distraught manner that he did not know. This made them think he was out of his mind. They examined him in more detail, and as the results of the examination were favorable, they came to the conclusion that he was merely eccentric. He overheard Madame du Colombier say to Madame de Larnage: "He is a queer fellow, but likable." From that moment he set out to prove that he was just that.

Unfortunately there was in their train a Marquis de Taulignan, not de Torignan, as the name is erroneously written in the *Confessions*. His presence was a constant source of annoyance to Jean-Jacques. He was a sickly old nobleman, who, if he was not actually paying court to Madame du Colombier and Madame de Larnage, was at least extremely attentive to them. He became inquisitive about the manners of this young boy whom his traveling companions seemed to be liking better and better, and took it into his head to make him talk about himself with the egotism of his youth, thinking to have a little fun at his expense.

Jean-Jacques was afraid of letting it be known that he was a convert, which might work to his disadvantage, and he did not care to be questioned. He gave out that he was an English Jacobite named Dudding. It must be noted that he could not speak a word of the English language and knew nothing of the people except what he had read in Hamilton and the gazettes, and in Voltaire's Philosophical Letters, whose spicy flavor he had learned to enjoy through Monsieur de Conzié. He was acting in a highly characteristic manner, with his passion for prevarication, his extravagant ostentation, and his need of complications; for he was running a huge risk of being caught and unmasked. The Marquis may have been as clever as the average man, with fair opportunities, but he cannot have been astute. He showed no surprise that Jean-Jacques spoke French with so little accent, and he talked to him about King James and the former court at Saint-Germain, carrying on the conversation mostly by himself.

Madame de Larnage, undeterred by her friend's presence, had continued the pursuit of Jean-Jacques or Mr. Dudding. But when Madame du Colombier finally bade her good-bye, she began to pay him her addresses with so much more coquetry than before that our novice, constrained by that shyness which is the extreme form of conceit, imagined she was making fun of him. He was so afraid of making himself ridiculous that he committed every possible blunder; and he would have discouraged any less experienced woman than the one he was dealing with, or any one less resolute on indulging her whim. The more Madame de Larnage complimented and coaxed him, the more firmly he believed that she was in league with Monsieur de Taulignan to lead him on. He made no response to her insinuations, though he hinted that he would have been overjoyed if he could believe she was inspired by any other motive than mischief. Confident of her charm, she grew more eager for the hunt, instead of being rebuffed by his resistance, of which she understood the motives and which she would not have heeded in any case except to keep an eye out for the first chance she could see or could make to overcome it.

The chance was not long in coming. Jean-Jacques has given us a detailed account of the culmination of his pursuit by Madame de Larnage. He ended by completely succumbing. He had amends to make, and he felt it was a point of honor to make them in full. Vaingloriously he declares that though it cost Madame de Larnage some trouble to bring him to heel, at least he gave her no cause to regret it. Nor had he on his part any complaints to make of her. He steeped himself in his affair with her; his rapture was undiluted and intense, disturbed by no haunting anxieties.

The understanding between Madame de Larnage and Mr. Dudding did not escape the eyes of the Marquis. But he was too polished a gentleman to act otherwise than as if he observed nothing. He pretended still to see in the young Englishman an abject suitor, and stubbornly persisted in his gibes, all in perfect taste. Jean-Jacques, after he had obtained the fulfillment of his hopes, and especially after he began to think that Monsieur de Taulignan gave him credit for having some intelligence, took the old fellow's pithy thrusts in good part. Occasionally he even returned the attack so neatly that Madame de Larnage felt justified in her good opinion of him.

The Marquis had assumed the responsibility for ordering their meals, and as they were traveling through a rich district at a good time of year, they fared exceedingly well. They would have been just as well pleased if Monsieur de Taulignan had kept his hands off the details of their accommodations at the inns, and had not always sent his lackey ahead for reservations. But his officiousness could not prevent them from keeping their trysts, and since they knew they risked nothing very serious even if they were by chance detected, they got more excitement out of their carefully planned reunions for all the difficulties they had to surmount and the secrecy they had to preserve. It was altogether delightful. However, it became even more so after the Marquis left them, a little before they reached Montélimar. Once free from his supervision, which, though it interfered with them so little, still kept them on their guard, the couple cast all restraint to the winds. Madame de Larange put her maid into Jean-Jacques's carriage and took him in with her. Then the days passed in joyous endearments, clasping of hands, caresses, heartfelt sighs, and kisses often prolonged far beyond the bounds of wisdom. These demonstrations distracted the attention of Jean-Jacques from the landscape, in which he would have found a tranquilizing interest, and excited his sensibilities to the highest pitch. In spite of the care of himself which Madame de Larnage enforced on her lover, he was laid low near Montélimar, with a serious attack of nervous exhaustion.

It was time for them to separate. Madame de Larnage knew how to do things properly, and as she judged by the way he traveled that the little Englishman was none too well off, she offered to divide the contents of her purse with him. He declined to be paid for his adventure—at least he assures us that he did; and I can believe him, for it is plain from the tone of his letters to Madame de Warens that he was pressed for money.

He left Madame de Larnage at the Pont du Saint-Esprit, between Montélimar and the town of Saint-Andéol, where she lived. She made him promise to rejoin her there after staying five or six weeks at Montpellier, so that she might have time to "get things ready," in order to "get ahead of the gossips." Jean-Jacques, whom she urged to observe minutely all the doctors' orders, was to complete his convalescence at her side; that is, he was to spend the winter with her. But he must have been seized with panic at the thought. Moreover, a craving for rest and peace made him averse to such a plan from the beginning, and he doubtless had a vague consciousness of something in himself whose conservation was worth the sacrifice of all worldly pleasures. Moreover, he was, like many abnormal intellectuals, frightened by the prospect of happiness and prone to make mountains, in their imaginations, of the duties and even of the efforts which it involves and which tie them down in bondage.

He had hardly settled at Montpellier, in the house of a Monsieur Barcellon, doorkeeper of the stock exchange, in the Rue Basse, when he began to have a very bad time indeed. To be sure, he gives us quite a different version of the story in the *Confessions*, where he says he lived like a son of the house in the family of an Irish doctor named Fitz-Moris, who "boarded a fairly large number of medical students." But his letters are extant to prove that he lied. They show that he was harassed because he had no money to pay his board or even his room rent; he borrowed, and pleaded with "Mamma" to send him directly the sum, two hundred pounds, which she had been kind enough to promise him.

What had come over her that she had been a month without letting him have any news of her? He feared the worst, and, suddenly perceiving his helplessness, clutched at the idea of returning to his old place beside his patroness. She had suggested that he enter the service of Monsieur de Lautrec, but, however promising might be the position that she wanted to secure for him, he could think only of the fact that she wanted to be rid of him.

"Oh, my beloved Mamma!" he writes. "I would rather be with D" (possibly *Vous*, you, abbreviated to *Vs* and looking like D, or possibly standing for *De* Courtilles), "doing the roughest farm labor, than be the possessor of the greatest fortune on any other terms. It is useless to think that I can live otherwise; I told you so long ago, and I feel it now more strongly than ever. If I can have that one benefit, I care about nothing else. To anyone of my way of thinking, I believe there can be no difficulty in getting around the important reasons you are unwilling to tell me. For heaven's sake, arrange matters so that I need not die in despair. I authorize anything and subscribe to anything, except to the one condition to which it is out of my power to consent, even though I should bring down on my head the most miserable of fates. Oh, dear Mamma! Are you no longer my dear Mamma? Have I lived just a few months too long?"

Evidently he was willing to accept any terms, even to put himself in the most humiliating position in regard to his successor, if only he might be received at Chambéry. If he really intended, as he notified Madame de Warens he did, to go for a short time to a charming little village two leagues from the Pont du Saint-Esprit to drink asses' milk, he gave up the plan almost at once. The dread of

Madame de Larnage was uppermost in his mind. A word from her that she would be ready to welcome him after Christmas would have been enough to send him posthaste over the Alps.

In view of his letter to Madame de Warens, we must consider as a mere literary effort the analysis which appears in the *Confessions* of his struggle with his conscience, which took place as he was leaving Montpellier. The struggle ended in his passing Bourg Saint-Andéol without a pause. He had certainly been corresponding with Madame de Larnage, but before he ever turned his back on Montpellier he had definitely made up his mind never to set foot in her house. Of the many reasons he states for his strong-minded decision, only two stick in my memory. The first is that he was afraid there might be someone in the lady's circle who knew English and who would enlighten her concerning his imposture. The second and stronger was that he was tired. He had doubtless imagined what life at Saint-Andéol would be like, and, dreaming on, as he always did, had taken into account that the daughter of his mistress, a girl of fifteen, might become infatuated with him and might find favor in his sight. As to the scruples with which he credits himself, they are too ingenious not to have been invented as afterthoughts. We are by now too well acquainted with Jean-Jacques to suppose that he would have resigned himself to a sacrifice for fear of compromising Madame de Larnage or of wreaking havoc in her family by seducing her daughter. When he preens himself on having carried off a victory over his own temptations, he looks very much like a man running away from a defeat.

CHAPTER VII

LES CHARMETTES

JEAN-JACQUES could hardly have returned from Montpellier with restored health for the excellent reason that no practitioner could have cured him of a nonexistent tumor. Moreover, he had languished in the town, which he thought dull and inhospitable, and where he had fared very ill, eating only bad mutton and fish cooked in evil-smelling oil; and where his lack of funds had precluded him from taking any proper course of treatment. The air, too, was too low and, as he said, full of "sharp, salty particles," so that it had not agreed with him. Consequently, when he returned to Chambéry, "Mamma" saw that he looked far from robust; and this was fortunate for him, because if her heart had not been touched by compassion, he would hardly have received even the chilly welcome he got.

"So there you are, Little One," said Madame de Warens, greeting him with a light and perfunctory kiss. "Did you have a good trip? How are you?"

He was given no credit, rather the reverse, for the speed with which he had traveled. Though he had been careful to announce the date of his return, he was given to understand that he had not been expected so soon. Wintzenried was there and had no scruples about letting him see that he was not wanted. So Jean-Jacques ate humble pie, and though he made himself out to be more ill than he actually was, he offered his services to "Mamma" and to Wintzenried, asking of the latter nothing but to be allowed to call him brother. Having already shown that he could do a secretary's work efficiently, and having perfected himself at Montpellier in mathematics, he saw no reason why Madame de Warens should not hand over to him the administration of at least some of her affairs. His wants were simple, as she knew. If she would only let him have a room in the farmhouse on the estate she had rented just outside of Chambéry, he could manage to live there on practically nothing, that is, on bread and salads.

His submissive manner touched "Mamma" and softened even Wintzenried's hard heart, so it was agreed without difficulty that he should settle early the following spring out at the Révil farm. However, when the time came, he departed to spend his exile, like a fallen monarch, not on that little property, which Madame de Warens was farming on lease and which was proving a costly venture, but at Les Charmettes. He owed the change of plan to an arrangement between "Mamma" and her neighbor, Pierre Renauld, made in June, 1738.

The famous retreat is so generally known as hardly to require description. There is an isolated house, "white with green shutters," on the slope of a dell; in front, a terraced garden; above, a vineyard, and below, an orchard; opposite, a small chestnut wood; a spring not far off; higher up on the mountain, meadows to pasture the herd of cattle, which consisted of two oxen, some cows, and a few sheep. The aspect of the place has changed very little since it harbored Jean-Jacques. The stony road ascending to the house between oaks and birches is the same that Madame de Warens mounted in her sedan chair. Only the slate roof has bleached, and the wistaria vine which suspends its purple clusters in summer over the lintel of the door, approached by a flight of six broad steps, has a knottier trunk now than then.

We may discount as mere fiction much of the idyllic legend which has drawn tears of sentiment from such different individuals as Francis Jammes, the Christian, and the pagan-souled Countess de Noailles, but there is no doubt whatever that Jean-Jacques tasted real happiness at Les Charmettes. He quickly adapted himself to "Mamma's" increasing coldness, for he had learned from Madame de Larnage that no man can hope to influence any woman, whoever she may be, except in proportion to the homage he pays her charms; and if his neglect of her arouses her resentment, it is less because she misses his attentions than because she is offended by his indifference to her love. He knew perfectly well that any effort he could make to sway "Mamma's" mind would be useless. He contented himself with the glow of tender emotion he felt when he saw her and the feeling of security which her presence gave him. Large and heavy as she had become, all the mystery of her being unsealed to him, he came to look on her truly in the light of a mother; a mother, to be sure, who neglected him and treated him somewhat as if he were a backward child, showing him indulgence tinged with resignation, if not with actual scorn, for he was past the age when sons are wont to be tied to apron-strings. But he could afford to endure injustice from her if she pleased to mete it out, and misunderstanding too; for by giving him cause for complaint, she still let him enjoy "the somber pleasures of a disconsolate heart."

Though he continued to be anxious concerning his future, his uneasiness was swept away in the floods of ecstasy which filled his heart at finding himself alone in communion with nature. "I had longed for the open country: I had it. Submission had been hateful to me: I was free as air. I rose with the sun, and I rejoiced. I went out into the open, and I rejoiced. I wandered in the woods and over the slopes. I strayed in the dells; I read and idled; I worked in the garden, and I gathered the fruits."

He came into his own, taking definite stock of himself,

perhaps achieving the process of molding his own personality and giving it the last touches. On the stem of his sensitive nature, refined by Madame de Warens, he grafted the misanthropy which became, as he grew older, increasingly bitter and savage. Monsieur de Conzié, who was his neighbor and who at that time went to see him nearly every day, was struck by his innate scorn of men and by his "persistent tendency to inveigh against their faults and weaknesses." The hurts which his vanity and his sensitiveness had suffered threw him back on himself or made him draw in his tentacles, though he continued to crave affection with an intensity which made him rave of it. Within the limits of the universe in which imagination holds sway, his knew no bounds. As he said: "All the grand passions are formed in solitude."

His own were never in any way trammeled at Les Charmettes, nor was his one overwhelming passion which included all his others. His happiness came from "nothing definable"; it was all within himself. In consequence, it was always with him, and he found, often subconsciously, inspiration for raptures in things of the meanest aspect. An anecdote in Book VI of the *Confessions* illustrates this point admirably. Madame de Warens, as she walked one July morning toward her country house, pointed out to Jean-Jacques "some periwinkle still in bloom" under a hedge. He paid little heed; but more than twenty-five years later, when he was botanizing at Cressier with his friend Peyrou, the sight of a pale blue blossom under a bush drew from him a joyous cry: "Oh! See the periwinkle!" His subconscious mind had retained in all its freshness his memory of that happy day when he walked with "Mamma" up the slope to the little hamlet of Les Charmettes.

The simple and monotonous tone of the happiness of his daily life was in accord with its ineffable character. No incidents or actions of his can be cited to illustrate it, much less to describe it. It consisted of sensuous experiences. The transports of emotion which interrupted the even tenor of the pleasant hours sprang from no other source than the whims of his emotional nature, to which he had entirely abandoned himself. Understanding his state of mind, one sees why he passed so easily over Wintzenried's scorn and insolence. On one occasion, after he had forgotten himself in the course of a dispute and made a rude remark which angered Madame de Warens, he wrote to her: "My beloved Mamma, I duly received the letter you wrote me last Sunday, and I have arrived at the honest conclusion that since you think me in the wrong, I must be so. Consequently I made no attempt at evasion and begged my brother's pardon with all my heart, and here I likewise most humbly beg yours. I assure you, too, that I have resolved always to turn to good account whatever rebukes you think fit to give me, whatever tone you choose to employ."

No one could appear better disposed or more docile. Of course he had to adapt his actions to the rôle of parasite he was playing—for since he had ceased to be the lover of Madame de Warens, one can hardly speak in other terms of his acceptance of her hospitality. If he fulfilled any secretarial duties whatever, he did so only at long intervals and in matters which required rather tactful handling. For instance, he was responsible for trying to collect money from her creditors, the Sourgels, to whom she had advanced sums borrowed at a high rate of interest, and he assisted her in drawing up a memorandum addressed to the governor-general of Savoy in which she petitioned a pension from the King. Wintzenried, who specialized in manual labor and supervised the "plowing, hay-making, stable-work, and poultry-tending," must have been well enough pleased to see Jean-Jacques struggling with the memorandum. No doubt he made pretexts to enter the room where the pedantic fellow he scorned was laboring to polish up his touching appeals, and listened with amusement to Jean-Jacques while he dilated on his own feeble health, his exemplary behavior, and the boundless charity of his patroness.

Sad indeed it is that Jean-Jacques had to purchase the tranquillity he needed at the price of such petty tribulations. His happiness may not have suffered from them, but his character was certainly corrupted and degraded. Because of them he became the mixture of hypocrisy and cynicism which was to make him the Tartufe-Diogenes combination that he was: one who, in accordance with a tendency already noted, came to consider his good intentions as good deeds, or to imagine that he had only to dwell with appreciation on the abstract idea of justice in order to announce himself a just man. We have already heard him priding himself on the delicacy of his feeling because he declined to share the favors of Madame de Warens with Wintzenried after he had already shown no scruples about supplementing Claude Anet. He had talked about sacrificing his pleasure to his duty, when out of prudence he left Madame de Larnage. Now we may hear him stating that the noble qualities already latent in him were stimulated by his troubles and first began to sprout at Les Charmettes—qualities "which had been nurtured in study and which needed only the leaven of adversity to begin to work." "The first fruit of that highly altruistic mood," he wrote, "was that I purged my heart of all hatred and envy against the man who had supplanted me. I wished sincerely to grow fond of that young man, to improve him, to labor over his education, to show him his good fortune, and to make him worthy of it if such a thing were possible."

Note the qualifying clause, and also the vanity with

which in his own mind he was attributing to forbearance his resignation to the affronts he had to suffer from Madame de Warens's new lover. But no doubt he had too accurate an understanding of Wintzenried to grant him any indulgence. He forgot none of the humiliations he suffered on Wintzenried's account, not even the painful experience, which made him boil inwardly, of being obliged to watch him sawing or chopping wood. He probably would have loved and embraced with warmth, every day of his life, the idealized being whom he constructed for himself in his mind without reference to the original, and whom he secretly continued to labor with, if that image had been substituted for the boisterous flesh-and-blood youth whose presence filled the house with sound and nonsense. But his resentment and irritation always got the better of his intentions. It pained him to see himself passed over in favor of a lout to whom his wisest and deepest speeches were "babble," and when he sought consolation by calling him "Taleralatalera," the harmless nickname concealed but ill the antipathy behind it.

The thing which exasperated Jean-Jacques and hurt him most cruelly was to see that Wintzenried succeeded by brutality where he had failed by gentleness. "Mamma" had ears only for the churl who, not content with flying out at her in rages, was quite capable of treating her roughly, and deceived her by having an affair with a slut of a servant, "an old red-headed thing with no teeth." However, I repeat, the "little one" got a bitter enjoyment out of his sorrows, would have lacked zest in life if he had been relieved of them, and cut a finer figure in his own estimation by thinking of himself as a kind of victim, if not as a martyr. Moreover, he had periods of respite from the torture of association with the man he hated. He spent the long winter months entirely alone at Les Charmettes, and though he complained to "Mamma" even before the return of spring that she was a long time coming, he still had occasional conversations with her at intervals, particularly on matters of religious belief, either early, in her own room, whither he went to wish her a chaste good-morning while Wintzenried was out looking over the stable or plowing; or after their noon dinner, when they had drunk their coffee in a bower of greenery behind the house, and he joined her in her survey of the flower-beds and the vegetable garden. He had made an effort to do out-of-door work like the others but was not robust enough, losing his breath at the least exertion, and he had to come down to taking care of the dove-cote and the bee-hives. But he was present at the vintage, if he did not take an active part in it, and it made a strong impression on him, as we can see from the descriptive passages of *La nouvelle Héloïse*.

On the whole, the life he was leading suited him physically, particularly after he gave up the diet which weakened him and again began to eat meat and to drink wine. He was up every day at break of dawn, followed a pretty footpath to the top of the hill, and said his prayers as he walked. He never said the same prayer twice, but composed it in accordance with his state of mind and his emotional mood of the moment, confessing his faith with more profusion of eloquence than lyrical inspiration. We must do him the justice to admit that the burden of them was praise to God on high, and that he pleaded less for favors than for virtue to make himself a worthy recipient of favors.

When he reached the crest of the rise, he stopped to gaze with delight never dulled by familiarity over the beautiful prospect which lay before him—the Alps, the Lake of Bourget, and the valley, a tossing sea of green. He filled his lungs with delicious air; then, after a few moments of peaceful meditation, he returned by a rather circuitous route for his breakfast. He particularly enjoyed the frugal morning meal, and would have taken even greater pleasure in it if he had not been obliged to put up with Wintzenried's sarcastic speeches and clumsy jokes. He finally reached his room, next to "Mamma's," on the second floor. There he studied until nearly noon; then, when he had dined and taken a little stroll, he returned to his beloved studies. But as he was a heavy eater and his digestion was sluggish, he worked without zest in the afternoons, attempting little except to entertain himself. He seized upon any sort of pretext to leave his books —a visit from Monsieur de Conzié, or one from Monsieur Salomon, his doctor and Madame de Warens's, "a fine man and intelligent, a devoted disciple of Descartes." He derived more benefit from this man's agreeable and informative conversation than from his prescriptions.

Once in a while "Mamma" expressed a wish to walk a little in the country in order to work off some of the excess flesh which she continued to gain; and he went with her, from hill to hill, from forest to forest, bordering the swift brooks. The breeze blew fresh, the air was clear, no clouds barred the horizon. They returned to the subjects they had been discussing early that morning or in the course of the preceding day—the Supreme Being, the life after death. There is no doubt that in this interchange of ideas with his benefactress the deism or natural religion of Jean-Jacques was strengthened and crystallized. "Mamma" was far from orthodox in her beliefs—how could she have been, when her manner of life necessitated for her the existence of a God merciful to sinners? Her God may have been a just God, but He was not one to condemn without remission of sins. In her opinion He did enough when He created Purgatory on the other side of Heaven, and there was no need of His having created Hell besides. She subscribed to the doctrines of the Church but lent faith only to those which suited her individually.

The statement cannot be definitely made that Jean-Jacques modified his religious ideas under the influence of Madame de Warens. Say rather that he became aware of the beliefs he was elaborating for himself when he put them into words and discussed them with this woman, who was, to be sure, loose in her morals, but was intelligent, and who had read and meditated. At Turin he had been affected by the beauty of the Catholic ritual as he followed it in the Royal Chapel, and a short time before he went to stay at Les Charmettes, when he thought his life in danger, he had solemnly testified in writing to his faith in the Holy Apostolic and Roman Church. He believed in miracles and was terrified by the thought not only of death, but also of that Hell whose existence "Mamma" denied—or tried to deny, if it is true, as Monsieur de Conzié said, that to speak of it gave her "goose-flesh."

He saturated himself with the writings of the Port-Royal group, and was continually preoccupied with the problem of grace, wondering: "In what state am I? If I died at this moment, would I be damned?" According to the Jansenist doctrines, there was no question but that he would, yet it seemed to him that according to his own conscience he would not. To relieve his doubts, he resorted to expedients of the kind conceived by superstitious souls, which may conduce to madness. For instance, one day he cast a stone towards a tree, saying to himself: "If I hit it, that is a sign that I am saved; if I miss, it is a sign of damnation." He hit it fair and square, though it must be admitted that he had chosen a very large tree and had stealthily approached very close to it before he threw the stone—and so he felt that he would be saved.

At the same time his terrors were calmed by interviews with Jesuits, particularly with Father Hermet, a "good and wise old man," who used to come to Les Charmettes to see him, and also by the reading of books in which "piety and scientific knowledge" were combined. These books, to be sure, offered him little that was consonant with his general state of mind, at that time a sort of tranquil languor. He had an odd lot of second-hand books, purchased at Chambéry from a bookseller named Bouchard, patronized by a number of men of letters, and he was also free to use the library of Monsieur de Conzié, consisting of no fewer than twenty-five hundred volumes. It included every kind of work, even treatises on the art of warfare, but books on literature and history predominated, mixed in with books on religious doctrine, agriculture, physics, and chemistry. Jean-Jacques conceived the ambitious idea of mastering all human knowledge, and in order to realize it he began by trying to amass the general information presupposed in the reading of one serious work. He soon saw, however, that he was on the wrong track; for, turning of necessity first to one reference and then to another, he wasted an infinite amount of time and lost himself in an endless labyrinth. All his thoughts became confused and conflicted with one another, so in fatigue and discouragement he made the wise decision to systematize his study. Being a man of his time, it goes without saying that he steered his way with the help of Chambers's Encyclopædia. Though the rule of study he adopted was still far from having any real method in it, he continued his education, from that time on, to some purpose, delving separately into the different branches of knowledge. However, he developed no exclusive devotion to any one subject. He was not capable of doing so. Steady concentration prolonged for any period of time wearied him so that he felt dizzy if he worked more than half an hour on the same thing, "especially following any other man's trend of thought." He had to renew his interest or refresh his mind by changing its preoccupation, and

LES CHARMETTES

so he turned from one subject to another, not without seeking other distractions meanwhile out of doors or in the bosom of his circle.

He assimilated his learning in a passive intellectual spirit. In his first attempts to tackle them all head on, he had felt stirrings of a desire to reconcile the different philosophical systems of Locke, Malebranche, Leibnitz, and Descartes, but here again he became convinced of the folly of his undertaking, and he then set to work to assimilate them all as completely as possible without comparing or questioning them, "almost without reasoning." For nearly five years he went on gorging his mind with different, often contradictory ideas. He made a sponge of himself and soaked up everything. But if one considers the feminine quality of his genius, one need not be at all surprised at such assimilativeness marked by no intellectual reaction. Indeed, it is hard to see, in spite of his all-embracing quest of knowledge—or rather because of it—that any virile thinking guided his learning. He said: "I was eager to absorb ideas about everything, partly to feel out my natural inclinations, and partly to put myself in a position to judge what was best worth cultivating." He made no effort to strengthen or to establish by proofs any truth, or what he thought was a truth—keeping in mind that he might have to modify it later. He did not collect any arguments in its favor. He was laying up a store for the future, without knowing what that future was to be. But his emotional nature, distrusting its own weakness, needed reasoned foundations as material for the specious speculations which it would embark on when the fever came upon him. I might put it that he was preparing culture-beds in which any stray germ might find an excellent foothold, to bring forth a swarm of sophisms and paradoxes.

Nevertheless, he was, of course, unconsciously swayed

by some theories rather than by others. Incidentally, the thinkers who made the strongest impression on him were not the most vigorous, but those who conformed best to his own vague aspirations or unconfessed tendencies. To understand his intellect aright, it is essential to know that he studied the natural sciences, as I have said, in the works of authors who subordinated them to religion or who were most skeptical of their results, pointing out their lapses and denouncing their contradictions, revealing their incapacity to see through the veil of mystery which enshrouds our being.

Pierre-Maurice Masson discerned clearly that Father Lamey touched a weak spot in Rousseau's Catholicism, already tending to run into rationalism and later transformed by slow degrees into theism, when he taught him to "look toward God in his studies, and study only for the purpose of knowing and serving Him"; that Le Maître de Clairville found a response in Rousseau's own love of country things when he preached that man can find no happiness except by withdrawing into himself, and can attain wisdom and virtue only in the solitude of the fields; that the Marquis of Saint-Aubin consoled him for his incapacity to grasp the experimental sciences when he demonstrated their hollowness to him; and that finally Rousseau was comforting his own soul, bitter in the consciousness that he was a parasite, when he affirmed that "the happy equality and simplicity of primitive times were vastly preferable to the tyranny of money which weighs upon us." This last author also awakened in him memories of the reading he had done, some time since at Annecy, in the works of Samuel Pufendorf, a German pamphleteer, who was thoroughly imbued with the doctrines of Grotius and who pleaded for the natural rights of man.

But to realize how heterogeneous was the reading of

Jean-Jacques in his retreat, one must look at the very poor poem he composed under the title of *Le verger des Charmettes*. He must surely have been consumed by the love of study, or else have been driven on to pursue it by an impelling inner voice, not to have weakened a hundred times in face of the task he had set himself. Besides the handicap of an unstable temperament, he had that of a poor memory. Not only was he prone to drop off into reveries, and so absent-minded that he was capable of leaving under a tree or on a bench, where it rotted away, the book he had taken out into the garden, but he also found it impossible to make anything stick in his mind without the most laborious efforts. Even his persistence could not overcome this difficulty, and he no sooner committed to memory the *Eclogues* of Virgil, for example, than he promptly forgot them all again. Incidentally, he was a lifelong rebel against the classical languages. It is beside the point to speculate as to whether he had any aptitude for algebra or geometry or was curious about astronomy. The interesting thing about him is that he labored with intensity over his Latin and Greek, which he never mastered, just as he worked at Italian, which he learned to speak perfectly, not so much to make them another approach to knowledge as to break away completely from their harmonious methods of expression. The few bits of poetry he wrote suggest, to be sure, Voltaire's *Henriade*, which, when he first read it, swept him off his feet, but the discernible elements of his prose are lyrical, in keeping with his poetic nature, or, if you will, with his natural tendency to express his thoughts musically.

He took the Bible for his "customary evening reading," and states that he read it all straight through five or six times at least. No other work could have been of so much benefit in the formation of his style, with its prophetic eloquence, majestically unrolling sentence after sentence of consciously artistic cadences, always seeking to make an emotional appeal behind its imagery. I am aware of the defects of that style. It is sometimes ruined by bombast and given over to declamation. It achieves some of its charm at the expense of the virility of seventeenth-century style. Gaining in delicacy, it loses in logic, first and foremost by altering the connotations of words. But we must bear in mind how fresh and novel it was, and, when it weakens, consider how heavy is its load of charm! The literary stock-in-trade carried by La Fontaine seems meager in comparison with that of Jean-Jacques as he goes cropping his hay, to use his own words, almost at random during his solitary walks in the outskirts of Chambéry. I am well aware that dangerous illusions were the price he paid for the unrestrained liberty of his imagination in its communion with nature. I seek only to show the circumstances which led his illusions to stray off their natural course and fetter themselves in theories and systems. We owe to the stay made at Les Charmettes by Jean-Jacques the fact that the flowers he gathered, the notes of the nightingale which intoxicated him with joy, the first buds of spring which he saw with a rapture that "exalted him into Paradise," were all to live on in our literature, translated into perfume, melody, and loveliness.

As time went on, the situation between Jean-Jacques and Wintzenried, even between Jean-Jacques and Madame de Warens, became no better, but rather steadily worse. Not only did the churl treat him with ever greater insolence, but "Mamma" began to refer increasingly often to her financial straits aggravated by the necessity of feeding a useless mouth. "Little One" realized at last that he was allowed to stay on only out of consideration for the past, and that he was a heavy burden. Instead of renewing with him the tenderly confidential relations which had been theirs, Madame de Warens kept her affairs secret from him and did without his companionship, if she did not actually avoid him.

"Little by little," he says, "I grew accustomed to keeping out of everything that was done in the house, and even to keeping away from the people in it; and in order to save myself constant heart-burnings, I shut myself up with my books or I went out to sigh and shed tears at pleasure in the depths of the woods."

It was absolutely necessary that he make up his mind to leave the shelter of Les Charmettes. Madame de Warens remembered that she had a friend at Grenoble named Madame d'Eybens, whose husband was associated with Monsieur de Mably, provost marshal at Lyons, and she suggested to Jean-Jacques that she secure him the position of tutor in that dignitary's household. He accepted it. Possibly he imagined that he now had not only the talent, but also the necessary learning, to figure as an educator. But Monsieur de Mably had two distinguished brothers, Condillac the philosopher, and the Abbé de Mably, and this circumstance weighed most heavily in his decision. Among his belongings he had the manuscripts of two comedies, *Narcisse* and *Les prisonniers de guerre,* by which he hoped, thanks to the good offices of these men of letters, to forge a way to fame.

He was just entering on his twenty-eighth year, so the fact that he had already composed two plays in prose and one in verse, besides a number of poems, including *Le verger des Charmettes* and an epistle "in praise of the monks of the Grande Chartreuse," does not necessarily prove that he showed any remarkable precocity, but does prove the truth of my statement of some time back that he did not wait to become an author until his feet were on the downward slope of life.

Monsieur de Mably was a fine man, of hard exterior, as he had to be in his position in the mounted police force, but high-minded and of wide experience. He at once came to the conclusion that Jean-Jacques was no better fitted to educate his children than a deaf man to conduct an orchestra, but he would have hesitated to discourage such good intentions as were apparently manifested by the young man. Consequently he handed over to him the care of his two sons, who in mind and temperament differed as widely as possible. The elder was lively, scatter-brained, mischievous, and merry; the younger was sluggish and stubborn. Jean-Jacques exhausted his scanty store of patience in trying to concentrate the attention of the one and waken the other from his torpor. Sometimes he sentimentalized over them until he wept, at other times he burst into fits of fury. Between the two extremes, he gave the youngsters plenty of latitude to escape from his control, and they did not fail to take advantage of it. Jean-Jacques tried in vain to make up by arguments and sympathy for the authority and firmness he lacked. The fact is, as he recognized, that there can be no true judgment or depth of feeling in a child who is all instinct and passion. Jean-Jacques had enough penetration not only to read the young minds under his tutelage, but even to realize his own defects. Unhappily he could not escape his tendency to accept reasoning as if it were reason, and was sometimes taken in by the arguments, often highly ingenious, of his elder pupil. The younger one was an even greater problem. He never heard anything nor gave any answer. One might have battered in one's own head against such apathy without obtaining any effect whatever.

It took Jean-Jacques a year to see that he was wasting his time. He might sooner have realized his ineptitude as a teacher if he had not, in the hope of getting on his feet at last, played with the idea that Madame de Mably might become attached to him. For she was pretty, and, according to his custom, he had at once fallen in love with her.

At the request of Madame d'Eybens, the kindly lady had attempted to polish the manners of her children's tutor and to teach him the ways of the world. But it goes without saying that where Madame de Warens had failed, she could not succeed. She undertook in particular to train Jean-Jacques to receive her guests, but he proved so recalcitrant that she grew discouraged and left him to sigh and ogle by himself. During his long months of rustic life, his natural awkwardness and shyness had grown on him, and his piercing regrets for what he had left made him feel less at ease than ever among the social acquaintances of the provost marshal.

He was wont to console himself by retiring to his own room with a book, a bun, and a pilfered bottle of Arbois wine. He delighted above everything in browsing through a volume, munching and sipping on his way. But he played Monsieur de Mably false, having been entrusted with a key of the wine cellar, which was summarily taken away from him when the use to which he put it was discovered. This man, so lightly putting himself in the wrong, laying himself open to being beaten or at least of getting his ears boxed like a common scoundrel, was the same who gave Monsieur d'Eybens, during the interview in which the latter asked him, for Monsieur de Mably, on what terms he would undertake the education of the magistrate's sons, the dignified response: "Sordid considerations matter very little to me, but kind treatment matters a great deal"; and the same man, again, who simulated a passionate enthusiasm for his task. But one contradiction more or less need no longer surprise us in his actions.

Between times he was writing to Madame de Warens, who sent him shirts, books, and on one occasion a silver jug which he was to sell for five louis. He sold it for only four and a half, but when he returned her the money, he increased the sum by "as much as his wretched circumstances permitted him to add." He was still too closely attached to "Mamma" by bonds which entered the very fibers of his being to be forgetful or ungrateful. His special delight was to hear news of the things in which he was particularly interested, his "chickies," the garden, the trees, and the fountain. And as he dwelt with loving memories on all these things, the desire to see them again gradually got the better of him. Perhaps, with absence and the passage of time, he misrepresented matters to himself, and fed his hungry heart on illusions, quenching the remembrance of the unpleasant features of his former situation, fanning to life only the memories of its joys. In any case, after the spring began, he was unable to resist any longer. He handed in his resignation to Monsieur de Mably, who had been deterred from requesting it sooner only by charity and who accepted it with alacrity. Then he returned to Chambéry. Wintzenried, who by now had definitely abandoned his own name and had become Monsieur de Courtilles, received him with his usual coarse chaff, but Madame de Warens scarcely spoke to him. Her heart had turned to ashes, ashes from which the last warmth of the embers had died. She was discouraged, finally sick to death, after all her disappointments, after his failures and fresh starts which came to nothing, now that her fortunes had begun to fail, and she felt he had come back only to complete her ruin.

"She was spending her pension before she got it, she was in arrears with her rent, and her debts were piling up." She may not have set out to undeceive Jean-Jacques, but her coldness was enough to make him perceive that he was no longer anything but an outsider in her house. "Consumed by vain regrets, sunk in the blackest melancholy," the unhappy young man resigned himself to spending his days alone except at mealtimes. He could no longer have the pleasant strolls with "Mamma" which he had enjoyed even the year before, but shut himself up in his room, seeking distraction in his books and trying to think out a way to shake off his humiliating yoke. In ceasing to teach music, he had not abandoned the practice of it. On the contrary, he had delved deeper into its theory while he pursued his other studies, and he now conceived the idea of trying to find some solution for the difficulty of learning the notes, a difficulty he himself had experienced, by inventing some system of numerical notation. The idea attracted him, and he lost no time in putting it into execution. His task finished, he lived with but one thought, to make enough money to get to Paris. To this undertaking he devoted the winter of 1741–1742, which he spent alone at Les Charmettes. The only way open to him was the selling of books. These books, though they were not the exclusive property of Madame de Warens, in whose library they were, certainly belonged as much to her as to Jean-Jacques. But he was persuaded that he was on the road not only to glory, but also to fortune, and that he could repay to his benefactress whatever he thus took from her. When he had saved up fifteen louis, he said a fond farewell to "Mamma" and even to his "beloved brother," and on a cool April morning, sparkling as brightly and gladly as his own hopes, he set out on his way.

CHAPTER VIII

PARIS SOCIETY

AS the reader will remember, one of the reasons why Jean-Jacques accepted the position of tutor in the household of Monsieur de Mably was that he hoped to make the acquaintance of that gentleman's brothers and through them to obtain entry into literary circles. But the Abbé de Condillac, the one of the two whom he met in the provost marshal's house, doubtless explained to him that no author could make any headway except in Paris, and he had decided to wait for a better opportunity to further his ambitions as a dramatist. He thought, now that he was starting for the capital, that the opportunity was at hand, and he decided to go through Lyons in order to obtain letters of introduction to some important men of the day in the Parisian salons. Monsieur de Mably and the Abbé de Mably, to whom he had the good fortune this time to be presented, gladly gave him the introductions he desired, including one to Monsieur de Fontenelle and another to the Count de Caylus. He took pains, besides, to communicate with his former acquaintances, particularly with Monsieur Bordes, who had already done him many favors, and through whom he was enabled to pay his respects to the Duke de Richelieu and to obtain an invitation to call on him in Paris.

Lastly, he went to the convent of Les Chazettes, where Mademoiselle du Châtelet lived. During the previous year he had been several times to see Madame de Warens's friend, whose kindness had meant so much to him at the time of his adventure with the Master. But this visit to her was made with no disinterested motive. He wanted to see Mademoiselle Serre, whose charms had blossomed since the already distant time when he had first met her, and whom he had assiduously courted while he lived in Monsieur de Mably's house. Mademoiselle Serre's heart had been touched by his attentions, but when he yielded to the attack of homesickness which drove him back to Les Charmettes, he had suddenly announced to her that he was giving her up in order to "spend the rest of his days like a philosopher, in solitary retreat." With her hopes thus dashed, Mademoiselle Serre had given ear to the honorable proposals of a young merchant named Genève, and was on the eve of a formal betrothal. Then Jean-Jacques, whom she had supposed forever lost to her, returned, apparently more enamored than ever.

As she had no dowry and he was practically penniless, it went without saying that he had no idea of marrying her. He took the precaution of telling her so. But he had made extensive inquiries about her and had learned that she had had "affairs," so he flattered himself that, as he obviously appealed to her, she would be willing to have one more fling by which he would profit. In order to persuade her, he wrote her a letter which, if it is not worthy of first prize as the trickiest and most unscrupulous epistle ever penned by a man in the throes of an infatuation, at least does no credit to his character—nor yet to his taste. Not only did he lie outright to her, saying that he had undertaken the trip to Lyons for her sake alone, but, with consummate lack of delicacy, he dilated on her former lapses in order to induce her to fly into his arms. All was padded with protestations of consideration for her and encomiums on his own kindness of heart and his loyalty.

Possibly Mademoiselle Serre saw through the bluff of the young man who boasted that he could show her the way to "true felicity" and who promised to cherish her all his life—being actually resolved to continue his journey before exhausting his scanty funds, that is, almost immediately. In any case, after having hesitated for some time, long enough to show that she really felt warmly towards Jean-Jacques, she cast her decision in favor of an honorable marriage, sacrificing the precarious happiness he offered her; and she let him depart laying the flattering unction to his soul that he was giving her up from generous motives.

The first time Jean-Jacques had seen Paris, the city had filled him with loathing. His second impression of it was far more favorable, the reason being simply that his mood had changed. He left the stagecoach on which he had managed to procure a free lift, at the Rue des Cordiers, near the Sorbonne, and put up at the Hôtel de Saint-Quentin, of which Monsieur Bordes had told him. The Rue des Cordiers was a filthy street, or rather blind alley, and the Hôtel de Saint-Quentin was a house of evil appearance. But worthy men before him had chosen to stay there, and he was confident that his good fortune would soon enable him to move on. He set his letters of introduction to work, and at least three of them brought him results. Monsieur Damesin secured him two pupils in music; Monsieur de Boze invited him several times to dinner, which would have been delightful except that Madame de Boze, who was pretty and full of mischief, made fun of his country ways; and finally Monsieur de Réaumur introduced him into the Academy of Sciences, where he had the honor of obtaining a hearing for his thesis. The reading was well received, but unfortunately it led to nothing. He had hoped for something better than the shower of compliments with which Messieurs de Mairan, Hellet, and de Fouchy, members of the committee appointed to report on his numerical method of musical notation, condescended to favor him; and he was mortified by their conclusion that the method had no practical advantage nor any original value.

Jean-Jacques may have had truth on his side when he claimed that the representatives of the learned assembly behaved like donkeys in the matter, and that not one of their objections to his system was valid. I am not competent to judge in such a question. But although Rameau demonstrated to him that his figures had the disadvantage, while they replaced notes, which the eye takes in directly, of obliging the mind to perform an arithmetical calculation, he persisted so stubbornly in his idea that he went to the lengths of getting his thesis published, appealing to the public to bear witness to the error of the Academy. All in vain. Not only did he arouse no enthusiasm: he failed to excite any interest whatever. From indifference or indolence, as he tried to make it appear, or else in a fit of the sulks, like a spoiled child who takes out on himself his irritation when others underestimate his talents, Jean-Jacques set out to squander his little remaining substance, idling away his afternoons among the chess-players after spending long mornings strolling in the Luxembourg gardens.

However, his frantic efforts to win success for his invention left him no poorer in acquaintances. He had in general met with a cordial reception, for, as I have already several times had occasion to remark, he had the gift of making people like him, in spite of his awkwardness and his halting speech when he found himself in a brilliant gathering. Servan, who made his acquaintance during his stay at Grenoble in 1768, and who helped and encouraged him, said that he was not a clever talker and that he had a "heaviness of jaw which was surprising in view of his reputation. But he had an eloquent eye which made up for his paucity of speech, and it was invariably recognized that the eye was that of no ordinary man." Servan also was obliged to note that he never talked in a slovenly manner and "always brought out his words singularly well." But when enthusiasm animated him, he came entirely out of himself. "At those times he talked with warmth, not excitedly, but with a concentrated inner fire which caused his arms and legs to twitch," and which affected his audience powerfully.

As Jean-Jacques had occasion to learn, a man who is unaccustomed to society and mixes with people disposed to judge him by manners alone, is likely to make a fool of himself; but let a reputation for brains or talent precede him, and let him then make his appearance in a circle where originality is at a premium, his peculiarities, instead of harming him, enhance his attraction. In the salons open to Jean-Jacques, the general consensus of opinion was that he was delightful. His shyness lent him grace, by reason of the gentle manner and cajoling air in which he had learned to cloak it, at least where women were concerned. His ingenuousness completed the conquest of the sensitive sex, by reason of the contrast it presented to the audacity bordering on impertinence which was affected by men of letters and philosophers; and as for these gentlemen, Jean-Jacques gave them no cause to complain that he was stealing their thunder. The aged Fontenelle, a meeting with whom opportunely reminded our hero that he had studied the stars in the orchard at Les Charmettes, found in him a respectfully attentive listener; Diderot, then a young man, found him an ardent music-lover and an enthusiastic supporter of his plans for books. Marivaux thought him a psychologist and, having given Jean-Jacques permission to read him the comedy *Narcisse*, was so gracious as to suggest a few improvements. Finally, by the advice of Father Castel, a good Jesuit who duly took note that Jean-Jacques was of the type more likely to make his way with the assistance of women than with that of authors and scholars, he was introduced to Madame de Bouzenval.

She was a worthy lady of mediocre intelligence, inordinately proud of her illustrious Polish lineage. She would have committed the blunder of sending Jean-Jacques to dine in the servants' hall if her daughter, Madame de Broglie, had not interfered. The ladies had no reason to repent of their courtesy to him, and they liked him all the better when he crowned the favorable impression he made at table by reciting to them after dinner an epistle in verse and—very properly—happening to have a neat copy of it ready to present. His epistle, dedicated to Parisot, was his regular stand-by. He liked to capture the limelight in the salons by reading it aloud, rolling out his phrases with contagious fervor. This time it did not fail to produce its effect; indeed, it actually moved his hearers to tears. Not that it was anything much. Its bombast alone would have been enough to brand it a mediocre performance. One may well smile at the favor with which it met, and at the thought of Jean-Jacques declaiming with scathing irony against social prejudice and against the degradation of men who sue for favors at the hands of this world's great, for the benefit of people whose patronage he was soliciting and who, in their inmost hearts, felt that they were of quite another breed than he.

But we must not be too hard on him. While the aristocracy has amused itself by playing with the Utopias and radicalism of the authors, the authors for the most part have been pleading not so much the cause of their kind as their own cause in particular by the parade of their speculations—which is simply to say, in other words, that the Revolution was strictly a middle-class and intellectual affair. In any case, Jean-Jacques, at this period of his existence anyhow, cherished no hatred of the great as such, either born or made. He was simply looking up, like his fellow-authors, and hoping to rise by his talents above his natural station. He was asking that his plebeian origin be overlooked for the sake of his genius and that he be given the consideration to which it entitled him. We shall see in time that his rancor and his espousal of the cause of the oppressed was the result of his feeling that he personally was being obscured and downtrodden. His quest of sympathy, beginning as I have indicated, led him on by natural stages from the contemplation of his own misfortunes to that of the misfortunes of others, and reminded him of instances such as that of the peasant who was hiding his little store to evade the persecution of the tax-collectors.

He suffered, not at this time only, but doubtless his whole life long, because he could not appear to the salon born. He longed for a graceful manner. We may hear him when he wrote his *Confessions*, that is, nearly twenty-five years after this incident, dwelling on the fact that the neatness of his attire and the dignity of his bearing should have warned Madame de Bouzenval that he was no man to be sent out to eat with the lackeys. But he was impressed by the successes attending his first appearances in society, and the change of heart he had been able to effect in his favor with Madame de Bouzenval after she had been on the point of putting him to shame, together with other similar experiences, convinced him that he could and should, even though he did not shine with the luster imparted by more showy gifts, make his way by sheer intelligence and force of character in the circles where elegance and formal manners reigned—for he loved these things in spite of his rustic tastes. He could not rival Marivaux in subtlety, Diderot in wit, or Bernis in courtesy, and he made no such pretensions. But to make up for "the small talk of Paris, full of witty little chaff and clever little allusions," which he was incapable of acquiring, though he shows in *La nouvelle Héloïse* that he appreciated all its polish and aptness, he felt that he had an exceptional gift of eloquence and he believed in the outstanding forcefulness of his logic, the nobility and breadth of his ideas, and the magnanimity of his sentiments. He considered himself mortally insulted if these signal distinctions were not properly respected and esteemed, and as years went on he became increasingly exigent. Men who set themselves up as arbiters of opinion are peculiarly liable to become impatient of contradiction, and Jean-Jacques, with his pride, his hypersensitiveness, and the lyricism which made him identify himself with his work until he failed to distinguish any difference between what he had written and what he was, or between his determination to carry conviction and his personal craving for sympathy, was exasperated to the point of fury when his conclusions were disputed or even when his dictates were not unanimously acclaimed and applauded. Without anticipating too far, one can already see with what a simple mind he deluded himself, on the one hand, into thinking he was irresistible, and, on the other, into taking seriously the expressions of the worldly in professing liberal convictions—in spite of disappointments he had already experienced.

Let us follow him into the salon of Madame Dupin, a lady destined to be the grandmother of George Sand. She had two sisters, Madame de la Touche and Madame d'Arty, the three being known as "the Graces." Of the group, Madame Dupin was by repute not only the most beautiful, but also the most virtuous. On the day when Jean-Jacques first called on her, armed with another of his letters of introduction from Father Castel, he found her at her toilet, with her hair loosened over her bare shoulders. The sight of her disordered dress, which he compared in his mind to that of the courtesans in the fashionable prints of the period, together with her exquisite elegance and fragrance, went to his head and he immediately fell in love with her. It must be admitted at once that he was dreaming again of worming his way into the affections of some great lady, discounting entirely Father Castel's prudent warning, "Women are the curves to which men are the asymptotes," and that his dreams were still tinged with romance at the same time that he was hoping to find a comfortable home. Why should he not in a new mistress meet a second Madame de Warens? Unfortunately Madame Dupin, though she gave him an extremely courteous welcome, made no sign of feeling disposed to grant him her favors. Her indifference in letting him see her before she had dressed was largely due to the disdain felt by any woman of high rank in that period for persons of humble origin, the same sentiment which prompted one such lady, whose name I have forgotten, to appear entirely unclothed before her lackeys with the remark that there was no telling whether they were human.

Madame Dupin talked with Jean-Jacques of his plans "like a bluestocking," sang to him and played her own accompaniment on the harpsichord, and, after having kept him to dinner, seating him at her side, invited him to come again, but in all this she gave him no grounds whatever to imagine that she was leading him on. As he took such advantage of her invitation as to abuse it, calling on her every day and staying to dinner two or three times a week, she preserved a cold and distant manner. He was aching to declare himself, but refrained from doing so for fear of getting himself turned away from "a rich house where fortune might be met." Her salon was, as a matter of fact, one of the most distinguished in Paris. Its *habitués* were all dukes, ambassadors, men eminent in one line or another, including famous authors, or women of beauty or influence, who frightened Jean-Jacques of course, but also stimulated to the highest pitch both his ambition and his erotic imagination. One can imagine the struggle between his hopes and fears which constantly tore him to pieces and which he prolonged with melancholy pleasure. Finally his timidity inspired him to write what he dared not express orally; he resolved, whatever the consequences, to address a letter to Madame Dupin containing an elaborate declaration of love, and he put his resolution into effect.

For forty-eight hours she behaved as if she had no knowledge of its existence; then she handed it back to him, holding it deftly between the tips of her fingers, and accompanying its return with a short lecture, full of prudent counsels, delivered in an icy tone of voice. She could have hit on no better method to put back in his place the upstart who would doubtless have preferred out-and-out severity to this rather contemptuous indulgence. From that time, on he behaved with the most exemplary reserve, but before he settled down he saved his face by one final outburst in which he composed the following quatrain:

> O Reason, fear not lest thou stray,
> In her mayst find thy source;
> Though wise men lose thee on their way,
> Thou art found in her discourse.

Any other man would presumably have made less frequent calls after the lesson he had been given; not so Jean-Jacques. He continued as regularly as ever to appear in Madame Dupin's salon, until finally she instructed her son-in-law, Monsieur de Francueil, to inform him that his attentions were too marked. After that he went less often to her house, and might perhaps altogether have ceased to go there if, by a change of heart which was less a whim than a kindly impulse, she had not asked him to tutor her son for a week.

I presume that the influence of Monsieur de Francueil

had something to do with his being taken back into favor. This young man, an ardent music-lover and a student of the sciences, had grown fond of Jean-Jacques, and it is probable that he pleaded his cause. He may have argued that our Genevan was not always entirely responsible for his actions; in any case, he had reason to know so. One evening they had been together at the Palais Royal, when Monsieur de Francueil said: "How would you feel about going to the opera?" Jean-Jacques replied: "I should enjoy it immensely." When they arrived, Monsieur de Francueil took two orchestra seats, gave one ticket to his companion, and, keeping the other, led the way in. A sudden push from the crowd separated him from Jean-Jacques, who immediately conceived the idea that he might lose his way in the confusion or at least leave Monsieur de Francueil to suppose that he was lost. He went out, turned in his coupon, and received his money back, that is to say, Monsieur de Francueil's money, and straightway departed, never stopping to think that his companion would be sure to notice his absence as soon as he reached his seat and the audience had taken their places. It is difficult to pass judgment on such a performance, to call it pilfering or actual theft, yet thoughtlessness is not a sufficient explanation for it in a man of thirty. The "bashfulness" to which Jean-Jacques attributed his lapses, itself a result of his pride, actually did prevent him from expressing his desires and, even in his later years, led him to filch small objects rather than ask for them. Occasionally, when he was overmastered by his craving for a particular thing, he lost his head in dismay and resorted to the most petty expedients to save his imperiled dignity. It may even be said that his desire to appear an honest man made him commit most of his flagrantly dishonest acts, though he was guilty of others in order to be thought unselfish.

He was keeping up his music all the while. Most of the

reputation which he enjoyed at this period was due to it, and he aspired to rise to fame as much by its means as by literature. At Chambéry he had composed a grand opera called *Iphis et Anaxarète,* which he had wisely decided to destroy, judging it to be of poor quality; then, at Lyons, he had written a second, *La découverte du nouveau monde,* which he had sent the way of the first for the same reason. During an attack of pneumonia which confined him to his room in a feverish condition favorable to inspiration, or, as he put it, to "the frenzy," he seized the opportunity to compose a heroic ballet in three acts, on three different subjects, which he called *Les Muses galantes.* Before he had finished it, his friends Madame de Bouzenval and Madame de Broglie, whom he had been neglecting for Madame Dupin and who were trying to find some regular employment for him, suggested that he become the secretary of the Count de Montaigu, French ambassador to the Venetian Republic.

The matter was not easily arranged, for Jean-Jacques raised plenty of objections. Penniless as he was, he scorned the wages, or the salary, offered by Monsieur de Montaigu. The ambassador finally fell back on a man named Folleau, who then left him in the lurch, and after this episode both parties to the transaction agreed to compromise. In May, 1743, Jean-Jacques left for the City of the Doges by the longest route, that is, by the Mediterranean, not so much "because of the war or for reasons of economy," as to seek some advice from Madame de Warens on his way. The expense account which he submitted to Monsieur de Montaigu testifies to these facts. He reached Venice about the middle of July, and immediately set to work, showing an ability which commands our admiration. His correspondence reveals what he was about, and recent researches into the period of his association with Monsieur de Montaigu confirms the impression we must glean from it—namely, that he was admirably fitted to carry on diplomatic negotiations. Doubtless his intimacy with "Mamma" had been an excellent foundation for his work. He may have exaggerated the importance of his rôle; it is not worth while to discuss the question. Needless to say, he did not by his unaided efforts save the kingdom of Naples, as he states. But he did literally fill the place of Monsieur de Montaigu, who did nothing but append his signature to documents drawn up by Jean-Jacques.

This personage, an ex-captain of the Guards, chanced to be both an ass and a blackguard, with a dash of the miser to boot. He was far from pleased with the sometimes excessive ardor of Jean-Jacques, who doubtless was overzealous at his task, and he called down the proud young man in a manner calculated to mortify him cruelly. Jean-Jacques assumed more importance than he could justly claim by giving out that he was a secretary of the embassy, whereas he actually was only a secretary to the ambassador, but Monsieur de Montaigu insulted him by treating him like a lackey—and, at that, a lackey towards whom his insolence took the form of paying no wages. It is a thousand pities, as Jules Lemaître has rightly said, that Jean-Jacques broke with the French ambassador at Venice. The rupture was more than an episode in his life: it proved to be a crisis. One need only take account of his exultation, when he felt he was somebody, to realize how desperate must have been his disappointment when Monsieur de Montaigu dismissed him. If his ambition had met with any encouragement, even though he had been obliged to trim its wings to some extent—and Monsieur de Choiseul actually did consider the possibility of being able to open a career for him in diplomacy—he would have settled down in the enjoyment of his official position and very likely would have written conservative treatises on political economy with no detriment to his other purely literary work, for he was of the caliber to attack successfully two such different kinds of composition. As it was, he found himself precipitated from the dizzy heights of his dream into the abyss of nothingness, and the violent rage engendered in him by his experience turned to rancor and to a conviction of the absurdity of all civil institutions when he got back to Paris and attempted in vain to obtain redress against his employer. To be sure, he presented his case in an entirely false light. In the first place, he was not a French subject; in the second, the controversy which had arisen between him and Monsieur de Montaigu was of a purely personal nature. He made the mistake of appealing to the king and of arousing, or endeavoring to arouse, against the ambassador the ladies with whom he was in good standing. But the reader must bear in mind the susceptibility of our hero, and also the fact that he was deeply in debt, owing to Monsieur de Montaigu's failure to fulfill the terms of the contract, after he found himself fallen from the high estate to which he thought he had risen—an estate in which he believed he had figured "in the high estimation of the Republic," and the "affection of every French resident of Venice." He was in the depths of despair, and I am inclined to think that in the extravagance of his attitude one may detect precursory symptoms of the persecution mania from which he later suffered. His health, moreover, had been precarious during the period of his residence beyond the Alps. When he left for Venice, he had still been somewhat run down after the attack of pneumonia some months earlier, and the fatigue of his journey and the excessive heat he had encountered brought on, as soon as he began his work with Monsieur de Montaigu, "a terrible burning of the urine and backaches," from which he suffered intensely. It is surprising that Barrès, conjuring up the glorious shades of "Amori et Dolori Sacrum," made no inquiry into the harmful effects of the waters of Venice on the health of Jean-Jacques. He might perhaps have discerned a malarial tendency in the fever which heated his blood and inflated his pride, even if he sought in vain for any signs of a uræmic attack.

Jean-Jacques was quite unmoved by the picturesque charm of the city. The reader will not have forgotten that he was blind to architectural beauty, doubtless because his faculties were engrossed by natural beauty, which he was the first man of his century to realize. However, he went out constantly, and was to be seen not only in the homes of French, Italian, even English acquaintances, but also in public amusement places, at the theater, in the gaming halls, and at the masquerades. However little he may have relished showy entertainments, which dazzled and tired him, he was obliged to attend them because of his position in the public eye. He had to let himself be seen, and he felt, moreover, a need of distraction which was the price he paid for his ardent labors, not only at his official task, but also at his private undertakings. He was passionately affected by Italian music, so admirably adapted to satisfy his love of melody, and he went into raptures, sometimes at the opera or in church, sometimes in the street, when he heard the boat-songs of the gondoliers, sometimes even when he heard the young girls of the lower classes singing in the hospices, or *scuole*.

He was intensely excited by the light and insinuating melodies which touched his emotions through his senses. One day he expressed a desire to see the young women whose voices had charmed him in the "Mendicanti," behind their iron gratings—only to be disappointed in them. Then, in that unimaginable Venice, the Venice of Casanova, where gallant courtliness and license were found hand in hand in every rank of society, his curiosity had egged him on, mastering his preference for affairs of a gentler and more discreet kind, to try commercialized love.

The anguish caused him by two highly unsatisfactory encounters with courtesans, and the strain on his nerves, aggravated the condition induced by his rage against Monsieur de Montaigu. In a letter he sent to the Foreign Secretary, Monsieur de Theil, on August 8, 1744, in which he asks in outraged terms for redress, he states that he is in poor health and much run down. He must have been at least feverish, before he left Venice, to indulge in follies as he did, and to stay on after the ambassador had dispensed with his services. For he undertook to show his independence for a time by appearing everywhere with ostentation and making numberless farewell calls with the maximum of publicity. When he finally realized the uselessness of his claims to justice, and the futility of his lamentations, he became so utterly disheartened that he began to think of sacrificing all ambition and retiring to Geneva, "there to wait for better fortune to remove the obstacles," until he could eventually rejoin his "poor, dear Mamma."

After his return to Paris, his spirits sank to the lowest ebb. On February 23, 1745, we find him writing again to Madame de Warens from the Hôtel de Saint-Quentin, where he stayed, and to which she sent him some soap and some chocolate, to say that he loved her and was thinking of her and had no higher ambition than to have the happiness of spending the rest of his days at her side. No doubt she, with her financial affairs causing her the gravest anxiety, could think of other ways to be happy than by reassuming the burden of an embryonic diplomat who had just made a failure as a secretary of the embassy, or a secretary to the ambassador. In any case, she made no reply to the "little one's" hint. His bitterness was accordingly deepened. He found, doubtless, much agreeable companionship in Paris, but no practical assistance in the struggle he had undertaken against Monsieur de Montaigu. Madame de Bouzenval, as was to be expected in anyone with her caste consciousness, rebuked him, and Father Castel, beneath his "soft Jesuit talk," gave Jean-Jacques to understand that he made no exception to "one of the cardinal maxims of the society, which is always to sacrifice the weaker to the stronger." Consequently it was in wretchedness and despondency that Jean-Jacques again set to work on his opera, *Les Muses galantes,* for he had to live and he hoped, though he did not estimate his work too highly, to be able to make something out of it.

He nursed a grudge against society, but dared not break off relations with people in high places. He allowed his friend Gauffecourt to introduce him into the circle of Monsieur de la Popolinière, the well-known revenue commissioner, whose house was called "the zoo" because of the strange assortment of guests one met there, but who was the patron of Rameau. To do so much was to put his head into the lion's mouth. For Rameau was of course anything but pleased with the appearance in the house of his special Mæcenas of a nondescript young man claiming to be a musical genius, and he did everything in his power to cast aspersions on the upstart. He affected to see in him nothing but a sponger without taste or talent. Luckily for Jean-Jacques, the Duke de Richelieu, who had expressed the wish to have a hearing of the *Muses galantes* in his house, did not share this opinion. He was particularly pleased to annoy Monsieur de la Popolinière, whose wife was secretly his mistress. He pronounced Jean-Jacques's opera "melodious to a degree," and promised to have it performed for the king.

CHAPTER IX

THÉRÈSE LEVASSEUR

AS we have seen, Jean-Jacques returned from Venice to stay again at the Hôtel de Saint-Quentin near the Luxembourg. There, in the spring of 1745, he met a little laundress, twenty-three years old, whose name was Thérèse Levasseur. The woman who managed the hotel gave her work and let her take her meals at the general table. The girl, who was not particularly remarkable in any way, belonged to a respectable middle-class family, but was so retiring in manner that she appeared a nonentity; however, to make up for her lack of intelligence and distinction, she was attractive and had an appealing little face which might have been called pretty. Jean-Jacques liked her for her very shyness, or for the shy air she put on, and particularly for the embarrassment she apparently suffered at the vulgar speeches made by the other boarders, Irish clericals and Gascons, all more or less foul-mouthed, who delighted in making free before her. When they made her the butt of their gibes, he was sorry for her and took up her defense, whereupon the "lewd fellows" turned on him, and his championship of her brought them closer together.

If he had deliberately planned to seduce her, he could have thought of no better method of going about it than the one he adopted without any ulterior motive—at least, so he believed. The girl appeared grateful for his protection and expressed her gratitude at first only by glances. Later she summoned up the courage to speak to him. The vehement displeasure of the hostess, who put in her oar, when she perceived the understanding between them, gave them still more in common. Thérèse looked to Jean-Jacques, or appeared to do so, for comfort when the vixen abused her, and he became her sole friend and supporter in the hotel. Things went their natural course. But not so fast nor so smoothly as one might suppose. Though she lacked wit, Thérèse was cunning. She was far from being the simple child Jean-Jacques believed her to be, and she concealed her true motives, craftily playing a close game. Later on she proved herself a schemer, and the universal testimony of her contemporaries is enough to condemn her. She reasoned that the gentleman who had risen so gallantly to her defense might well serve to extricate her from her other difficulties, her father having lately lost his position in the mint at Orléans, and her mother having been forced to close the little shop she kept there. Thérèse understood that her attraction for Jean-Jacques was in her modest manner; consequently she played the sanctimonious hypocrite for his benefit and pretended to be deeply moved by his grandiloquent speeches. What she understood of them was chiefly to the effect that he wanted to make her his mistress. Not his wife; he told her as much in unmistakable terms. But he also vowed that he would never leave her. She was willing to believe his protestations; her instinct told her to believe him, for she sensed that he was weak if not sincere, and that assurance was all she needed.

He had intended merely "to get some amusement out of her." He soon perceived that he had done more and had got himself a permanent companion. Thérèse had been right when, putting no hard and fast faith in his fine promises, she had concluded that she would be wise to act as if she believed in them. She quickly bound him to her by the strongest of ties. It is surprising to me that there should have been so much question among the commentators as to what these were. There is no mystery in the continued intimacy between Jean-Jacques and Thérèse. The first point to make is that love had nothing to do with it. As we shall see, the fact that he lived with Thérèse did not deter Jean-Jacques from straying in his dreams. But he remained at her side in the flesh even when his heart parted company with her, and it was only in a figurative sense that he returned to her after a night of orgies like the pigeon with the lame wing in the fable.

He liked to contrast Thérèse with the noble ladies who had offended him or against whom he fancied he had grievances. When he went out into society, he exaggerated the devotion she gave him and the affection he felt for her. He played with the relationship in his mind, and she played with his enmities by adding fuel to their flames. He did not want it to seem that he resorted to her only for lack of anyone better. He delighted in railing with her at his enemies, real or imaginary; thus she satisfied all the petty and misanthropic side of his nature. People of vulgar extraction are much given to slandering those of whom they are afraid, those whom they need, and those who are superior to them, and Thérèse had the soul of a servant. She belittled Jean-Jacques's friends and patrons, assured him that they were conspiring against him, and encouraged his persecution mania. Moreover, she was neither surprised nor disgusted by his ailments and physical infirmities. She established herself as his mentor and guide, his "governess," as he put it, or his trained nurse. According to his own avowal, he needed "someone to succeed Mamma." He found her. In Thérèse he had a docile and responsive girl to share his happy hours or his "triumphant mornings." Inevitably he tired of her companionship; but once the association had been established and the habit of her acquired, she became necessary to him, absolutely indispensable in fact, both morally and physically.

His meeting with Thérèse was a turning point in his life. Here was someone on whom he could lean, a prop which grew stronger as years went on, to support him against the hostility he sensed or fancied among the aristocratic and upper-middle-class people with whom he continued to mix. If he had had Madame de Warens to guide and counsel him as time went on, his life-story would have been quite different. Instead of sharpening the edge of his susceptibility, "Mamma" would have made every effort to blunt it, and would have softened every hurt his pride received. Not so Thérèse. If ever there was a day when Jean-Jacques was not included among the men of letters invited to dine at the house of Monsieur Dupin, Thérèse showed such surprise at the omission that it appeared she thought it an insult. Monsieur de Francueil employed Jean-Jacques jointly with Madame Dupin as secretary, at a salary of eight or nine thousand francs, and required him to lodge within call. Thérèse never ceased bemoaning the whim which involved them in expense, for Jean-Jacques had rented an apartment for her in the upper part of the Rue Saint-Jacques, whence he had to depart each night to sleep in a furnished room in the Saint-Honoré quarter. He got so that he never went to Monsieur de Francueil without cursing and sulking, and when he got into difficulties with the *Muses galantes,* his temper grew no better.

It must be remarked here that Thérèse had imported to Paris all the members of her family. With Madame Levasseur came the whole tribe, sisters, sons, daughters, and granddaughters, eight souls in all, for whom Jean-Jacques had to provide, since his mistress' small earnings were not sufficient to feed and clothe them. On his father's death

THÉRÈSE LEVASSEUR 143

he inherited fifteen hundred francs, but he felt under obligation to send a fraction of this sum to Madame de Warens, who by this time was completely destitute and who sent him appeals of distress. He would have liked sincerely to do more for her than he did. But he was torn between "Mamma" and Thérèse, the one in the clutches of her creditors, the other of her family; he was himself divided between fear of abuse from the Levasseurs and desire to give expression to his gratitude, and was at an utter loss what to do.

He suspected Monsieur de Francueil of obstructing his rise in the world, imagining that Madame Dupin's son-in-law was unwilling to let his reputation rise for fear that when he should publish his own books he would be accused of plagiarizing from Jean-Jacques. So he began to think of nothing but achieving his independence, and redoubled his efforts to obtain a presentation of his opera. He did not get it performed until 1747, and then with only mediocre success. In the meantime Voltaire had occasion to need the services of a musician who was also a poet, to work over *La Princesse de Navarre*, an opera of which he had written a versified libretto for Rameau's score. The Duke de Richelieu suggested Jean-Jacques, and Voltaire was willing to use him, unknown though he was. Thus Jean-Jacques had the opportunity, which he was not slow to seize, of becoming acquainted with the illustrious author of *La Henriade*.

"For fifteen years," he wrote, "I have worked to be worthy of your attention and of the consideration you accord to young aspirants in the arts in whom you recognize some talent." He then pointed out to his famous elder the fact that, though he had indeed figured as a musician, he took his abilities as an author more seriously and thought of himself in that light. Voltaire, who supposed Jean-Jacques stood on a much better footing with the Duke de

Richelieu than was actually the case, answered him in an extremely courteous letter. But Rameau's jealousy spoiled everything. The old composer was incensed to discover in his disciple a potential rival, and put every possible obstacle in his path. Jean-Jacques was so deeply affected by the spite, or, if we elect to use his own word, the "sorrow," which Rameau's actions caused him, that he fell ill.

No sooner had he recovered than he undertook to found a little periodical called *Le Persifleur,* but produced only one number. He then set to work at his Greek, and began to edit articles for the *Dictionnaire des arts et des sciences,* turning restlessly from one thing to another, with his nerves jangling more and more violently. But he paid no attention to them. Irascibility gave him strength, and he turned on those who had hurt him, "hounding them," to use his own expression, "from the rear." Actually, the people who most stood in his way were the Levasseurs, who were squeezing Thérèse, while she in her turn extracted from him everything she could get.

Whenever he escaped for a brief respite from that flock of harpies, he put on flesh, became less of a hypochondriac, and grew sociable once more. In 1747 he went to spend the autumn in Touraine at the Château of Chenonceaux, of which Monsieur Dupin was at the time the fortunate possessor, and there he once more blossomed out into a society man. Life was delightful indeed in that charming spot, where feasting and music were the order of the day. He contributed his share by composing trios for three voices, short poems, of which the best—that is, the least bad—is *L'Allée de Sylvie,* and by improvising a comedy of manners, in the style of Marivaux, called *L'Engagement téméraire.* Touched by the deference accorded to him, he was courteous, gentle, almost affectionate. He was introduced by de Francueil, who was her recognized lover, into the circle of Madame d'Épinay, and was invited by her to La

Chevrette, a château near Saint-Denis. It was there that he first met Mademoiselle de Lalive de Bellegarde, soon to become the Countess d'Houdetot.

Returning from his visit in the country, he found Thérèse in the advanced stages of pregnancy. He was greatly troubled and perplexed, though, no doubt, less so than he would have us suppose. But no man of thirty-five can learn of the approaching birth of his own child without considerable emotion. True, Jean-Jacques appears to have been devoid both of paternal instinct and of moral scruples. At the time he was bound by no social ties, but allowed himself to be swayed entirely by his momentary impulses; he was all emotions, which, though not invariably bad, he judged to be invariably good, and he had no principles whatever. He never put his faith in any except those which he himself later elaborated and combined into a system. When he called himself a republican, in his epistle to Monsieur Bordes, he was acting in hatred of "arrogance" and scorn for "the rich upstart." As the reader will remember, his verses to Parisot reeked with rhetorical praises of independence and denunciations of the injustice of social conventions. He never stated in definite terms what that virtue was which he found to be the concomitant of poverty, but used the word in a vague and all-embracing sense, content to believe that his own conduct in every circumstance was in accord with it, or that he could justify his conduct by invoking it.

I doubt whether he actually felt as firmly resolved as he says he did to remain forever with Thérèse. In any case, one may be quite sure that he had no intention of bringing up her progeny. To begin with, he had not enough money, and, further, he did not wish to incur responsibilities or to trammel himself for the future. He needed free elbow room, which he could not have if he were burdened with a child. As he puts it, "he did not feel like entering into an everlasting contract." He had no conception of duty. We must keep in mind that he had expressly told Thérèse he would never marry her. He would live under no obligation in regard to her, and if he stayed by her, his adherence would be due to magnanimity, not to compulsion.

The difficulty was to persuade Thérèse to abandon her child and leave it in the foundlings' home. It was unnecessary for him to cite in the *Confessions*, as his own excuse for this dastardly plan, the loose morals of the age and the influence on him of the group of debauchees he was in the habit of meeting where he took meals, at the table of a Madame La Selle, opposite the entrance to the blind street which led to the opera. I do not understand why his followers have been at such pains to explain away his cynicism or his lack of human feeling. They contend that the author of *Émile* could never have acted like an unnatural father. The truth is, they say, that he never had any children, but laid the calumny at his door from fear lest he be thought to be impotent. He so dreaded ridicule that he chose to impute this infamous deed to himself. The explanation, however, does not hold water.

He was not inconsistent in inducing Thérèse to have the child left at the orphanage, for the excellent reason that, being so far neither a philosopher nor a sociologist, he could not be inconsistent. Eventually he overcame the objections of his mistress, who took the situation far more seriously than he, and who yielded only under combined pressure from Jean-Jacques and from Madame Levasseur, for the old wife dreaded "a new swarm of brats." Thérèse went through her confinement secretly in the house of a Mademoiselle Gouin opposite Sainte-Eustache. Jean-Jacques took her a number which he had written in duplicate on two cards, one of which he attached to the swaddling clothes of the infant; and the midwife deposited it in due form at the office of the foundlings' home.

In 1748, Thérèse bore a second child, and again he resorted to the same expedient "as far as the numbering, which was neglected." A third child in 1750 went the way of the first two. Thus, beginning with the second, Jean-Jacques deliberately took no means to establish the identity of the baby by which he might some day prove his paternal claim. There could be no more complete exhibition of cold indifference. But I repeat that at the time he was perfectly incapable emotionally of experiencing the remorse from which he later suffered in all sincerity; and that he was equally incapable mentally of devising the sophistical arguments with which he later glorified his conduct. For, not content with excusing his behavior, he went so far, without fear of appearing to contradict himself, as to claim that in abandoning his children to public charity because he was unable to support them himself, and in thus determining their fate, ordaining them to become workmen or peasants instead of adventurers or fortune-hunters, "he was acting as a citizen and *a father*, and considered himself a member of Plato's Republic."

The Rousseau who wrote these lines was the Rousseau of his famous days. He was the exponent of a doctrine and was unwilling to have it appear that he himself had ever acted in opposition to its dictates. He had insisted with stubbornness, in the meantime, on abandoning in their turn two more of his children by Thérèse, bringing the total up to five. His philosophy must appear to be a rule of life by which he had regulated his own impulses. In this connection, we must recall his well-known dictum, with its amazing pretension: "I have only to consult my own self concerning what I wish to do. All that I feel to be good, is good; all that I feel to be bad, is bad."

Making a halo for himself of his sensitiveness, in this manner, he would naturally find it impossible to confess that he had ever behaved as a hard and feelingless man, "deaf to the call of nature." Not at all; he had refrained from proclaiming his deed from the housetops not because he was in the least ashamed of it, but because he was considerate of Thérèse's feelings. It is a pity that the woman on whom such consideration was lavished, perhaps an unworthy object of it, was so cruelly grieved at being defrauded of her maternal rights! But Jean-Jacques cannot disguise the fact that he did not conceal his abandonment of his children from a single friend who knew of his relationship with Thérèse. As a matter of fact, that would have been a very difficult matter. He would have had to send Thérèse away. And Madame Levasseur had no compunctions whatever, as Jean-Jacques himself says, about telling anyone and everyone of her daughter's confinements and of their conclusion.

But we shall drop the discussion, although it would clear the air somewhat to consider in turn each of the arguments later advanced by Jean-Jacques to extenuate his wrong. It is enough for me not only that he did the wrong, but that he did it repeatedly, the last two times from pride; and, another point against a philosopher regardful, as he claimed to be, of the rights of the individual, that he paid no heed to the just reproaches of Thérèse, who resisted him to the end and submitted only with tears. Thanks to Madame Levasseur, the unhappy mother gained at least a material advantage from her sacrifice. Without the knowledge of Jean-Jacques, Madame Levasseur made the most of her daughter's pitiful plight to melt the heart of Madame Dupin. She and Monsieur de Francueil together not only raised Jean-Jacques's salary from eight hundred francs to fifty louis, but also helped him to make a home. Madame Dupin helped him to settle in a little apartment in the Languedoc building in the Rue de Grenelle-Saint-Honoré, and a kind of second honeymoon began for the couple.

Jean-Jacques, who continued to see Diderot because

they were collaborating on articles for the Encyclopædia relating to music, compared his mistress to her advantage with the philosopher's Nanette. The companion of Denis, "a scold and a fishwife," was indeed no better than the companion of Jean-Jacques. At least, so Jean-Jacques says, thereby showing that he could be deceived by appearances. In the early stages of their relationship Thérèse, though she was hard and shrewish by nature, may well have attempted to continue in the rôle she had played to captivate Jean-Jacques. In any case, he considered her at that time an exquisite creature, "an angel," and no joy to him was comparable to that which her company gave him. Their pleasures were indeed simple, of a kind suitable to their station. They made little excursions to the outskirts of the city, where they squandered in princely fashion "eight or ten pennies in a wine-shop," or, more humble still, they supped together at home. Seated at their window, they enjoyed the meal prepared by Thérèse, to whom cooking was an art, and Jean-Jacques in his greed relished it all the more for its informality. They sat opposite each other on chairs set up on a trunk which filled the window space, the sill serving as their table. They drank in deep breaths of fresh air, looked out on the surrounding streets and down on the passers-by. "Though it was on the fifth floor, we could gaze right into the street while we ate. Who can describe," exclaims Jean-Jacques, forgetting that he was not always so frugal, "who can describe and who can experience the delights of those meals, consisting of naught but a loaf of coarse bread, a few cherries, a bit of cheese, and a half-measure of wine, which we drank together? Companionship, confidence, intimacy, sympathy, what seasonings for you! Sometimes we sat till midnight, not thinking of the time nor suspecting the lateness of the hour unless the old wife reminded us of it."

The "old wife" was Madame Levasseur. The pestiferous

old thing, who prided herself on her fine manners and polite ways, apologized for sometimes breaking up a love-scene. She would go out rubbing her hands and muttering that the silly girl knew at least enough to keep her hold on Jean-Jacques. She was a shrewd and clever woman, nicknamed by that good old soul, her husband, who was too soft with her no doubt, and feared her as he did the plague, the "lieutenant criminal." She had a mind to make all she could out of Jean-Jacques, whom she considered impractical indeed, but whose talents she appreciated. Her one fear, knowing that women adored him and that he was extremely susceptible to their charm, was that he would suddenly become infatuated with someone else and would desert Thérèse. So she kept her eye on him. She realized how great was her influence on Thérèse, and he loathed what he called her wheedling whispers. He never knew what was going on in his own house. Whenever his friends came in to see him, she took them off for confidential chats behind his back. "You should advise him—tell him to do this or that. Why did you let him do so?" He flew into rages, all in vain. Nothing but calm and inflexible firmness would have served his need, and these he could not command. "I could make scenes, but I could do nothing," he confessed. "They let me have my say out, and then they went right on."

We have reached the year 1749, and in that summer, on July 24th, an event took place which stirred Jean-Jacques to his depths. Diderot was arrested on the King's order, was taken to the dungeon of Vincennes, and there confined on the fifth floor. The only charge against him was that on the first page of his "Letter concerning the Blind, for those who have Good Eyes," he had inserted a little jest, harmless enough in all conscience, at the expense of a lady of the Pré de Saint-Maur. True, the lady was an intimate of Monsieur d'Argenson, and she had demanded the punishment of the offender. General sentiment in high places was not at all averse to tormenting the editor-in-chief of the Encyclopædia, and her wish was speedily complied with.

Jean-Jacques, who supposed that Diderot had been condemned to life imprisonment, nearly went out of his mind. He even wrote a letter to Madame de Pompadour, to which, it goes without saying, he received no answer. But he was soon calmed by hearing that the philosopher, far from being kept in secret confinement, was allowed to leave the dungeon and to wander anywhere he pleased within the bounds of the castle and the park, as a prisoner on parole. Monsieur du Châtelet, the governor, even gave him permission to see his friends and invited him to eat at his own table. Jean-Jacques hurried to Diderot's side. Several times a week, in the afternoons, he made the two leagues between Vincennes and Paris, in spite of the extreme heat, which again brought on his bladder trouble. For Diderot was his Aristarchus, and his persuasive speech and sound advice were to Jean-Jacques the staff of life.

Imprisonment weighed noticeably on Diderot, but whenever he got to talking with Jean-Jacques his spirits revived, and, with his spirits, his insatiable curiosity and the instant response to any topic which was characteristic of him and which made of him the most stimulating and encouraging of friends. At this time, though he was nearly forty years old, he was in love with a certain Madame de Puisieux, whom he suspected of carrying on an intrigue behind his back with a young rake. In spite of having given his word of honor to Monsieur du Châtelet, he was determined to make a break out of prison bounds in order to get to Champigny, where someone had hinted that his lady was to meet her gallant at a party, and where he hoped to take her by surprise. At the worst, he would be sure of his misfortune, and the certainty might cure him of his foolish infatuation, worse than foolish, since it incited him to write licentious stories for the sake of earning more.

One day Jean-Jacques came in sight in the distance waving his arms about excitedly. Whatever could have come over him? Suddenly he saw Diderot and gesticulated frantically in his direction with a gazette he carried in his hand. He was streaming with perspiration, though it was autumn —perhaps he had been hurrying, even running in spurts. But as he approached, Diderot saw that his face glowed with the expression he wore only when he was on fire with some emotion or conviction. His eyes shone, and he panted as he shouted:

"Denis! Look here! The *Mercure de France!* The Academy at Dijon has set this subject for next year's prize discourse: 'Whether the progress of the sciences and the arts has tended to corrupt or to improve morals.' I am going to compete."

"Quite right!"

"Can you guess which side I shall take?"

"The side you take will be the side no one else will take."

"My turn to say 'quite right.' Your answer has removed my last doubts, if I still had any. But don't you think—"

"What I think is that you have no chance of winning unless you go at it in paradoxical fashion. I know what your ideas are. You are full of them, and you are burning to advertise them. Go to it!"

In connection with this conversation, we must glance at Jean-Jacques's letter to Monsieur de Malesherbes:

"I happened to see the subject proposed by the Academy of Dijon. . . . If ever a man felt a sudden inspiration, I felt it when I read that article. At once a great light beamed into my mind, dazzling me with a thousand rays, and ideas crowded into it all together, in such profusion and with such violence that I was indescribably upset. I felt my head turning round, as dizzy as if I were drunk. My heart beat so violently that I was in distress and my chest heaved; I could scarcely breathe as I walked; I dropped to the ground under one of the trees that border the avenue, spending half an hour in such acute excitement that I got up with the front of my vest all wet with tears, though I had not been conscious of weeping."

Allowing for his usual exaggeration, one sees that he is giving a fairly accurate account of the occurrence. But the fever which seized him on his way to Vincennes became still more violent after his interview with Diderot. And it was on his return, not on his way there, that he wrote under an oak tree—if he wrote it at all at that time—the famous apostrophe: "O Fabricius, what would thy great soul have thought—"

When he reached home, he could not sleep. His brain teemed with emotions and ideas; he glimpsed the truth, reached out for it, and was enveloped by it. In his enthusiasm he consecrated his sleepless night to putting his oration into shape. Unhappily, when he attempted in the morning to write down on paper the sentences which he had constructed with infinite pains, working them over and over until he felt he had attained perfection before he committed them to memory, he was unable to do so. He had forgotten everything during the time it had taken him to get up and dress. But there was Madame Levasseur, who came in each morning to light his fire and do his little household chores, in order to save him the expense of a servant. It occurred to her that in this prize theme which so distracted her daughter's lover there might be the makings of a fortune. Now was the moment for her to make the best of her education in the household of the Marquise de Monpipeau, and to show that she could wield a pen as well as anyone. She proposed to Jean-Jacques that she act as his secretary, and he accepted the offer, dictating to her thenceforth from his bed, in order not to lose the inspiration, all that he had composed during the night.

Diderot left Vincennes on November 3rd. By that time

Jean-Jacques had finished his discourse. He submitted it to his friend for criticism; Diderot liked it and suggested a few improvements. When these had been made, Jean-Jacques sent the manuscript to Dijon without having spoken of it to anyone else except possibly to Grimm, whom he had recently met and who had become his intimate friend.

Once each week Jean-Jacques dined with him, Diderot, and Condillac in a Palais-Royal restaurant called the *Panier Fleuri*. He invited the group to his own home too, either together or, more often, singly by turns, "for a picnic." He was also in the habit of seeing Alembert, the abbé Raynal, Baron d'Holbach, Marmontel, Helvétius, and the chaplain Klupffel, a German like Grimm and an exceedingly clever man. Thus his circle was one of philosophers, and it may be said that he was one of them. He was not considered an outstanding figure among them; no doubt he lacked as yet any qualities which would entitle him to special esteem among those reformers and thinkers. But they thought well of him, took care, knowing how sensitive he was, not to hurt his feelings, and gave him credit for the fanatical enthusiasm which his eccentricities covered. "A peculiar fellow" they called him, especially when he became expansive and excitedly spun the tale of his adventures. Duclos alone recognized his genius, and said of him: "He is as ill-tempered as a bulldog, but give him time and he will set the world on fire; you'll see." The group in general looked on him with the indulgent kindness accorded an unfortunate member of the fraternity who, at thirty-seven, was nearly old enough to be classified among the failures.

To them his musical gifts and accomplishments seemed his chief distinction. Grimm frequently persuaded him to sing Italian melodies and barcarolles, doubtless compositions of his own too, and accompanied him on the harpsichord. For an idea of his appearance at this period, one need only turn to the famous pastel drawing made by La Tour in 1753, which Diderot criticized as giving an incorrect impression of his age. There is nothing in this portrait to indicate that Rousseau was the violent misanthrope that later generations considered him to be. A well-rounded countenance smiles out frankly from under a wig; the chestnut eyes sparkle with intelligence. His complexion is rather dark. On the whole he is an agreeable-looking man, one whose charm will be most felt in his animated moments.

Marmontel assures us that he was treated with something more than consideration, and that he was generally petted "with the attentiveness and forbearance granted a pretty woman who is particularly difficult and vain." He notes Jean-Jacques's politeness, savoring occasionally of obsequiousness. This description is not inconsistent with the later one written by Madame d'Épinay: "He pays compliments without being polite." This peculiarity explains the strong attraction he had for women, already noted, which, as the reader understands, lay chiefly in the contrast between his customary timidity and reserve, and his spontaneous outbursts, if not of passionate sincerity, at least of confidence, self-forgetfulness, and rough-spoken frankness.

Jean-Jacques tells us that he had actually forgotten all about his discourse and the prize he had had the ambition to covet. As a matter of fact, he had not talked of it at all, but perhaps this was because he feared the judges of the Dijon Academy might fail to appreciate his eloquence, and in that case he would prefer to have no one know what high hopes he had entertained for it. His delight can be imagined when he heard on July 18, 1750, that his manuscript had been awarded the first prize. With that prize he had at last achieved the fame he so yearned for, and the chance to be a success. So overjoyed was he that he succumbed to his emotions, as he had formerly succumbed to grief, and he fell ill again with bladder trouble. This time the attack was exceedingly serious. It kept him in bed five or six weeks, and he continued to suffer agonies all through the autumn. He thought he was going to die, again an indication that his illness was largely a matter of nerves. He speaks in the *Confessions* as if he had contracted it by getting overheated on one of his trips to Vincennes, but attributes its severity partly to the increase of work and the anxiety caused him by the position Monsieur de Francueil had recently given him, of household treasurer—recognizing that his ailments had a mental as well as a physical foundation.

Madame Dupin sent Morand to him, but with all his skill the famous surgeon succeeded only in inflicting fearful suffering on him and failed to relieve his symptoms. Morand then recommended that he try Daran, who helped him. When Morand made his report to Madame Dupin on the condition of her protégé, he definitely stated that Jean-Jacques could not live six months. Jean-Jacques heard of the statement later on, when he was taking a new lease of life and knew quite well that the doctor was mistaken. It intensified the conviction, however, at which he had arrived during his illness and convalescence, that with his weakness and his ill health, it was useless for him to try to act as if he were an ordinary, that is, a normal, man.

As Jean-Jacques was confined to his bed, Diderot undertook to get his manuscript printed for him. "It is taking everyone by storm!" he announced in a note sent to inform the author of its publication. "Never was such a success." The success soon assumed the proportions of a triumph. It determined Jean-Jacques in the resolution he had been constantly turning over and over in his throbbing head, while he lay on his bed poisoned by toxins of one sort or another. A new existence was about to begin for him.

PART TWO

CHAPTER I

THE PEASANT OF THE DANUBE

IF any reader asks whether the *Discours sur les arts et les sciences* is a masterpiece, the answer must be "no." It cannot even be called original, for Rousseau got most of its arguments out of what he had read. But that is not the point—the eloquence of the style is its distinction, eloquence tainted with rhetoric, to be sure, but spontaneous, powerful, poetical. The public made no mistake in applauding it—that section of the public to which Jean-Jacques addressed it, the little handful of leading spirits among whom he would have liked to be numbered, from whom he had not hitherto obtained the full recognition he craved. His readers relished the definite accents in which he denounced civilization, despising its amenities and condemning its lights, so proudly hailed by mankind and cherished under the name of progress.

"Fancy our little Rousseau," was Madame Dupin's comment, which summed up the general opinion. "Who would have thought it of him?"

According to Garat, the world was seized by "a kind of shock." Jean-Jacques was quite aware of it, was puffed up by a sense of his own importance, and immediately convinced himself that he must live up to the truth as he perceived it, live up to it in every respect, moral and physical, while he was revealing it to mankind. His spirit suffered a sudden change, like the change effected by a touch of grace. He fell into a state of exaltation such as he had been in when the ideas for his discourse took possession of him, but the exaltation was greater because the success of those ideas persuaded him they were sound. He believed himself inspired by God, appointed to fulfill a divine mission. A frenzy seized him in which he felt freed from all the contradictions which had baffled him all his life.

The whole trouble with him had been the fact that, kind-hearted, simple, well-meaning, in short, natural as he had been, he had conflicted with schemers, men of complicated psychology, frivolous and artificial, and had attempted without success to conform to their ways. He, though he was better than they, had made the mistake of trying to model himself on them or at least to bring himself down to their level, to allow them to think that they were in the right, whereas they were obviously and patently wrong. Like a fool, he had prostrated his genius before these knaves and idiots, and had let himself be intimidated by their fine manners and deceived by their false appearances. Henceforth, instead of making useless efforts to adjust himself to them, he would force them to adjust themselves to him. In his own words: "My foolish, morbid shyness, which I could not overcome, arose from my fear of violating polite conventions; so I resolved to take heart by setting myself against all conventions. Shame made me a cynic and a scoffer. I pretended to scorn the courtesy I was unable to practise."

This was really rather clever, to make a show of his weak points. And what a relief it must have been to him to cast off with one sweep of his hand all the fetters which had bound him!

"My temperament greatly influenced my maxims," he said. But it worked inversely as well, for he framed maxims to fit his conduct. His imagination soared until he stood on the heights of Plutarch's heroes, who had been the delight of his childhood. I am not exaggerating in hazarding the opinion that he aimed to set himself up as an example, to gather a following, to found a school, possibly to create a sect.

Any attempt to dispute him merely strengthened his opinions or led him to defend them with more violence. For a couple of years he conducted a polemical correspondence, answering the arguments of his opponents, among whom were King Stanislaus, Professor Gauthier, and his former friend Bordes of Lyons, in a long series of letters superior even to his discourse. They show him to have been an adept in paradoxical dialectics. Of course he had to compromise somewhat, stating his paradox in milder form, but this did not rob his essential idea of any of its force, and increased its effectiveness. This idea gained in weight and depth as he contended in its defense, for as it lost here and there by his conceding a point, it expanded in other directions. The fact that refinement of manners corrupts men's hearts does not imply that luxurious living results from the advancement of knowledge. Not at all. The two begin at the same moment, and the one cannot exist without the other. "The first cause of evil is inequality." He grew more vehement as he argued: "Because we must have meat-juice in our sauces, many of the sick must go without broth. Because we must have powder for our wigs, many of the poor must go without bread."

His fashionable audience was tickled with delight at his thunders, but his friends among the philosophers were only mildly amused by them and surprised by his eagerness to exploit his success, considering that he was "going it rather hard." But he cared not a whit for their skepticism. He put on the armor of conviction which the sharpest shafts of their irony failed to pierce. It did not matter to him whether or not they liked the lesson he set them by his behavior. His reform of morals began with a material transformation in himself. He discarded his gold lace and his white stockings, wore a round wig, and laid aside his sword, the same sword that had made a gentleman of him, and for which Madame de Warens had given him the silver handle. He also sold his watch. But he was not satisfied with this sumptuary revolution. He sent in his resignation as cashier to Monsieur de Francueil. To keep books for a capitalist was unworthy of a "free and honorable man, with a soul above fortune and the opinion of others."

In order to earn the "forty pennies a day" which he must have to live, he decided to copy music. Grimm jeered: "It would be better to peddle lemonade. All Paris will run after you, and you will grow rich." Grimm was an officious fellow. He had come to Paris with very little money but high social ambitions; he was conspicuous among the crowd one met in the salons chiefly because of the Germanic expressions with which he larded his conversation. But he had the acumen to foresee Jean-Jacques's popularity with the public. As a matter of fact, he was completely swamped with work and was offered more copying than any human being could possibly do. All sorts of people suddenly discovered in themselves a passion for music, and came in droves to ask him to draw for them pages of notes with elaborate clefs. His little room in the Rue Grenelle-Saint-Honoré was never empty; from morning to night an endless procession passed up and down his stairs, inquisitive visitors of both sexes and every social degree thronging almost superstitiously, as they would have reached out to touch the hump of a hunchback, to catch a glimpse of him at any cost, and to hear him speak.

He raved and cursed, but was actually less annoyed than he pretended to be, for though the crowd bothered him, he was secretly delighted with the admiration he received. Besides, the more rudely he behaved, the more stubbornly the invasion proceeded. People showered courtesies upon him and brought him armfuls of presents. These he indignantly rejected, but Thérèse and the "lieutenant criminal" were on the spot and needed no bribe to accept what Jean-Jacques had declined. There were baskets of fruit, once in a while a chicken, a bottle of good wine, and firewood.

The reader must not be misled into thinking that he turned his back on society. Though he preached asceticism, his manner of life had nothing of the eremite about it. He could hardly have enjoyed setting himself above the rabble had he cut himself off from mankind, and he could never have uprooted from his nature his deep-seated love of the companionship of cultivated men, and especially of fashionable women, in whose sympathy he basked and in whose flattery he reveled. He continued to wait on Madame Dupin and on Monsieur de Francueil, whose wife wrote to ask him whether it was true that he had left his children at the foundlings' home, and whom he answered in an avowal phrased with incredible arrogance. He went elsewhere as well—for instance, to the houses of Madame d'Épinay and Madame de Créqui. He was also to be seen at the weekly dinners of Baron d'Holbach, "Mæcenas d'Holbach," as Diderot called him, but less frequently than before. He did not relish the kind of conversation encouraged by "God's personal enemy," conversation, according to Morellet, who had a sly tongue, "which would bring down a thousand thunderbolts on the house—if they ever struck for that kind of thing." But Jean-Jacques took atheism more seriously than did that ecclesiastic. On one occasion, when he was a guest of Mademoiselle Quinault, he even broke out, on overhearing some blasphemous remark against God: "If it is base to let evil be spoken of an absent friend, then it is a crime to speak evil of one's God, who is present."

Moreover, as he was not satisfied even when the philosophers treated him on an equal footing, he was incensed when he felt they were looking down on him. Not because their irony hurt him; ah, no! a mind like his is far above the reach of their attacks. But they were too much inflated with a sense of their own importance. They even turned his sentiments to their own advantage, as Diderot had done when Jean-Jacques embraced him and shed tears over him at Vincennes in the presence of the treasurer of the Sainte Chapelle; and all that Diderot had been able to say to the dignitary was: "You see, Monsieur, how dearly my friends love me."

To satisfy them, Jean-Jacques would have had to put himself under their orders, to think and write as they directed him. They were always out for themselves. They suppressed him and spoiled his effects. He could not converse unless he was listened to, and he was unable to hold up his end in a symposium. To Alembert, however, he had no objection whatever as an interlocutor, for Alembert was a straight and serious-minded man. He wrote to the Marquise de Créqui: "His presence will not drive me away, but I beg of you not to think ill of me if any other third party causes me to disappear." He preferred to be received alone, and fled when he found company. Madame de Créqui was praised for the art with which she "tamed wild animals" because she begged him to take supper alone with her. A long "conference" with her was to him the height of joy. She was the first to hear the contents of his letter to Professor Gauthier, and later he went through his opera for her. If she spoke of going to see him in his "garret," he attempted to dissuade her, not because he declined to give her credit for "enough philosophy" to do him the honor, but because he feared he himself might not have enough to receive it without embarrassment. In short, he played the gallant with this lady. He liked her nearly as well as he did Madame de Chenonceaux, young and pretty as was the latter, a woman who had preferred to renounce her pleasant social life rather than play second fiddle to Madame Dupin. Such women have true discern-

THE PEASANT OF THE DANUBE 167

ment. They know and esteem true worth, and are not deflected from their admiration of a sage by interest in the hero of the latest fashionable scandal. Grimm was such a one. He, having failed to worm himself into the favor of Mademoiselle Fol, had had the idea of falling for several days into a coma. Though the doctors could make nothing of his strange malady and smiled up their sleeves at it, it had once more brought Grimm into prominence before the footlights of high society, and simultaneously the relations between him and Jean-Jacques had cooled perceptibly.

Occasionally Jean-Jacques reached a point when he sighed for open country, and at such times he fled from Paris and his friends in quest of its delights. He went to spend a few days at Marcoussis, where Madame Levasseur knew the vicar, and he accepted the hospitality of Monsieur Mussard, his fellow-townsman and relative, at Passy. This man, a retired jeweler, entertained theories like those of Monsieur de Buffon on the origin of fossil shells, and played the cello passably well. While staying with him, Jean-Jacques conceived the idea of writing a comic opera adapted to French taste. He composed both the words and the music of *Le devin du village*, which was performed in October, 1752, in the presence of the king and the court at Fontainebleau. It is a slight thing, a highly artificial pastoral, in the spirit of *L'Astrée*, where an aged peasant who is supposed to be an enchanter shows a girl the way to win back her fickle lover by making him jealous. But the music is melodious and deliciously sensuous.

During the performance, Jean-Jacques occupied the box of Monsieur de Cury, superintendent of the palace menus, over the stage and directly opposite the higher box in which sat his Majesty and Madame de Pompadour. Far from making any effort to appear at his best in honor of the occasion, Jean-Jacques had made a point of showing his usual self, "neither better nor worse," as he said. I can vouch for the fact that it was worse rather than better. He wore a full beard, and his wig was unkempt. He mistook his lapse in propriety for heroism, and he had seldom enjoyed anything more than feeling himself an object of curiosity to that highly aristocratic audience. His satisfaction increased as the performance went on. From the end of the first scene, which Rousseau describes as "really touching in its childlike innocence," a flattering murmur rose, at first from stray quarters of the auditorium, but soon from the whole house, gradually swelling into an uproar. Except for the fact that applause in the king's presence was forbidden, everyone in the theater would have been clapping. Enthusiasm waxed the greater because of the restraint put upon its expression, and Jean-Jacques was soon bathed in a subtle atmosphere which went to his head. He was, however, less susceptible to the plaudits of men, even though he might realize that they represented a chosen few of the best judges, than he was to the appreciation of women. He might be deeply moved in his vanity as an author, but still not so much as in his vain glory and his sensuality as a voluptuary. He was faint with emotion at overhearing the whispered comments of the women, who appeared to him "as beautiful as angels" as they exchanged opinions: "It is delightful!" "It is charming!" "Every note in it speaks to one's heart!"

When the performance ended, Monsieur de Cury brought from the Duke d'Aumont the message that Jean-Jacques's presence at the château was required next morning at eleven o'clock for a presentation to the king. A pension was to be conferred on him, and his Majesty, who had been delighted with the piece and had left the theater humming Colette's aria all off the key, wished to announce the good news himself to the fortunate composer of the *Devin*.

This sign of favor cast Jean-Jacques into the most agonizing perplexity. He would rather die than disgrace himself. What would happen if he proved unable to combat his overwhelming timidity, and if he could not express proper gratitude for the honor done him by "so great a king" without losing the dignified manner in which he had clothed himself? He would cover himself with ridicule unless he could embody "some deep and useful truth in a fine and well-deserved speech of praise." In short, he trembled lest he be scoffed at for some blunder and risk the loss of his hard-won reputation as a sage.

He called in his pride as an excuse for his weakness, and appealed to sophistry to extricate his groveling soul from its predicament. He writes in the *Confessions*: "To be sure, I stood to lose the pension which had been in a way proffered to me, but in losing it I freed myself from the yoke it would have imposed on me. Farewell to truth, to liberty, and to courage! How could I thenceforth dare to preach independence and fair-mindedness? If I were the recipient of a pension, I would be left no choice but to flatter or to keep my peace; moreover, what assurance had I that it would be paid? How many calls I would have had to make, how many appeals! I would have had to take more trouble, of a much more disagreeable kind, to hold on to the pension than to support myself without it."

Was ever a man deluded by a stranger conception of his own dignity? In order to preserve the independence which he insisted was indispensable to him and which he would have been able to attain at such trifling cost to himself, whatever he may say about it, he mortgaged his future and subjected himself to the most unworthy bondage. We shall see him pass in future from one master to another, from patroness to patron, a feather blown hither and yon at the mercy of every breeze, wandering from shelter to shelter, never achieving security and repose.

Thus he left Fontainebleau without having been presented to the king. When Diderot heard of his friend's incomprehensible behavior, he broke out in a frenzy. The mad fellow was simply impossible! Diderot pursued him to Madame d'Épinay's door one evening when Jean-Jacques was to take supper with her, and insisted on his getting into the cab with him. Having himself taken on the onerous task of the Encyclopædia in order to bring up his children, Diderot could not allow Jean-Jacques to add to his cynical irresponsibility as a father such contemptuous indifference to the lot of the woman with whom he lived. Carried away by his impetuous sympathies, which led him to concern himself with the affairs of other people even against their will, Diderot roundly berated his friend and issued orders, slapping his thigh to punctuate his remarks, to retrieve at all costs the pension he had forfeited. But he did not yet realize the whole extent of Jean-Jacques's obstinacy. Any attempt to force him to adopt a line of action simply made him recoil from it with violence. Ready at all times to take umbrage, he was prompt to take the bit in his teeth at the slightest suspicion that anyone was planning to dominate him or even to influence him. Diderot was presuming to lay down the law to him; he took a stubborn stand; and they were near to quarreling.

With *Le devin du village*, Jean-Jacques performed the nearly impossible task of reconciling the factions among the supporters of the opera, the one group, who sat beneath the queen, sponsoring Italian music, the other, under the king, favoring French music. But so strong was his desire to avenge himself on Rameau, who pursued him rancorously and took every opportunity to proclaim him a plagiarist and an upstart, that he could not resist destroying the harmony he had himself introduced, by publishing his "Letter on French Music" in 1753. In it he undertook to demonstrate that "the French have no music and are incapable of having any," thus showing himself unjust to his own age and false to the future, and he added that what music they had was "like a galloping cow." The pamphlet raised the storm on which Jean-Jacques counted. He was beside himself with delight. If we accept his own statement, there had never been an upheaval to equal it and no one but Tacitus himself could have described it. The *Devin*, in the meantime, had been honored with a second performance, this time in Paris. Louis XV bore no grudge against Jean-Jacques for his insolence, and chose to regard it as nothing worse than eccentricity. He sent him a draft for a hundred louis, and Madame de Pompadour, who had herself sung the rôle of Colette in the Bellevue theater, sent him fifty louis on her own account, in order not to lag behind her royal lover in munificence. In addition, Jean-Jacques was paid five hundred francs by the opera and five hundred more by Pissot, the publisher, so that his total profits rose to a very pretty sum.

At last, it seemed, his fortune was made. In the portrait by La Tour already mentioned, which was painted during this year, 1753, he is shown, as I have said, smiling happily. He appears as he had looked four years earlier, for by this time he wore a beard, which he had shaved off for the sittings, and he had also had his wig specially curled, suppressing the moral reformer and revolutionary philosopher in himself in favor of the composer and the man of letters. True, his little comedy *Narcisse,* which was anonymously performed at the Théâtre Français, was a failure, but he found consolation for his mortification by remarking in loud tones to a group of his friends at the Café Procope, whither he had fled during the performance, that he had written that wretched play which was being hissed down. The fact was already suspected anyhow. He knew it, but was no less impressed by his own courage, and he published *Narcisse* with a preface in which he supported a second time the theme of his prize discourse for the Dijon Academy, modifying it in some respects, so that it is evident success had made him more amenable. The substance of his argument is as follows: Since the harm has been already done, that is, since the arts and sciences have already debased the world, it is perhaps "better, after all, to keep them." They have given rise to vices, of course, but at the present time they are necessary to prevent those vices from running to crimes. It is proper to use them as antidotes or to turn them to account, as we do "the beasts we train to the bit." Apparently Jean-Jacques cherished no illusions concerning the vanity of men's ambition to make their mark, especially in literature, pointed out before his time by Alceste. But since there could no longer be any possibility of turning mankind back on the virtuous path, he thought it advisable to keep men occupied with "foolishness" in order to prevent them from occupying themselves with evil. Here we have a strange spectacle—Jean-Jacques resigning himself to play the part of a comedian and entertainer, after he has declared in his discourse that all abuses come from preferring talents to virtues, and that the true philosophy is "to withdraw into one's self and to listen to the voice of one's own conscience amid the silence of one's passions." Noble words indeed, these, words by which we wish that he had himself abided for his own glory and the benefit of mankind.

But the Academy at Dijon was on the alert. Possibly, as Jules Lemaître suggests, there was in that staid body of pedants some rebellious spirit, or one, as I am more inclined to believe, affiliated with a secret society, who noted the sleep of Brutus, planned to awake him, and to slip the murderous weapon into his hand. In any case, the fact is that in November, 1753, the members of the Burgundian Academy, mindful, one may suppose, of their laureate of 1750, published in the *Mercure de France* the following topic for a thesis: "How did the inequality of man arise? Is there anything in the law of nature to authorize it?"

Jean-Jacques heard the call, felt that it was being made to him. He was struck, as he says, by this great question, and since the Academy was so bold as to propose it to him, he persuaded himself that his duty lay in taking up the challenge. But in order to do so, he had to have leisure to think, and he must be in the country. Only in natural surroundings could he fashion his eloquence to accord with the ideas which fermented in his mind. He could do nothing in Paris, where he was disturbed and distracted, made restless by the artificial city life which he was soon to condemn. No conception could take form until he found peace and escaped from the chaos which so wrought him up that he had palpitations.

He packed his bundle and departed for Saint-Germain, not alone, but in company with Thérèse and her boarder, whom he describes as a good kind of woman, one of Thérèse's friends. But lest it be supposed that it was he who shouldered the expenses of the little party, I hasten to state that his traveling companions not only paid his way, but handled all details of the trip as well. Our philosopher might be proud indeed, but he could also be adaptable when he had to be, and could put his scruples to sleep. The women filled their time with domestic affairs, and left him alone with his thoughts; at meal-hours he turned in care-free fashion from his meditations to make merry with his companions. I surmise that Diderot, who had not long remained on chilly terms with Jean-Jacques, was looking out for the Levasseurs and had advised them how to handle him. He had already attempted to detach them from him by dangling before them the bait of a salt-shop or tobacco-booth to which he could set them up at the expense of Madame d'Épinay. Failing in this attempt, he had urged them to watch him well. He rejoiced when Jean-Jacques embarked once more on philosophical speculations, and encouraged him to give free rein to his love of nature, hoping to see him advance on the road to naturalism and lose his deism in pantheism. He continued to advise him, even at times to inspire him, and, as Jean-Jacques says, imparted to what he wrote the "hard, dark tone" which his work lost when Diderot no longer influenced it.

Jean-Jacques claims that he sought in the solitude of the Forest of Saint-Germain the vision of man's primitive state which he was attempting to describe. But it is a question whether he succeeded in obtaining any picture of it beyond the one his own imagination created. He attempted no critical study. His introduction to his subject begins with the words: "I set aside all facts." He gave himself up to feelings and to dreams, confusing the wild state of man with the pastoral, even the bucolic, state, representing primitive life in colors suitable for a picture of the Garden of Eden. To be sure, he adopted the Christian conception of the fall of man, and the error which he attributed to the human race is most closely related to the sin imputed in Holy Writ to Adam and Eve. According to him, the evil originally grew and fell into the hands of man from the tree of science. On the day when men linked themselves into society, they acted counter to the laws of nature and began to fall into evil ways. The state of society produced the state of reflection, which finally debased man by giving rise to inequality. How simple it all was! Only note and appreciate, for in this fact lay all the effect produced by Jean-Jacques's discourse, that in his sophistical argument, the idea of equality slid easily off the spiritual and moral plane where Christianity had placed it, and entered the sentimental and material plane.

He undertook to dissipate whatever misunderstanding might persist in the minds of his readers, by an appeal to revolt, which he termed the most sacred of all duties. He anathematized all property rights: "The first man, who, having fenced in a bit of ground, thought of saying, 'This is mine,' and discovered that other men were so easy as to take him at his word, laid the foundations of civil society. Think of the crimes, the wars, the wretchedness, and the sufferings which would have been spared the human race if one man had pulled up the fence posts, filled in the ditches, and cried to his fellows: 'Beware of this impostor! You are ruined if you lose sight of the truth that the fruits of the earth belong to all and the earth to no one!' "

This represents his tone, a tone which to us moderns seems fit only for a child's primer. But his rhetoric tingled with even more passion than that of his first discourse, and all of 1793 is in his vehement and unrestrained denunciation. The Academy at Dijon did not dare to crown the *Discours sur l'inégalité* as it had crowned the *Discours sur les science et les arts*. The member whom I have suspected of being responsible for the subject did not raise his voice to protest against the award of the prize to a certain Abbé Talbert. This time, Jean-Jacques passed over the heads of the learned body, which he no longer needed, since his reputation had been made. He printed his thesis, and addressed it to "The Republic of Geneva," with a dedication begging the "great lords" of the free city to testify their consideration and gratitude to the working people and lower classes, all their equals by natural right and the rights of birth.

His dedication is dated from Chambéry on the road to Geneva, whither his old friend Gauffecourt had invited him to go, attended by the inevitable Thérèse, whom his health required him to trail about on all his travels. Remembering the humiliations which he had suffered in his native city, he had burned, ever since he became famous, to be accorded a distinguished reception by the Genevans. But before he made his triumphal entry, he parted at Lyons with Gauffecourt, who had not hesitated to lay violent siege to Thérèse on the way. At least she complained that he did, either to flatter her vanity or, more likely, to stir up a scandal, which would have been more in keeping with her character. Jean-Jacques could not possibly have been jealous of Gauffecourt, who was over sixty years old and gouty, shriveled with fast living. But the ugly means employed by the old fellow in his attempts to seduce Thérèse, and his disloyalty, disgusted and grieved him. "What a sweet and holy illusion is friendship," he cries in the *Confessions*. He had no feeling that a woman should not share her favors, but he did not think the sharing should be done behind the back of either of the men concerned. If Gauffecourt wanted Thérèse, who was, to be sure, no longer "either young or pretty," why did he not say so to Jean-Jacques? Jean-Jacques would certainly have surrendered her to him with tears of tender emotion. But when Gauffecourt took advantage of Jean-Jacques's descents from the chaise, in which they were traveling by easy stages, in order to read to the poor woman from "an abominable book," or to show her "infamous pictures," then he felt Gauffecourt's conduct to be unworthy of a natural man. Jean-Jacques said nothing, but was hurt to the quick. The sight of Madame de Warens, on whom he paid a call, and the new grief, of a different sort but no less poignant, which his visit to her caused him, hardly sufficed to make him forget his woes.

"Mamma" had been abandoned by the "beloved brother" Wintzenried, finally translated into Baron de Courtilles, when he married. She was still living in the Savoyan capital, but was dragging out a truly wretched existence. Jean-Jacques at various times had sent her small sums of money, but all these had merely been swallowed up in the flood of debts in which her improvidence had involved her. Her pension was still punctually paid, but was invariably mortgaged in advance. It cannot be said in all conscience that Jean-Jacques failed to do enough for her. He was hardly in a position to relieve her, and one can understand how, knowing her difficulties to be insoluble, he made no greater efforts than he did in her behalf. But since all he did was to give her a little money, when he saw with his own eyes to what straits she was reduced, and then abandoned her to her fate, why does he say that he considered "devoting his life and that of Thérèse to making hers happy"? Why attempt to convince us of the self-evident fact that it would have been an act of madness to identify his own existence with hers, and that he gave proof of magnanimity enough when he invited her to come and live in obscurity with him —if he did anything of the sort? We must take all this with a grain of salt, as well as the affecting episode he narrates of the little ring which "Mamma" slipped from her finger on to that of Mademoiselle Levasseur and which Mademoiselle Levasseur returned, kissing her hand and shedding tears as she did so, in a manner worthy of her lover. Jean-Jacques was certainly deeply moved to see Madame de Warens again, "in such a state, good heavens, in such destitution!" But I do not believe for a moment that, seeing her grown old and helpless, he thought at all of the radiant vision she had been that Easter morning in 1728, beside the Annecy cathedral. His eyes were on the future, not on the past. He was burning, as I said, to be back in Geneva among his kinsfolk. Madame de Warens professed a faith not tolerated in the Calvinist city, a faith which he himself must abjure before he could be reinvested with his rights as a citizen.

If he suffered from any lingering compassion for her, it was drowned in the excitement of his reception at Geneva. He was fêted, flattered, and celebrated. He glowed with patriotic and republican enthusiasm. We may picture him, dressed with extreme simplicity, as became a sage, confessing his errors to the commission of five appointed by the consistory, holding his head high all the while, in order that he might appear again as the representative of his own faith and his own family. Can this be, indeed, Jean-Jacques, the son of clockmaker Rousseau? Yes, for this is the man who, though still a child in years, was in pride the equal of the free man he is now, the same who chose flight and vagabondage rather than a flogging at the hands of the engraver Ducommun.

It took Jean-Jacques four months to get his fill of celebrity in Geneva. He made the accquaintance of a number of outstanding men of the town, including a pastor and several professors, but he soon found that the arena in which he had once dreamed of confining his ambition was too barren and too cramped for him. Honors were showered upon him, but he missed Paris and France, men of letters, philosophers—above all, fashionable ladies. The Danube peasant could not be at his best without an audience to whom he appeared as rough as a bear. A "bear" was what he was soon to be called, and one of the most conspicuous of the ladies at whose feet he fawned was soon to expend her utmost efforts in taming him—Madame d'Épinay.

CHAPTER II

THE HERMITAGE

MADAME D'ÉPINAY, to whom, as the reader will remember, Jean-Jacques had been introduced by her lover, Monsieur de Francueil, could not have been over thirty years of age in 1754, having been born about 1725. She was the daughter of Tardieu d'Esclavelles, a brigadier of infantry, and had been married to her cousin, Lalive d'Épinay, a dissipated rake who abandoned her shortly to enjoy himself in his own way. As she appears in the little portrait of her by Léotard of Geneva, dressed in a blue corsage, a white cap, and lace elbow sleeves, she cannot be called pretty, may even be called plain. Her complexion was muddy, her forehead protuberant, her nose lacked dignity, and she was short and scrawny. In her own self-portrait which she made after the fashion of the time, she describes herself as having had a good figure; but her saving features were the intelligent sparkle of her dark eyes, her sensuality or loose morals, which she took for emotional responsiveness, and her alert interest in every kind of topic, making her—at once romantic and logical as she was—one of the most typical exponents of the eighteenth century, that century in which the intellectual curiosity of the women stimulated to the highest pitch the scientific zeal of the men.

From the first she liked her lover's secretary and "took delight" in chatting with him during that autumn of country life which he spent at Chenonceaux. She must have been kind, at any rate she could not have been touchy, for she paid scant heed to Jean-Jacques's bursts of ill temper. He helped her to compose letters to her thirteen-year-old son, and played on her sympathies by telling her his troubles in "a queer, innocent way," so she forgave him his gruff manners and perhaps actually liked his snubs. He had no scruples about implying that she would have been his mistress had he put himself out to pay court to her. Probably she would. But every physical circumstance tended to keep them apart, and he allowed Grimm to take the place of Francueil, who was neglecting her, in her affections. That sly Grimm, moreover, took up her defense with heat on one occasion when she was accused of making away with some papers in a financial matter. His intervention involved him in a duel, from which he emerged with a wound. Such chivalrous conduct gave him a claim to her gratitude which Jean-Jacques would have been ill-advised to dispute. Moreover, Jean-Jacques had no intention whatever of pursuing onto high ground such an adept in fashion as Grimm, who, we may appropriately remark here, had once been reader to the Crown Prince of Saxe-Gotha. It was hardly Jean-Jacques's place, having discarded all such trumpery, to draw his sword in behalf of a lady; and even though he might still condescend to take part in one of his own comedies on the stage of the private theater at La Chevrette, Madame d'Épinay's château above Saint-Denis, where she spent a large part of the year, he became constantly more scornful of all the tomfoolery called "fine manners" in order to disguise its silly pretentiousness. The very sight of Grimm, all painted and powdered, over-elaborately dressed, as his countrymen usually are when they attempt to adapt themselves to French social ways, overdoing his courtesies too, fluttering from group to group, was enough to turn our hero's already dark misanthropy deep black. Why, indeed, should he prostrate himself before Madame d'Épinay's aristocratic friends? He was no noble, to be sure, according to French standards, but all the same his newly acquired title of Citizen of Geneva elevated him to the front rank in a country recently recognized as a sovereign state by the king of Sardinia. He insisted that he "thought much more of the duties than of the privileges connected with this distinction," but a little knowledge of the constitution of the Calvinist city shows that in flaunting it before the eyes of society he was not wearing a mere chicken-feather in his cap. Diderot remarked with great truth: "Rousseau wished the title of Citizen only because he could not aspire to that of Monseigneur." But he had never before been so aggressively himself nor lived so consistently up to the rôle he began to play after his first discourse. "I was quite transformed," he wrote, betraying his megalomania in smug complacence. "My acquaintances and friends no longer recognized me. I ceased to be the timid soul, shamefaced rather than modest, who had dared neither to put himself forward nor to raise his voice, who quailed before a gibe, who blushed at the glance of a woman. I was bold, proud, dauntless, and I went about with an assurance all the stronger because it was natural and resided in my soul rather than in my manner. The scorn which my profound meditations engendered in me for the customs, maxims, and prejudices of my time made me impervious to the ridicule of men who shared them, and I crushed their witty little jests under my pronouncements as I would have crushed an insect between my fingers. What a change! All Paris quoted the tart and biting sarcasms of the same man who, two months earlier and ten years later, could never think of the right thing to say nor of the proper words to use."

He broke with Baron d'Holbach, then renewed the friendship with him when his wife died. But he realized that the Baron's coterie continued to look at him askance, especially since his abjuration of faith at Geneva, and that the incorrigible materialist Holbach never spoke of him otherwise than as "the little bluestocking." Consequently, though Jean-Jacques had the magnanimity to pretend to carry on frank discussion with him when they met at Madame d'Épinay's house, he let slip no occasion to oppose his ideas. He cast a gloom over the brilliant gatherings at La Chevrette, where cleverness and corruption went hand in hand and where everyone was as busily occupied in spinning adulterous intrigues as in unraveling the world's most serious problems, social, philosophical, and political, all with the same flippancy. The only man esteemed by Jean-Jacques was Duclos, to whom he dedicated the *Devin du village,* out of gratitude for his having secured its production. Diderot, who became more and more officious in his rôle of mentor, exasperated him all too often, and Grimm, whose ways and manners he detested, put him out of all patience by never addressing him except with a sneer or an out-and-out snub. Grimm's rapier wit baffled him as completely as the heavy pedantry of Baron d'Holbach; and he could never see old Gauffecourt without recalling his satyr-like performance with Thérèse.

While the forest of Montmorency reëchoed with the winding horns and baying hounds of the pack of the Prince of Condé pursuing the stag, Jean-Jacques sought solitude in the very depths of the Park of La Chevrette. There Madame d'Épinay occasionally joined him, slipping away from the gay circle who made much of her and vied in efforts to please her. Her malicious cousin Mademoiselle d'Ette, Valory's mistress, as Madame de Lismore was Marmontel's and Madame d'Houdetot Saint-Lambert's, said to her with a bitter-sweet smile: "Look out, my dear, your bear has gone and poked his nose into another hive. You will get a gruff welcome from him." But, quite the other way, the "bear" was docility itself when he was left alone

THE HERMITAGE

with the young woman. He chatted freely of himself, his plans, his health, his troubles. Just at this time Tronchin, the illustrious Genevan physician who was visiting Paris, offered him a position as public librarian in Geneva at a salary, large for the time, of twelve hundred francs a year. He hesitated whether or not to accept it; at least he feigned hesitation, the truth being that after his recent experience in his native city he had firmly decided never to live there. In the *Confessions* he writes that his reason was he could not have endured living near Voltaire, who had settled at Les Délices, close to Lake Leman. But, as a matter of fact, his relations with the Arbiter of Letters were, up to this time, still perfectly courteous, even cordial. The two had even been drawn closer by a misunderstanding, quickly cleared up, which arose from Voltaire's resentment of an attack on him by a different Rousseau. Jean-Jacques had assumed that he must address his second Discourse to his "chief," as he called Voltaire, and the "chief" had replied in a jocular letter, doubtless intended to sting a little, for he invited Rousseau to "come and browse in his pastures," but, for all that, praising him extravagantly. Certainly the propinquity of Voltaire was not the reason for Jean-Jacques's refusal to accept the lucrative post he was offered. One actual reason was that he felt he was not in the odor of sanctity at Geneva. If he had not liked the town, it was because he was aware that before long he would not be liked by it. His work on inequality had in general made a bad impression, and Thérèse, who felt no desire to pass the rest of her days away from France, in the gloomy Calvinist citadel, pointed out to him that he would be unwise to put his trust in men inimical to his ideas. As we know, she had been quick to detect Jean-Jacques's tendency to suspect anyone and everyone, and she toadied to him by pointing out enemies all about him—rescuing him, according to his statement, from dangers into which he would have plunged blindly. Another reason was that he did not wish to sacrifice his personal liberty. The position which would have assured his independence gave him the shivers, like the sight of a prison, simply because it would have tied him to one spot. And a final and decisive reason was that he relished too highly his abhorrence of Parisian society.

One day, before his trip to Geneva, he and Madame d'Épinay had wandered through the park as far as the water-works, where there was a pretty vegetable garden and a small cottage in ruinous condition, known as the Hermitage. He said to her, with a sigh: "Ah, Madame, that is exactly the refuge I would love! What a delicious spot to live!" Madame d'Épinay did not respond to his hint. But she then and there came to a decision. With the reserve of women whose whole existence revolves around their emotional imagination, and who delight in planning and carrying out in secret elaborate preparations to spring a pleasant surprise on someone they love, she took advantage of the absence of Jean-Jacques to repair the Hermitage. And then, when her "bear" was wandering about with her from grove to grove, talking of Tronchin's offer, she led his steps imperceptibly toward the spot where he had formerly expressed a wish to seek refuge. There, instead of the ruinous hut he had seen, stood a one-story house, with a projecting wing, topped by a fine tile roof.

"What do I see?"

"There, my dear bear!" said Madame d'Épinay, smiling on him. "This is your den. It is yours for the sake of our friendship. And I hope you will have no more cruel thoughts of leaving me."

Jean-Jacques could not but be affected by such thoughtfulness. Never in all his life did he remember being so touched, and he fell at the feet of his benefactress. He shed tears, of course, over her hand—perhaps it shook a little—

as she held it out to him. But to have accepted on the spot the generous gift she made him would have been too fine, or too simple, or too unworthy of his "teacher and consoler, Plutarch." He made objections. Was Madame d'Épinay trying to make a lackey of a friend? He quibbled. But she knew that although she might not have achieved his conquest, she had at least gone far toward weakening his resistance. She labored to allay his last scruples, argued him down, enlisted the Levasseurs or attempted to do so. Perhaps he must have a letter to exonerate him in the eyes of posterity? She wrote it:

"You have often heard me speak of the Hermitage on the edge of the Forest of Montmorency. It has the loveliest of situations. There are five rooms, a kitchen, a cellar, a vegetable garden of one acre, a spring of running water, and all the forest for a garden. If you decide to stay in France, you, my good friend, are its proprietor. I remember well that you once told me you would not think of going anywhere else if you had an income of a hundred pistoles. This is my proposition: let me add what capital you need, over and above what your last book has brought you in, to make up your hundred pistoles, and I will make any arrangement that suits you in regard to it."

Jean-Jacques made his plans. The house was well arranged, "was very comfortable for a family of three," for he at once thought not only of Thérèse, his "governess," but of the "lieutenant criminal," his secretary, as well. Madame d'Épinay was to furnish the place. He would employ a gardener and would pay his wages out of the hundred pistoles which— But, as for that, why should he not again copy music? He would be within reach of clients, for Madame d'Épinay's own guests would surely wander out to see him in his rustic retreat, to kill time or to satisfy their idle curiosity. It was ideal; here he would have peace and the joys of country life which he had missed so sorely ever since he had lived at Les Charmettes, and he would have companionship to boot. He accepted.

"I have at last come to a decision, Madame, and you do not need to be told that you have won the day. I shall go to the Hermitage for the Easter festival, and shall stay as long as you will allow me."

So overjoyed was Madame d'Épinay that she could not restrain her exultation in Grimm's presence. She had concealed all her plans from him, but he had to know them in the end. Tactful as he was, he was unable to suppress his amazement and his disapproval.

"This is indeed folly! You will see for yourself that Rousseau cannot endure being alone, even for two weeks. That fellow must have the incense of the crowd and the amusements of the city."

Grimm's prediction, which showed that he understood only one side of Jean-Jacques's nature, was accepted at once by the band of philosophers, and especially by Baron d'Holbach and Diderot. The author of the two Discourses, distrusted as a disciple, was frowned upon when he elected to withdraw from the rest. They attempted to dissuade him from leaving Paris, suspected him of ulterior motives, jeered at him, rained sarcastic comments on him, stirred up Thérèse and Madame Levasseur to combat him— Thérèse, who loathed country life, and Madame Levasseur, who was seventy years old and very frail in health. In short, they did all they should have done if their object had been to drive him into going. He went.

On April 9, 1756, Madame d'Épinay went out of her way to meet Jean-Jacques, Thérèse, and the "lieutenant criminal" in her own carriage. Her farmer went to handle the scanty baggage of the three, who settled that same day on the edge of the Forest of Montmorency. And here I leave Jean-Jacques to describe his own impressions for I am incapable of doing it any better. He wrote:

"Though the weather was cold and there was still snow on the ground, the earth had come to life. Violets and primroses were out, the trees were in bud, and the night I arrived I heard the first nightingale singing almost at my window in a copse which bordered on the house. I slept lightly and awoke with a start, forgetting I had been transplanted, and thinking I was still in the Rue de Grenelle. The notes sent a sudden shiver through my frame, and I cried to myself: 'All my hopes are realized!'"

It goes without saying that he turned first, not to the task of classifying his notes and establishing a routine for himself, but of taking possession of the country which was his own domain, and of planning for his rambles. "There was no footpath, no thicket, no grove," not a single bower of greenery about his abode which he did not explore on the very first day after his arrival. The wellspring of his joy was a child's whole-hearted delight, and he would have risen to divine heights if in his bliss there had not been a tinge of feverish elation. His happiness was defiled by a kind of ignoble triumph and by outbursts of pride in which he saw visions of all those who had put him to shame, or who he felt were inimical to him, lying prostrate at his feet in his illusory omnipotence.

Remember that he had reached the critical age of forty-four. He arrived at the Hermitage and settled there just as the spring broke, and he felt himself again the Rousseau of his youth. The "burning but sterile flames" which had consumed him and had then died down in embers, flared up once more. He was conscious of the emptiness of his heart, unfilled by the presence of Thérèse at his side, and endeavored to persuade himself that he had made a mistake in not employing the first years of their intimacy in "adorning with learning and acquirements" the mind of the unfortunate girl. He must have forgotten that she was so dull she could not even read the hours on the sun-dial. He missed the companionship of a woman capable of thought, or at least of the appearance of thought, who would give heed to him, study to please him, and be the crowning reward of his glory. Thérèse, far from sharing his delightful excursions, more often than not sought pretexts to avoid the strolls he at first suggested that she take with him, but which he soon ceased to suggest to her. He even ceased to share her room, and began to treat her in every respect as his sister. He ate his heart out, craving affection. Madame d'Épinay could not be the one to satisfy his hunger, for he knew she loved another man, and was aware also that in spite of her delicate attentions to him and the wheedling caresses she showered upon him, she was entirely oblivious of certain shades of his complicated emotional nature. He said to her, on one occasion: "Some day you may come to realize that my heart speaks a different language from any other." All he did for her was to give her advice concerning the education of her son, "the scholar," as he called him, advice in which we can discover the seeds of those principles he was soon to elaborate in the *Émile*. He also sent her sheets of figures, for he kept accounts with her, in which he informed her that his gardener was robbing him and taking the peaches from his orchard to sell in the Montmorency market. He showed, too, some anxiety concerning her feminine indispositions, and particularly concerning a chronic indigestion from which she suffered, but all the time he felt secret regret that she was too simple to allow him to compliment her on her "darling idiocy." Her conversation, "pleasant enough in a crowd," was "uninspiring alone," and occasionally a silence fell between them which lasted so long that it became embarrassing.

He was writing, but the works on which he was engaged, *Paix perpétuelle* and *Polysynodie,* did not absorb him sufficiently to wean him from his erotic obsession. It pursued him into the chestnut grove near his cottage where he best loved to roam, a place which nowadays teems with refreshment stands. As he wandered over the heights of Andilly and Montlignon, or dropped down to the pool of Saint-Gratien, he was haunted by his memories. The fresh woodland air, the song of a redbreast or a finch, the murmur of a brook, carried him away until he was lost in "too seductive reverie," the mood to which he was born; and then he basked again in the unchanging graciousness and charming smiles of the women who had touched his heart in his amorous youth. Mademoiselle Galley, Mademoiselle de Graffenried, Mademoiselle de Breil, Madame Bazile, Madame de Larnage, all his delightful pupils, even down to vivacious Zulietta. He added to their number creatures of his imagination, "celestial in their virtues, as in their beauty." He would have liked to spend all his days in their society, and, leaving them only to snatch a hasty meal, he was wont to flee back to the groves they frequented. Houris or nymphs, whatever they were, figures painted by his feverish imagination, they exhausted him by the sensual excesses of chimerical delight in which he swam, and, after singeing his wings in the light of the heavenly bodies, he was forced to fall back on guttered candles.

He had at least begun work on *La nouvelle Héloïse*. In order to "give free rein to the need of love which he had never been able to satisfy and which was consuming him," in order to manufacture for himself a bliss which might compensate him for the bliss "which destiny owed him" but which it had always denied him, he conceived the romance in which he himself figured, exactly as he was, with all the faults and all the virtues he recognized in himself. In it his two "heart's idols," love and friendship, went hand in hand or were inextricably combined, each lending grace to the other. In it Jean-Jacques set himself free. To begin with, the scene of his story is Lake Leman, where he had wandered along the shore after his recent journey to Geneva, and which was the background for all his childhood. Then the principal figures of his story are, first, two women, Julie the fair, Claire the dark, the one so full of life, the other so gentle (shades of the luncheon at the Château de Toune!); and, second, two men, the one Wolmar, deliberate and thoughtful, the other, Saint-Preux, young, eager, passionate. But no simple pairing off—can one forget Chambéry? Julie and Claire are both there— but Julie alone is beloved, and by both friends. Claire loves Saint-Preux, but Claire is superfluous, and when Saint-Preux, Julie, and Wolmar have threaded their way through all the dangers of their incredible situation and run the gamut of its perplexities, why, then—one must remember that Saint-Preux, like the Jean-Jacques who waited on Monsieur de Gouvon, was the social inferior of the others and could no more marry Julie than Jean-Jacques could have married Mademoiselle de Breil.

He was dreaming over his romance, writing scattered letters to incorporate into it as the inspiration seized him, under Madame d'Épinay's wing, when a woman came into his life who gave to Julie the definite traits she had hitherto lacked. This was the Countess d'Houdetot, whom he had met almost ten years earlier, before her marriage. Her advent altered the nature of his fictitious narrative and infused into it all the life it contains. The Countess d'Houdetot was a less virtuous lady than the wife of Wolmar, more like Madame de Warens than like Julie, and she had a lover, the Marquis de Saint-Lambert. Saint-Preux was the friend of Wolmar, just as Jean-Jacques was the friend of Saint-Lambert, and as he had been the friend of Claude Anet. It seems there are men born to fill such a post! Madame d'Houdetot was twenty-six at the time. Her husband, a captain in the mounted police, did not bother his head to find out how she employed the hours he failed to spend at her side. She leased Eaubonne, a league from the Hermitage, a charming country place bordering on the estate where Saint-Lambert lived, in order to spin out the web of her idyllic love-affair with him, the former successful rival of Voltaire for the favors of the Marquise du Châtelet. But Saint-Lambert, poet though he was, author of a long didactic poem in imitation of Thomson's *Seasons*, was also a soldier and was for the time being on active service. Madame d'Houdetot had nothing to occupy her time.

She was an ugly woman, with a pock-marked yellow countenance, and round, short-sighted, and slightly crossed eyes. But she had charm, a dashing sort of elegance, high spirits, and a ready wit; on her lips there was always the suspicion of a jest or of merry laughter, both wholly spontaneous. She was cultivated too, had translated the *Pastor Fido* when she was fifteen, and had accomplishments as well, playing the clavichord, dancing, writing verses like her lover—but her verses, unlike his, were sprightly and graceful, never dull. One autumn day she suddenly and unexpectedly entered Jean-Jacques's sanctum, having left her carriage mired in the depths of a valley. She was wearing heavy boots, borrowed from one of her lackeys to replace the little slippers she had lost in the muck. How funny it was! With her pretty manner, all the more engaging for a touch of boyish awkwardness, she begged forgiveness for her intrusion and asked Thérèse for clothes into which to change. She bubbled over with laughter:

"See here! Your friend, Saint-Lambert, sent me to you. Apparently you are the only man in the world to whom I may talk about my feelings for him. He is the perfect lover. I simply must tell someone, just as soon as I think of them, all the passionate things he cannot hear just now. But what a risk he would be taking—except that you are a philosopher."

"I am a romancer as well."

While she shared a country supper and dried her stockings before the fire, he read to her bits from the *Héloïse*. How those pages tingled! He promised to copy them out so that she might know them better and lose herself in rapture. Ah, how she would love to talk of love to a man who wrote of it so feelingly!

She promised to return. But the autumn wore on, and then the winter passed, without his seeing her again. He thought of nothing but her, and to her Saint-Preux addressed his impassioned speeches. Though Jean-Jacques might have considered that a woman was at his side who would be hurt to think he cared more deeply for another than for her, he paid no attention to the idea. He sighed and squandered kisses on the dress the Countess had left when she wore away Mademoiselle Levasseur's cast-off frock. What would Jean-Jacques, "the grave citizen of Geneva," not have given to cut one single lustrum off his years, to be Saint-Lambert's age again! And yet what real difference is there between a man of forty-five and a man of forty? Alas! Saint-Lambert was an officer, Saint-Lambert was a nobleman, Saint-Lambert was a dandy and a society man; Jean-Jacques was a plebeian, and sickly, and nothing worth looking at in his rustic garb!

Mimie, as Madame d'Houdetot was called by her intimates, was apparently not coming back. Was the gay little thing afraid of the old bear in his den? Hardly. Like the swallow, she was merely waiting for the spring before she reappeared. This time she came through the grove which shaded the threshold of the Hermitage, on horseback, dressed like a man. Our Gruffanuff, though he boasted that he hated all that kind of masquerading, was unable to resist her romantic costume, innocent in semblance but artful in design. Madame d'Houdetot had been well aware of the impression she had made on Jean-Jacques when she appeared in her big boots. To make sure of an even greater success, she had arrayed herself in thoroughly masculine fashion and had bound her leather-clad legs in whip-lash.

When she left him, he was no longer tormented by the pangs of love, but consumed by devouring passion. He made her swear to let him meet her again. She promised. She was a flirt, of course, but she was kind, and the timid advances of her middle-aged devotee worried her not a whit. As she was a fine walker and enjoyed botanizing, she appointed frequent meetings on the terraced slopes known as Mount Olympus, where Jean-Jacques always arrived long in advance of the hour set, and, while he waited for her, scribbled incoherent notes, which he left for her in a cranny. They wandered together through the woods and fields, chatting and cooing. But that was not enough. As soon as they separated, they sat down to write long missives to each other. The author of the *Héloïse* was on his own ground when wielding a pen. He did not need even to change his tone to express the outpourings of his own heart after the outpourings of Saint-Preux. He addressed the Countess in familiar and in formal terms all in the same breath, calling her sometimes by her own first name, Sophie, sometimes, with execrable taste, Sarah, for a high-born damsel who falls in love with her lackey in a novel by Saint-Lambert.

He groveled, teased, domineered, dripped adoration. She had taken his arm as they walked, had let him kiss her cheek and even her lips—he reminded her of all this, and took advantage of these signs of favor to demand more. She talked to him of Saint-Lambert, and "with delicious shivers" he took deep draughts of the "poison cup." "The contagious strength of love"—ah! why would she not give him, if only for a moment, some of the affection she so lavished on another? His impassioned pleading wrung her heart. In order to please him, she took down her fine black curls, which rippled to her knees. All in vain. He fumed because he could not kindle "the least spark" in the heart of his idol.

The pitiable state of his emotions was intensified by the times he went to stay with her at Eaubonne. From the moment he left the Hermitage, the thought of the caress she would bestow on him when he met her was enough to turn him dizzy. His eyes dazzled, and he had to stop and sit down on a bank or by the side of the road to avoid falling senseless. His thoughts whirled ceaselessly and inevitably about in the same circle. She might have melted, but the hour of his closest approach to her was the hour of his totally fortuitous and definite defeat. For in the end, virtuous as Madame d'Houdetot might be, or rather loyal as she intended to remain to Saint-Lambert, she plunged down the headlong slope that leads to ruin. Any other man than Rousseau would have forced her to repent her rash behavior. One night, after a supper alone together at Eaubonne, they wandered into a grove where she had made an ornamental waterfall at his suggestion. Moonlight flooded the scene, the copses, the bank of turf on which Jean-Jacques sat at the feet of the Countess, a huge acacia laden with heavily scented flowers, the most subtle of love-potions. He talked and talked with vehemence, subsiding at exactly the right instant, and as she let her fingers play over his tearful face, he kissed her knees. She murmured:

"Never was a man so lovable, and never a lover who loved like you."

Her distress increased till she felt faint. He went on talking. He was "sublime." So sublime, in fact, that he let slip the moment; and a carter had time to drive his wagon along the road just outside the garden wall. A carter at night behind a wall! He suggested the Virgilian verses of *La tristesse d'Olympie*. But the fellow's horse was out of hand, and the Countess, suddenly recalled to earth, burst into a peal of laughter at the sound of his voice breaking burlesquely on the scene, as if at a cue:

"Get-ee-ap, you nag! Go on, old rack-of-bones!"

As may well be imagined, Jean-Jacques had not carried on his affair with Madame d'Houdetot with sufficient precautions to keep it a secret. He often met his adored Sophie at La Chevrette among the guests of Madame d'Épinay, and his attentions to her excited notice and set the gossips agog. The Levasseurs were especially active. Thérèse realized the transformation in Jean-Jacques which the Countess's first visit to the Hermitage had made, and she talked about it with Madame d'Épinay's lackeys in the servants' quarters, where she enjoyed herself much more than in her own cottage and whither she sped on every occasion as soon as the "bear's" back was turned. There is no incentive to free speech like a good bottle of wine, and Madame d'Épinay knew it well. Her jealousy was aroused, and though she may not herself have filled the cup of Jean-Jacques's companion, she managed to encounter her at times when she knew confidence would be easily won. Thérèse told her how she heard Jean-Jacques raving and sobbing at night and even getting out of his bed. He was writing letters and receiving them. Madame d'Épinay expressed a desire to know more about the correspondence, and so Thérèse rummaged among his papers, obtaining evidence to enlighten her. Madame d'Épinay notified Grimm, who was hostile to Saint-Lambert, of what was going on at Eaubonne. Madame d'Houdetot's lover heard the news at once. There was no necessity for an anonymous letter sent by Thérèse, as the legend has long run, and anyway no such letter from that ignorant woman could have remained anonymous, her scrawls being as good as a signature. The affairs of Jean-Jacques became still more common knowledge. It was an open secret that he had lost his head over

Madame d'Épinay's sister-in-law, and Baron d'Holbach came to La Chevrette for the sole purpose of enjoying the spectacle of his folly. Diderot exclaimed: "I knew it! His going off that way could come to no good end."

Diderot had done everything in his power to get Jean-Jacques back to Paris. He left him pretty well alone during the summer of 1756, but with the return of cold weather he renewed his scolding and his admonitions. He had young Deleyre, a fanatical disciple, write to him, and he wrote himself, reminding him of all the beggars waiting for his alms, and of Madame Levasseur, whose death might be on his head if he kept her in the country over winter: "O Rousseau, consider the woman of eighty!" As a matter of fact, she was only seventy, and one sees quite as many hale and hearty old women in the country as in the city. Rousseau told Diderot to mind his own business. Diderot was annoyed, and printed in the *Préface du fils naturel* the statement: "Only a wicked man lives by himself." There could have been a real quarrel this time if Madame d'Épinay, with whom her "bear" was for the moment in high favor, had not intervened. She exacted from both a promise to forget their grievances. But the reconciliation was tinged with resentment, ready to break out again on any pretext.

Before another break occurred, Diderot, knowing of Jean-Jacques's misfortunes, thought the time ripe to recall the strayed philosopher to the fold of the Encyclopædists, and got together with Holbach and Grimm. The three, who were hand in glove, and who went so far, some time later, as to collaborate in pawing over Madame d'Épinay's memoirs to find material for an attack on their former ally, by then their enemy, put their heads together to turn Jean-Jacques's benefactress against him. He was warned by Madame d'Houdetot herself that Saint-Lambert "knew about it but knew wrong," and he cleverly took the offensive in order not to be put in the position of having to defend his innocence. On September 4, 1757, he wrote to Saint-Lambert complaining that the Countess had changed: "She scarcely speaks to me, even of you; she finds any number of excuses to keep out of my way. She treats me exactly as though she wanted to be rid of me." What does it mean? Has Saint-Lambert issued instructions, and, if so, of what nature? Is it possible that he suspects his friend? Jean-Jacques unblushingly protests his innocence: "A thousand times no, Saint-Lambert! In the breast of Jean-Jacques Rousseau no traitor's heart beats, and I would scorn myself more than you imagine if I had ever attempted to rob you of her love."

Ah, the subtle Jesuit! It was the truth that he was not guilty of having attempted to oust Saint-Lambert from the affections of Madame d'Houdetot, but he had tried to share his dominion over her heart. We know already that he saw no harm in a woman's loving two men at once. We know he believed the two men could be the best of friends, and doubtless he dreamed of persuading Saint-Lambert to his point of view. There was no reason why Saint-Lambert should not feel towards Jean-Jacques as Jean-Jacques made Saint-Preux feel towards Wolmar; as Jean-Jacques would feel himself if he could cut himself in two and be both the husband and enamored lover of the same woman, or her accepted lover and her sighing adorer.

Whether or no Saint-Lambert believed Jean-Jacques is doubtful, but he acted as if he believed him, like the diplomat and experienced man of the world he was, in order not to excite further scandal. He answered from Wolfenbüttel, October 11, 1757, excusing Rousseau and apologizing for having taken alarm at an intimacy he had himself encouraged. When he left the army, he did still more. He went with Madame d'Houdetot to pay a call on Jean-Jacques at the Hermitage and invited him to dine. One does not treat a rival so. He was certainly a most tactful man, and intended by all means to silence gossip by his behavior. His demeanor was severe but kind, his manner firm though compassionate. And he avenged himself insolently by falling asleep and snoring when the author, resuming his rightful privileges, read him a long epistle to Voltaire after supper.

Jean-Jacques was mortified. Might he have to relinquish the hope of "sharing the intimacy of the pair as a third party"? He could not bear to give it up. He moaned and lamented. Madame d'Houdetot, sick of the whole affair, broke off relations with him and asked for the return of her letters. He implored Saint-Lambert to intercede for him with her "as a humane duty." He was overwhelmed and despairing. Never had he been so ill as he was at this time, and he suffered, besides all his other ailments, from a hernia of the groin, contracted at the feet of his too cruel Sophie at Eaubonne or at Montlignon. Saint-Lambert magnanimously gave him a kind answer, stalled for time, undertook to wear him out. But Grimm then returned from Brunswick, and the titled Teuton had less consideration for the troublesome sensibilities of Jean-Jacques. In spite of his ingratiating manner, Grimm had a tough heart, and his nickname, "Tyran le Blanc," aptly hinted at the hard crust concealed under his exquisitely powdered wig. He could defend Madame d'Épinay against the machinations of men like Duclos and Suard, but he did not always make things pleasant for her himself, and he was annoyed, perhaps even incensed, by her fondness for Jean-Jacques. He had long since plotted the downfall of that "madman" from her favor. The moment seemed to have come. He had known all along, he said, that "a hot-headed and unbalanced fellow like that" could not live alone without doing himself harm. An echo of Diderot is discernible in his words; and Diderot's hand can be felt behind the succession of blows now rained by Grimm on the hermit whom he had made up his mind to dislodge from his retreat.

He humiliated Jean-Jacques to the ground. Not only did he settle down at La Chevrette in the very room the former had been accustomed to occupy when he stayed there, but he kept him at arm's length and treated him with colder disdain than before. Then he elected to put to the test the devotion of Madame d'Épinay's protégé to her, the devotion on which she harped whenever his faults were shown up and she was hard put to it to defend him. Admittedly, Jean-Jacques's feelings for Madame d'Houdetot were entirely different from his feelings for Madame d'Épinay, to whom he had never been disloyal, properly speaking, still less treacherous. But now, since Madame d'Épinay was ill and was planning a trip to Geneva to consult Tronchin, why not ask Jean-Jacques to accompany her? She would thus try out his gratitude and affection, and at the same time would separate him from the object of his unfortunate infatuation.

The idea of making a journey with Jean-Jacques pleased Madame d'Épinay, who had perhaps been a little piqued and even a little stirred by amorous inclinations when she observed the absorption of the philosophic recluse in her sister-in-law. Everyone applauded her scheme, no one more than Madame d'Houdetot herself, whose mind would have been greatly relieved by the departure from Montmorency, for several months, of her too persistent adorer. Madame d'Épinay sent for Jean-Jacques. "See here, my bear," she said. "You know how ill I am. I must go to your own city to ask that clever Tronchin to use his skill against my ailments. I had an idea you would like to go with me and with the Scholar's tutor. Was I right?"

Jean-Jacques knit his brows. In spite of the fact—or possibly because of it—that his physical condition was extremely bad, he had never been more alert mentally, nor had his imagination been more prolific. He instantly suspected the worst. However, he forced himself to jest: "How useful for one invalid to help another along the way!" Madame d'Épinay did not urge him. And Jean-Jacques immediately made inquiries or set inquiries afoot by delegating Thérèse to the task. He could have had no better emissary. Thérèse brought him the news that Madame d'Épinay was with child. She got the information from the butler Teissier, who acquired it from the maid, who was of course in a position to find out whatever her mistress most wanted to keep secret. That was it, then! Madame d'Épinay wished to conceal her condition and was going to bear her child in secret at Geneva. Why did she need Jean-Jacques?—of course, to shield Grimm from the accusation of being the child's father, and to lay it to the charge of Jean-Jacques. There were smiles and shrugging of shoulders. Just the same, when Jean-Jacques suspected he was being persecuted, he was right.

Madame d'Épinay did not again request him to chaperon her on the trip for which she was speedily pushing her preparations, but Diderot wrote him a honey-sweet and perfidious letter, reeking with all the false appearance of sincerity, the appeals to magnanimity, to gratitude, to liberality, which will ever enter into the composition of what may be called the professions of faith of democratic ethics.

"My fate is to love you and to cause you grief. I hear that Madame d'Épinay is leaving for Geneva, but I hear nothing about your going with her. My friend, if you are fond of Madame d'Épinay, you must go with her; if you are not fond of her, all the more reason why you must go. If you feel burdened by the weight of your obligations to her, this is the time to requite her in part and to ease your mind. Possibly your health is less good than I suppose, but are you any worse just now than you were a month ago? As for me, I assure you that if I could possibly bear the journey in the chaise [all very well, but he went as far as Russia, just the same, to pay homage to the great Catherine], I would join the cortège and follow her. Aren't you afraid, too, that your behavior will be misunderstood? You will be suspected of ingratitude, or of some secret motive. I am quite aware that you will always do the right thing according to your own lights, but do you think your lights are enough to guide you without assistance? and do you think you have the right to pay no heed to what others think? Anyway, my friend, I must write you this to clear my conscience toward you and toward myself. If you dislike what I say, throw it into the fire, and all will be as if it had never been written."

Jean-Jacques was incensed, and I admit he had justification—all the more because Grimm had said to him exactly what Diderot had written in almost the same words, proof positive that Diderot's action, purporting to be spontaneous, was part of a concerted scheme. He answered that he knew his own business and that Diderot was "nothing but an out-and-out fool" to meddle with what did not concern him. It might as well be understood that the "bear" was allowing no one to muzzle him, nor to put a ring through his nose. He already considered that Madame d'Épinay was going too far when she required him to come to see her at La Chevrette every time she was left alone there. Consequently he no longer consulted her convenience when he called on her, but his own. And for him there could be no friendship without freedom. Madame d'Épinay was entirely mistaken if she thought she had a right to make a slave of him just because he had been willing to oblige her. He shouted it from the housetop: "Whatever happens, I am not going to be her lackey nor show myself off to my own countrymen in the trail of a *lady farmer-general!*"

A mean, rancorous, low speech! But we must remember all that lay behind and make excuses for him: his weak-witted, obstinate determination to stay near Madame d'Houdetot in spite of Saint-Lambert and of Madame d'Houdetot herself.

Grimm gave Jean-Jacques to understand that he was no longer wanted at the Hermitage and that he must pull up stakes. To gain time, Jean-Jacques wrote to Madame d'Épinay, whom he had allowed to leave for Geneva with her husband—with her husband? how so? then her journey was no such secret, after all? But Madame d'Épinay answered:

"Since you want to leave the Hermitage, and since you must leave it, I am amazed that your friends have tried to make you stay. As for me, I never consult my friends as to what I ought to do, and I have no remarks to make about yours."

There was no possibility of hesitating after this stinging rebuke. Although it was December, Jean-Jacques's pride would have obliged him to move out at once from his beloved haven, even if he had had to sleep in the woods on the snow which covered the ground. But he could not bear to go far from Eaubonne. He leased from Monsieur Mathas, financial adviser to the Prince of Condé, a little house in his garden, Mont-Louis, within the bounds of Montmorency.

CHAPTER III

THE KEEP OF GLORY

THE last weeks of Jean-Jacques's stay at the Hermitage were weeks of anguish. Diderot went to see him at the instigation of "Holbach's crew" in order to make a final effort towards a reconciliation, and found him in a state of cold fury, nursing a suppressed but overpowering rage which seemed to him terrible. He wrote to Grimm, on December 5, 1757: "The man is mad. I fear he is utterly callous. I fly to your arms like a man in a panic. I am trying in vain to write poetry, but the fellow keeps coming between me and my work, he disturbs me, and I feel as if I were in the presence of a lost soul. He is a lost soul—that is one thing certain." Strange language, indeed, for an atheist, but a moment's reflection will show us that the flames to which our materialist believed his friend was doomed were those kindled to roast men debarred from the heaven of philosophy.

"Diderot-Danton already had a vision of Rousseau-Robespierre," wrote Michelet rhetorically. But the truth was not that the "bear" in his solitude was plotting against the Encyclopædists, but that the Encyclopædists were out to flay the "bear" for his hide, since they had failed to keep him cooped up in their zoo. They broadcast libelous rumors about him in Paris at the Wednesday dinners of Madame Geoffrin, who was subsidizing the Encyclopædia, at Baron d'Holbach's Thursday dinners, at the Tuesdays of Helvétius. In vain did the soft-hearted Madame d'Houdetot, who dreaded for her wretched lover the storm of hatred gathering over his head, seek him out to warn him to take care. Her wise and gentle letters, instead of calming him down, added the last straw to his exasperation. "If you must leave the Hermitage," wrote Sophie, "at least do it quietly." Quietly! As if that were his way! He would leave it slamming all the doors and setting everyone by the ears!

He made his move with Thérèse on December 15th, having forced Mother Levasseur to leave for Paris in the mail-coach. All Montmorency was out to see his scanty baggage being carted through the steep and icy streets. As he owned practically no furniture himself, after giving to the "lieutenant criminal" all that she and her daughter owned in common, he hastily and "at great expense" bought a little. He settled in his new home, or rather in "the one and only bedroom" of his new home, with practically no household goods. He was not, however, cramped for space. At the end of a terraced walk in his garden, there was an open keep which looked over "the valley and the pool of Montmorency," and from which "the vista ended at the plain but perfectly good château of Saint-Gratien, the retreat of the righteous Catinat." To this tower, "sheeted in ice at the time," Jean-Jacques withdrew with the intention to write, and there, in less than a month, warmed by no fire except that which burned within him, he composed *La lettre à d'Alembert sur les spectacles.*

It must be realized that, as he said himself, he could not write in businesslike fashion, "as all other men of letters do," but had to write at white heat. He was ablaze with passion when he took up his pen to reply to the editor-in-chief of the Encyclopædia, whose article entitled "Geneva" had just appeared. Alembert had advised the authorities of Calvin's own city to establish a theater in it, and Jean-Jacques instantly recognized the influence of Voltaire behind the proposition. A suspicion that the master of Les Délices had a finger in the doings of the

THE KEEP OF GLORY

philosophic band had already stirred his resentment and made him furious; he had sent Voltaire fifteen lengthy pages of protest against his poem, *Le désastre de Lisbonne,* the same pages which had lulled Saint-Lambert into real or pretended slumber. Jean-Jacques, suffering from illness and the pinch of poverty, could not sit still when Voltaire, "that poor unfortunate, weighed down with glory and prosperity," declaimed against the miseries of human life. He could not endure to hear him impute to God the blame for the disastrous earthquake which had killed thirty thousand souls in Portugal; for to Jean-Jacques not God, but man, was responsible for it, at least man's accursed civilization which had herded so many inhabitants into one spot, in buildings of a height never dreamed of in man's natural state. Voltaire had postponed his reply, making none until the publication of *Candide,* that masterpiece of irony which had hit at Jean-Jacques in his pride and made him quail.

Thus, in exposing Voltaire's sly move to open the way for the representation of his own tragedies near Ferney, our grave Genevan citizen, while he persuaded himself that he was only doing his duty, was satisfying his personal animosity. In the *Lettre à d'Alembert* he inveighed with all the power he could muster against the theater, the most insidiously harmful of all the arts. Although he was suffering intensely from his ailments, and Doctor Thierry, whom he had called in, was trying all sorts of methods to relieve him, his spirits were so high that he wrote with effervescent joy, shedding "tears of delight" as he worked. He was not only pleading for the ideas he so fondly cherished; he was liberating his whole nature and soothing his soul. He remarks that he described, without being aware that he was doing so (though I cannot see how), the whole of his own situation at the time, with Madame d'Épinay, Madame d'Houdetot, and even Saint-Lambert.

No sooner had he finished his task, however, than he received a letter from Sophie telling him that all Paris knew of his passion for her and was talking of nothing else. "Diderot has given it away," said Madame d'Houdetot. "Diderot has betrayed me!" cried Jean-Jacques. He had confided in his friend, to be sure, but no matter how garrulous Diderot might have been, he could not have been the only one to chatter about Jean-Jacques's affairs. Just the same, Jean-Jacques held Diderot responsible for this crushing blow—the definite dismissal of him by Madame d'Houdetot. Saint-Lambert, who came to see him in order to mitigate the effect of the dismissal, confirmed his certainty of the philosopher's guilt. He did so through Mademoiselle Levasseur, for it chanced that Jean-Jacques was out when Saint-Lambert made his call. He talked to Thérèse (grief!) for two hours (how can it be?) while he waited for Jean-Jacques's return, told her that he was accused of having been the lover of Madame d'Épinay, and revealed a number of circumstances known "neither to her nor to Madame d'Houdetot," secrets which Jean-Jacques had told only to Diderot in the greatest confidence. They gossiped shamelessly, and for once Saint-Lambert appears in a truly sorry light, puddling with Thérèse, foul-mouthed fishwife that she was, in that mire of petty meanness.

Anyhow, it ended in the firm determination of Jean-Jacques to punish Diderot for his crime. He said nothing of what he was thinking to Saint-Lambert, whom he saw after he had made up his mind. He even let Saint-Lambert suppose that he thought himself mistaken in having suspected Diderot. For he planned a thrust which would be all the more deadly for being unexpected. Before his eyes he had an excellent example as his guide, in the classic manner dear to his heart: "When the illustrious Montesquieu broke with Father de Tournemine, he hastened to proclaim it openly, saying to everyone: 'Listen to nothing that is said either by Father de Tournemine or by me about the other one. We are no longer friends.' This conduct was widely applauded, and everyone praised the sincerity and magnanimity of it." Jean-Jacques conceived the idea of winning applause on his own account by inserting in the form of a footnote in his book the following passage from the twenty-second chapter of Ecclesiasticus: "Though thou drewest a sword at that friend, yet despair not; for there may be a returning to favor. If thou hast opened thy mouth against thy friend, fear not; for there may be a reconciliation: except for upbraiding, or pride, or disclosing of secrets, or a treacherous wound: for these things every friend will depart." In order to make certain the identity of the accused, Jean-Jacques wrote in another place: "I had a stern and judicial Aristarchus; I have him no more, I wish no more to have him; but I shall never cease to mourn him, and I miss him in my heart even more than in my writing."

After the publication of his letter, Jean-Jacques addressed a copy of it to each of his friends, and one even to the husband of Madame d'Épinay. Saint-Lambert was greatly perturbed by his. He was a military man, and it was certainly a mistake for him to be also a man of letters! Between Rousseau, for whom he felt a liking, even a kind of affection, and the Encyclodpædists, whom he admired, with whom he wished to remain on friendly terms, or of whom he was afraid, he was at a loss what stand to take. After long reflection he decided he must register anger at Jean-Jacques's performance, and sent him word that he could not accept his gift. "You seemed to me to be quite sure," he said, "that Diderot was innocent of the lapses in discretion of which you had suspected him. Possibly he has done you wrong—I know nothing about that; but I do know that he has done nothing to give you any right to insult him publicly. You and I, Sir, entertain principles which differ too widely for us ever to agree. Forget my existence. It should not be difficult to do so, for I have never done to any man either so much good or so much harm that it will be long remembered."

As soon as he had thus vindicated his courage, Saint-Lambert became a prey to scruples, possibly to fears. Jean-Jacques the Terrible might go to any lengths in his resentment. Already, choosing to regard Madame d'Houdetot as being in league with her lover, he had demanded that she send to his rooms to collect the money she had given him for a copy of the *Héloïse*. All Madame d'Épinay's circle took fright when they learned of the situation. They put their heads together and agreed that there was nothing for it but to pacify the "bear" with the utmost speed. They settled that Monsieur d'Épinay—not Madame—when he acknowledged Jean-Jacques's work, should invite him to dine at La Chevrette. The request went forth, and because he longed to see Saint-Lambert and Madame d'Houdetot, who were to be among the guests, he fell headlong into the trap. They showered attentions on him, leaving to Madame de Blainville, Sophie's sister, an intolerable woman, the pleasure of hailing sarcasms down upon him. Curiously enough, though entirely explicable in a man with such a pronounced feminine streak, he hung about the lover of the woman he had adored, not about the woman herself. Saint-Lambert had gone back on him, he must run after Saint-Lambert; Saint-Lambert had put him in the wrong, he would eventually apologize for it; Saint-Lambert despised him for the moment, but would come to admire him. He wrote, in the *Confessions:* "I can swear that although the sight of Madame d'Houdetot, when I first arrived, made my heart beat until I was ready to faint, after I turned away, I scarcely thought of her again; I was entirely absorbed in Saint-Lambert." He had

THE KEEP OF GLORY

discovered that his feelings were less altered than he had supposed, and it was not from self-abasement, but from jealousy, that he felt moved to neglect his mistress.

He returned to Mont-Louis pacified, almost serene. This really marked the end of his great passion, of his dream of love and friendship. From that time on, he let the noblest sentiments wither and fade, the tenderest of relationships wear off into indifference. Some time later, as he sat meditating in his tower-keep in the light of the setting sun, watching the pool of Saint-Gratien first reflect the last bright rays, then flush under the evening glow, he saw one final airy apparition of Sophie float for a moment over the surface, then sink down into it. And thus he was led to bring Julie to a watery grave, when he finished the *Héloïse*.

However, the clamor aroused by the appearance of his *Lettre sur les spectacles*, far from subsiding, swelled into an uproar. Diderot shrieked murder, and all the Encyclopædists, whose work had been suppressed by the government, followed suit. Voltaire was enraged, and began to wage against the "watchmaker fellow" who had dared to oppose his plans and attack his interests, a guerilla warfare of epigrams and gibes in which his sharp and malicious wit was at its brilliant best. The public, however, cheered Jean-Jacques on. His old friend Madame de Créqui, who had become his devoted disciple, wrote him: "Anything you say will always make a sensation." Visitors came from Paris to see him, and Deleyre once took out to Mont-Louis his mistress and a number of her friends just to gaze upon the amazing man who was so much talked about. In order to avoid the troublesome crowd, Jean-Jacques took flight. This time he was firmly resolved not to surrender his freedom and not to involve himself in any relationships where something besides pure friendship figured. With the addition of a handful of the faithful, such as

Monsieur and Madame Dupin, Lenieps of Geneva, Monsieur Reguin, and Monsieur Carrie of Venice, he could have as much of this as he wanted from his neighbors in the country, who included the young lawyer Loyseau de Mauléon, the publisher Guérin de Saint-Brice, the parish priest of Grosly, and the Oratorians of Montmorency.

No more going out into high society for him, with all its attendant exactions and financial burdens. A man alone, with no servant, is at the mercy of the household in which he is a visitor, and where he must make himself popular. Fine ladies who try to save a man money only bring him to bankruptcy. With all their cleverness, they are fools in this respect. One of them invites you to supper, and, instead of letting you send for a cab, orders her own carriage to take you home. There you are! Instead of having to pay twenty-four sous for your drive, you have to fork out a crown to tip her coachman or her groom. Or another writes you a note, and, to save you the four-sou letter-fee, sends one of her servants on foot, who arrives bathed in sweat, and you have to give him a dinner and a crown to boot, which he has surely earned. Still another suggests that you spend a week or two with her in the country, and informs you that you will save money on your meals all that time. She never thinks of your interrupted work, and of the fact that your household expenses, your rent, your laundry, and your clothes go on just the same, not counting the fact that living at her establishment costs more than living at home—for instance, the barber.

"I can honestly state," write Jean-Jacques, "that I spent at least twenty-five crowns at Madame d'Houdetot's house in Eaubonne, where I stayed overnight only four or five times; and over a hundred pistoles at Épinay or La Chevrette during the five or six years when I was a constant guest. Expenses of this kind cannot be avoided by a man of my temperament, who can never provide things for himself nor get along without anything, nor bear the sight of a servant grumbling or serving you sulkily." It is certainly true that there is nothing more unpleasant to a poor but sensitive guest than the sorry faces of servants, and Jean-Jacques, who had lived among them, knew from experience the kind of thing that would be said about him in the kitchen. Besides the lordly chef, who had to serve his dinner while the others were having supper, and his supper while the others were asleep, there were all the poor wretches to whom he dealt slaps in the face, as he put it, while they watched his choice bits with hungry eyes, and who sold him, to save him from dying of thirst, their master's adulterated wine at ten times the price he would have had to pay for better in a wine-shop.

With the coming of spring, elated at recovering his independence, he again began his tramps through the woods, stopping occasionally at a little clump of cottages where he partook heartily of chervil omelet, and listened to the far-away "rustic refrain of the bleating from the meadows." If he stayed at home to work, inspiration was there, fiery and prolific, almost miraculous. From his pen flowed a torrent intended to overflow the mildewed old earth and wash it clean. It seems as if there must have been a presentiment in the fascination with which nobility tiptoed to the keep, which was soon to radiate like a beacon the glory shed upon it by Jean-Jacques. For he had had to submit to the closing in of the circle about him once more. Gradually, stealthily, his citadel was besieged. Grimm remarked, with a touch of spitefulness: "To take our place, he had the very best people." One might say more accurately that they had taken him up again, putting their best foot forward, so as to run less risk of being snubbed in the end.

First came the Marshal de Luxembourg and his lady,

who arrived to spend the summer at the château of Montmorency, with their friend Monsieur de Malesherbes. Then came the Prince of Conti, the victor of Mons, who lived apart from the court, did not dabble in philosophy, and made flattering overtures of friendship to Jean-Jacques. Lastly came the sweet and understanding Marquise de Verdelin, who lived at Soisy, close to his abode, and who wrote him delightful letters, as full of wisdom as of noble sentiments. In short, neighbors, and still more neighbors. Jean-Jacques quite justly felt that he would commit no more flagrant breaches in his self-imposed rule by acknowledging their advances than by acknowledging the attentions of Mauléon the lawyer and Guérin the publisher. But because in his secret heart he was more delighted with them, he owed it to himself to resist them more rabidly. Such was his nature, and such was his pride. He laid the flattering unction to his soul of saying that "times have changed" and that the day was long past since Madame de Bouzenval had sent him to dine in the servants' hall—witness the fact that Monsieur and Madame de Luxembourg sent him their congratulations and invited him to take supper with them whenever he felt like doing so. How he must have prided himself on his exclusiveness! They seized the opportunity presented by the visit at Montmorency of Madame de Boufflers, whom he knew and who was extremely intimate with La Maréchale, to return to the attack. He never budged. The Chevalier de Lorenzi, a member of the suite of the Prince of Conti, came several times to see him, and urged him to go to the château. He did nothing of the sort. The Marshal had to take the trouble to come himself, followed by five or six subordinates, before he made up his mind to call on the lady who had sent him her compliments.

For all his airs and graces, however, it was not without trepidation that he presented himself to Madame de

THE KEEP OF GLORY

Luxembourg, who had a glittering if somewhat obsolete reputation for beauty and for numberless love-affairs. She had been left a widow by the Duke of Boufflers, and had made a second marriage, with her former lover. She was said to have a sarcastic wit, and Jean-Jacques entered her presence with all the anguish which he liked to have women inflict upon him. But if she was really mischievous, not to say malicious, and a Machiavelli for cunning, she took great pains not to frighten him by betraying it. She showered the most gratifying compliments on him, all the finer for appearing to be spontaneous outbursts of emotion. She had him at her feet in no time. She knew how to make him feel he was appearing to advantage, and he left her overcome with admiration for her tact, completely charmed by her unaffected graciousness.

The geniality of the Marshal, unspoiled by his merely moderate intelligence, and mingled with a little shyness, delighted Jean-Jacques no less. The illustrious officer was perfectly at ease the day he honored the "bear" with a call in his wretched den, amid his dirty dishes and nicked pots and pans. He was in no wise disgusted, but was able to fuss tactfully over the ruinous condition of his bedroom, where the rotten floor-boards were falling in, and he offered to let him stay at the château while the necessary repairs were being made. Jean-Jacques, with his customary rudeness, laid down certain conditions. He was flattered at the Marshal's behavior, affected by the kindness the couple showed him, but he smarted from recent hurts and had no intention of submitting again to any kind of servitude. Since the Marshal had spoken of accepting him on an equal footing, he took him at his word. "I speak only one language," Jean-Jacques said to him brusquely, "the language of friendship, of familiarity." All right, they had no objection to friendship, none even to familiarity. And Madame la Maréchale was on the spot to smooth things over when Jean-Jacques's ill temper upset them for a moment. Not once or twice, but innumerable times, was the unhappy wretch assailed by sudden scruples, worried over the falseness of the situation in which his intimacy with "a man greater than himself" involved him. She calmed him every time, wrapped him about in attentions. Her affection made her confidential and jealous. "You say," she wrote him, "that you feel freer with Monsieur de Luxembourg than with me. I tell you, Monsieur, that at my age a woman is no longer of her sex; all that remains of me is a heart which feels no age where you are concerned." How could anyone resist such inexhaustible kindness?—extending not only to the philosopher's mate, but to his tabby cat, Doyenne, and his dog, Duke, whose name he had thought fit to change to Turk.

So, from May 15, 1759, he was settled at the château of Montmorency in a secluded summer-house of the park where Watteau had painted. There he wrote the fifth book of the *Émile*, which he had begun immediately after finishing the *Héloïse*. As he composed it, he was thinking, I'll be bound, of Madame d'Épinay, for whose son, as the reader will remember, he had framed some maxims on education. She doubtless regretted, when his book appeared, that she had lost the friendship of the great man who could produce so epoch-making a study in pedagogy.

Never in the world did a man have better morning coffee than that which Jean-Jacques drank with Thérèse in his little suite of rooms, while the birds sang to him in chorus, while his eyes rested on the neighboring sheet of water, and while he inhaled the perfume of orange-blossoms. But as summer wore on, Monsieur and Madame de Luxembourg paid so much attention to him that he was obliged to respond "by seeing them constantly." This meant abandoning his supposedly inalterable resolve to preserve his independence. Fortunately, these people were less exacting, or more tactful, or more sensitively discerning, than Grimm's mistress. They treated a man so that he simply could not resist advances which would be very embarrassing from anyone else. Madame de Luxembourg kept Jean-Jacques constantly on the jump with excitement and delight. She talked only of him, gave all her time to him, fed him all day long with compliments, and wheedled and caressed him continually. She insisted on having him "within reach" at meals, that is, at her right hand, and if some aristocrat—note the "some aristocrat" —made a move to dislodge him, she protested and told the upstart to sit down somewhere else. If he took offense with her—for he had to have spats—she knew how to appear affected without being angry. She scolded him for his morbid sensibilities while she made him feel she attributed them to extraordinary refinement of feeling. His only fear was that he might be found wanting in the conversation she expected from him. He knew that she was extremely critical in this respect, far more than the Marshal, who was well enough pleased with his sententious pronouncements. But he thought up "an aid," or, as we should say to-day, an expedient, to solve the problem of how to talk in her presence. He read aloud to her, read her his *Julie* letters. She was entranced. There was nothing else in the world to compare with it—he absolutely must make her a copy of it, as he had once done for Madame d'Houdetot. The faithless fellow set himself to the task. But Madame la Maréchale chatted to everyone she saw about the masterpiece of whose existence she had just learned.

In the meantime Madame d'Houdetot, who was handing the manuscript about to all her friends, had already spoken in the most enthusiastic terms of it; and while Monsieur de Malesherbes was working to put it into shape for publication and making the necessary corrections to insure its uncensored circulation in France, a throng like that which had invaded the Rue Grenelle-Saint-Honoré flocked to his reteat. "Even though he hated their ranks and titles," Jean-Jacques could not refuse to greet the noble callers who condescended to "climb the fatiguing slope on the pilgrimage to Mont-Louis." For he had returned to his little haven, now thoroughly repaired and suitably furnished. Among his visitors were the Prince de Tingry, the Marquis d'Armentières, the Duchess de Montmorency, the Countess de Valentinois, the Duchess de Boufflers—indeed, the Prince of Conti himself, whom Jean-Jacques, recalling his passion for chess, challenged to a game and beat, to the consternation of the courtiers.

He had a fancy to make a flower-bed on his terrace, already beautified by a double row of lindens as shade-trees, and had a stone table and bench made for the place, which may still be seen. Whenever he felt in the mood to stay at home on a bright day, to write or read, he sat out there and received whatever callers might arrive unexpectedly to pay him their respects, provided he was willing to be disturbed. There could surely have been no better answer than such unaffected republican simplicity to the calumnies of the Diderot-Grimm-Holbach cabal. If we are to believe his own assertion, he cared nothing whether or not he was petted and indulged. But to have his personality a humanizing influence, to make men better by the example of his life, filled his heart with joy and good will. One day Coindet of Geneva came to show the Marshal sketches for the illustrations of the *Héloïse*. The Marshal invited him to stay for dinner, and, as Coindet had to be back in Paris early, offered to escort him there as soon as they had finished eating. So they set off along the Saint-Denis road with Jean-Jacques following behind, all in tears like a child, "dying to kiss the footprints of the wonderful Marshal." "Ah, Monsieur," he said, "before I knew you, I hated all the great of this earth, and I hate them even more since you have shown me how easily they could have made themselves adored." Amazing man! His gratitude to Monsieur de Luxembourg was all because he gave himself no airs, as humble folk say, in spite of his newly acquired fortune, and sat down to supper with his neighbor, Pilleu the mason, after he had dined earlier in the day at a table graced by dukes and princes.

Julie, ou la nouvelle Héloïse, was published in the early spring of 1761, at the beginning of the carnival season, and was received by the public with even greater enthusiasm than by the inner circle. The publishing houses in the Rue Saint-Jacques and the one in the Palais-Royal were mobbed, women being more in evidence than men, while avid readers quarreled for a copy and snatched it from one another. So great was the demand that the volume was rented out by the hour, for one hour only, though five or six hours were required to read it through, not counting the time lost in wiping away the tears it provoked, tears abundant enough "to make you ill, to disfigure you."

The Princess de Talmont first turned the pages as she was about to start for the opera ball. At midnight her carriage was announced. She went on reading. After waiting some time, her servants perceived that she had not stirred, and came to tell her that it was two o'clock. Without raising her eyes, she answered that there was no hurry. Later still, she noticed that her watch had stopped, and rang her bell to ask what time it was. Four o'clock. "Then it is too late to go to the ball," said she. "Order the horse unhitched." She had her maids undress her, and spent the rest of the night, or rather of the morning, as if in a blissful trance, absorbed in her reading.

Madame de la Tour de Franqueville, one of Jean-Jacques's admirers, wrote him confidential letters, at first anonymously, signing herself "Claire d'Orbe." They charmed him to begin with, but soon annoyed him by demanding prompt replies. The Countess de Boufflers, young and pretty, who expressed a desire to see the *Héloïse* printed in "letters of gold," was spurred by unwholesome curiosity to take Thérèse aside and draw her out, hoping to extract indiscreet revelations concerning the private life of Saint-Preux's creator. In fact, the general opinion was that expressed by the Countess de Blot, who declared that no woman of any feeling could resist anything whatever to the author of the best romance ever published in France.

We in modern times cannot understand without a stretch of the imagination such rapturous admiration of a work which is certainly the wildest attempt ever made to set the emotional life on a plane above rational life, and of which the psychology, subtle though it be in places, and the sentiments, sincere if not always true to life, are elaborated with the most tedious flow of words. But it must be realized that Jean-Jacques was restoring to its place in literature love, or rather romantic passion, and through literature was restoring it to the social customs from which it had been banned. He was shattering the narrow bounds of libertinism and opening the light of day to lovers who hitherto had been cramped within the restricted limits of a one-room apartment furnished with a day-bed.

The enemies of Jean-Jacques could not but be abashed and annoyed by the success of his romance. They went on with their task of disparagement, but in the meantime he had added to his own score at least two offenses against them. First, he had written an extremely insolent letter to Voltaire concerning his *Épître sur le désastre à Lisbonne* (a letter to which I have already alluded), which, though it was not intended for public consumption, had been published by Firmey in Berlin without consulting Jean-

Jacques, probably at Grimm's instigation. Secondly, he had felt obliged to return to Palissot the copy of his *Comédie de philosophes* which that unimportant author had sent him, making the excuse that in it he was exalted while Diderot was besmirched and calumniated. This display of magnanimity, instead of touching his old friend, had greatly vexed him, as he might have known it would.

Voltaire had believed for a time that he could rid himself by one good kick of this "bastard cur of Diogenes' dog" who barked at his heels. By this time he realized that his glory was at stake and depended on his snuffing out the rival who threatened to eclipse him. Under the pen name of the "Marquis de Ximénès," he wrote a parody of the *Julie* called the *Aloïsa*. From then on he took up other weapons than irony to attack the wretched fellow; he launched pamphlet after pamphlet against him, never appearing in person, but signing assumed names, as was his honorable custom—"Monsieur de la Poupillière," "le R. P. d'Escarbotier"—and even going so far as to attribute some of his productions to authentic authors—for instance, the *Lettre au Docteur Lausophe*, which he professed to believe came from the Abbé Coyer, then from Monsieur Bordes.

"One must lie like the devil—boldly and continually," he wrote to Thiriot. "Strike on the sly," he advised d'Alembert. And he treated Jean-Jacques meanwhile like an untouchable outcast. The deist of Geneva was put in the same boat with the Jesuits.

Jean-Jacques blazed with a fire kindled to ever greater intensity by his aggravated ill health, and all he thought of was following up his recent victory with another. In turn he finished the *Émile* and the *Contrat social*, while Brother Côme, called in by Madame la Maréchale, was inflicting great pain on him with his examinations. The verdict was encouraging. He had no gallstones, as he feared; and though his trouble was probably incurable, it was not fatal. The assurance affected his imagination so joyously that he immediately felt better and declared that he suffered much less from that time on.

But it was ten years later that he wrote his account of his feelings at this period. In point of fact, he could not have been cured; his condition was like that of a man who stammers, and who, after a respite, long or short, from his sufferings, invariably becomes afflicted anew. The high nervous tension at which he lived soon brought him lower than he had ever been before. He watched for the publication of the *Émile*, which seemed to him slow in appearing, with frenzied impatience, mingled with dread, as if he had a presentiment of the misfortunes which awaited him. He worried more over the *Émile* than over the *Contrat social*, which was published by Rey in Amsterdam on April 25, 1762. He received warnings from every side, and sensed increasing hatred for himself, which aggravated his anxiety. The letters which he wrote at this time to Monsieur de Malesherbes, containing the germs of his *Confessions*, seems to me to betray his distressed state of mind. His urgent need to open his heart and bare all its secrets reveals a sense of helplessness, of being at bay. He was not satisfied with confessing himself to Monsieur de Malesherbes, who was then director of book sales and who was taking great pains to prepare the *Émile* for the press and to correct the proofs with the zeal of a devoted friend, but went on to confide in Madame de Luxembourg, acknowledging to her that he had abandoned his children to the foundlings' home. She at once took steps to trace the first of them, at least, by means of the mark sewn into the infant's swaddling clothes. Her efforts were all in vain; and Jean-Jacques, who nowhere reveals the exact nature of the sign by which he would have been able to identify his child, rejoiced at her failure. He was by no means eager to be called on to make reparation to his offspring at the moment when his own treatise on education was about to appear, containing in black and white the statement that "no degree of poverty, no lack of time, nor any human tie" can excuse a man from the duty of supporting his own children and bringing them up himself.

He indulged in rosy-colored dreams while he fretted. He aspired to be free from all the cares imposed by his work, to abandon literature, and to retire with Thérèse to the depths of some province, preferably Touraine, calculating that with the proceeds of the books he had already published, and possibly one or two more, such as *Essai sur l'origine des langues* and a *Dictionnaire de musique*, he might buy an annuity and settle down to spend the rest of his days in good works. He dropped all ambition to stun his adversaries, and began to think only of justifying himself in the eyes of posterity by writing his own memoirs. This desire for self-abnegation at the height of his triumph is another indication that some instinct warned him of the afflictions he was shortly to suffer.

The *Émile* at last appeared in the spring of 1762, a few weeks after the *Contrat social*. The latter was printed only in Holland, but the *Émile* was published simultaneously in Amsterdam and in Paris, by the house of Guérin and Duchesne. The Marshal and Madame de Luxembourg had arranged the transaction between Rey and his French colleagues without the knowledge of Jean-Jacques, whose frame of mind was such that he preferred to confine his work to a foreign edition. Hardly had it been put into circulation before a disturbing rumor arose. Jean-Jacques sent word to Moulton on June 7th: "It is said that the Parlement of Paris, in order to justify its proceedings against the Jesuits, is about to persecute those who do not agree with them as well. For several days my friends have been making mighty efforts to frighten me; I am offered hiding places everywhere." Those friends knew what they were talking about. During the night of June 8th–9th, while Jean-Jacques was, as usual, reading his Bible before dropping off to sleep, Madame de Luxembourg's house-servant, La Roche, came running to warn him that he was to be arrested at sight and that his work was condemned to be destroyed and burned by the common executioner.

CHAPTER IV

THE REFUGEE OF MÔTIERS-TRAVERS

MADAME DE LUXEMBOURG, who had just retired, was waiting for Jean-Jacques, not wishing to fall asleep before talking over with him the blow which had just been struck him by the Parlement. He must get up, dress with speed, in spite of the fact that it was two o'clock in the morning, and hurry to the château. There he found Madame la Maréchale in a frenzy of grief; the Marshal, as befitted a man who had been under fire, somewhat more collected, but still in despair; and Madame de Boufflers, who had just come from Paris, extremely anxious. The Prince of Conti had written to the Luxembourgs that, thanks to his influence, Jean-Jacques would not be pursued if he left Montmorency, but that he would certainly be put under arrest if he stayed. He must flee, then, but where? Madame de Boufflers suggested the Temple, which belonged to the Prince de Conti and which was a sanctuary. The Marshal offered to keep him in hiding for a few days. But Jean-Jacques refused to consider either of these expedients, both of which merely served to postpone his inevitable acceptance of the only way open to him—exile. He realized that his protectors were at heart afraid of being compromised, and desirous to be rid of him. After making a brief show of resistance to his decision to leave France, they fell to discussing solely the question of where he should go. Madame de Boufflers was in favor of England; Jean-Jacques thought of Geneva. But he knew that the French minister was as powerful there as in Paris, and, moreover, he had many enemies in the city. He resolved to flee to Switzerland, postponing, for the time being, any definite decision as to where in Switzerland to settle. He spent the morning and part of the afternoon sorting out his papers with the help of the Marshal de Luxembourg, then said his last farewell to his friend. They all wept, especially Thérèse, who had been kept in doubt as to his fate, and who did not know that he was to flee until she actually saw him getting into the post-chaise. She wished to go with him, but he begged her to stay behind, to settle his affairs and collect the money owing him, promising her that she should shortly rejoin him.

"My child," he cried, "you must be brave. You have shared my prosperous and happy years; now, since you wish it, you shall share my misery. But remember that you can expect nothing but insults and misfortunes if you stick by me."

As he drove off in a light gig with the top down, he met, on the road between Montmorency and La Barre, a livery coach containing four men dressed in black. They saluted him and smiled. They were the four officers who had been sent to arrest him. In Paris friendly gestures greeted him from the people in the streets. He was recognized and his presence reported all along his route, but although he traveled by easy stages, he reached the frontier not only without molestation, but even without being once followed or spied upon. Such was the spirit of the time.

In point of fact, the Parlement of Paris was only too glad to have him get away. He had guessed right in thinking that his condemnation was nothing more than a move against the Jesuits, to silence good churchmen. He should have stayed at home. Not being a French citizen, he risked nothing worse than deportation from France after a short period of imprisonment, which would have increased his popularity. But to a nervous temperament like his, the most painfully difficult of all necessities is that of facing the unknown perils of the future. He always apprehended the worst. As he said himself, he was victimized by "dark designs," and saw their effects all about him. He was haunted by thoughts of the fate of Calas, and foresaw that arrest would end in his being put to the torture and led to the executioner's block. We must also give him credit for his unwillingness to endanger the Luxembourgs, the Prince of Conti, and Malesherbes, by standing in his own defense. This exhibition of moral courage on his part is not incompatible with the physical cowardice he showed from this time on, the effect of the persecution mania from which he suffered. It is going too far to charge him with having lightly brought down upon himself the rigors of the law by signing his name to the *Émile*. As we know, Voltaire acted differently, publishing his philosophical works anonymously and disowning them if the necessity arose. But in my eyes, Rousseau, reckless in his pride, is a more admirable figure than Voltaire, covering his smirking conceit with sly prudence. In this case the plebeian sets an example of nobility to the middle-class adventurer aping the squire.

If we inquire into the exact nature of Jean-Jacques's offense against the laws of France in writing the *Émile*, and the reasons why this work rather than the *Contrat social* excited the authorities against him, we find that the *Émile*, venturesome and chimerical though it is, is something better or worse than a practical exposition of an educational method. It expounds an ethical theory of the development of the human being from birth to maturity. Jean-Jacques founds his argument on the Utopian idea he so fondly cherished. "Everything is good," he says, "as it leaves the hands of the author of nature; everything deteriorates in the hands of man." The pedagogue should limit his efforts to helping the child to feel and think according to his own instincts; in other words, his rôle is negative. The teacher has no business to abandon his subordinate attitude to his pupil even in matters of religion. He should make no attempt to introduce the child to his Creator until the child has reached man's estate, or, rather, he should not until then help him to the discovery of God within himself, and should summon no dogma to his assistance. It is God's will that He be worshiped in spirit and in truth—that is the essential. No other teaching is of any avail. "The infallible authority of the Church, for which Catholics argue, leads nowhere," says the Vicar of Savoy in his profession of faith. This is not a negation of the supernatural nor of miracles, but amounts to indifference to them; and if it is not a rejection of Revelation, it is at least a rejection of any obligation to take it into account.

It was on this point that Jean-Jacques was condemned. The authority of the Church had actually less to fear from his deistic opinions than from Diderot's atheism or Voltaire's anticlericalism. If his subversive ideas caused anxiety, why was no heed paid to the fact that he was propagating more dangerous theories in the *Contrat social* concerning the organization of the State than any he had pronounced affecting Catholic orthodoxy? In eighteenth-century France, the Parlement was the only militant political authority; and, as we have seen, this assembly, eager to assume the position of a permanent legislative assembly, desired to wipe out the Society of Jesus. It condemned the *Émile* in order to appear to be defending the Church. For this one time at least, the Parlement was acting in agreement with the views of the philosophers and its old enemy Voltaire, who wrote to Alembert:

"Have you read Master Jean-Jacques's prosy stuff? His *Vicaire Savoyard* is worthy of every kind of punishment. That Judas is deserting us, and look at the moment he has

THE REFUGEE OF MÔTIERS-TRAVERS 227

chosen for his desertion! Just as our philosophy was on the eve of victory all along the line."

The Parlement was not in the least hostile to the proposal of the *Contrat social* to substitute "through the mechanical means of universal suffrage," to use Proudhon's expression, a government which should come from below for the government which came from above, thus aiming at nothing less than the abolition of the existing order. Since the King and his ministers or counselors were willing to have the end of his sovereignty predicted, since its end was eagerly anticipated, and steps were being taken to hasten it, the Parlement, conservatively minded though it was, but opposed to absolute power and probably honeycombed from beneath by Freemasonry, had no call to hurl thunderbolts at Rousseau's revolutionary work.

I do not agree with Émile Faguet in thinking it strange that our reformer should have produced the *Contrat social*. Faguet is correct in his statement that the principles enunciated by Jean-Jacques in his famous political treatise not only have no connection with his ideas in general, but run contradictory to them. The point he overlooks is that their basic sentiments are the same. It is true that the preaching of Rousseau's whole life upheld the individual, that in the *Émile* he opposed the man to the citizen—"one has to choose between making a man and making a citizen; one cannot make both at the same time" —and that he then turned about in the *Contrat social* and sacrificed the former to the latter. Here the individual is subordinated to an all-powerful social body. "Man is born free, and is in fetters wherever he goes," postulates the opening sentence of the *Contrat social*. As one reads, one expects that at the end the author will have broken the chains of captive man and will display him, finally set free, in a world where his development can flower unhampered. But nothing of the sort occurs. New bonds are forged, stronger than those which have been struck off; man falls under the domination of a new and harder master than the one whose yoke he has succeeded in evading—the State. The State is a rabid enemy of the civilization which flaunted the independence of man *in puris naturalibus*, reducing man at one fell stroke to a dependent creature, dependent in body, mind, and spirit or soul, on civil law, political law, and religious law.

It hardly seems worth while to deliver man from civilization only to subject him to an all-powerful organization. As this organization is, even in its inflexibility, the "expression of the general will," man always has a master, no longer a master in his own image, but a power, an anonymous abstraction. Jean-Jacques would have it so, pushing his reasoning to absurdity in his hatred of superiority, his hatred of aristocracy, his consuming passion, as it was that of the Cordeliers, of the Jacobins, and of all his demagogic successors. Once he attempted to show his adversaries, after having undertaken to refute them in ethical argument, that he could also be a leader in political thought, he could not possibly have worked out any other kind of book than the one he wrote, at once discordant and systematic as it is. He was an individualist when he conceived of man in his uncivilized state; he became a socialist when he conceived of him in the civilized state. For the liberty of primitive times, when no art or science existed, and consequently no talents, no advantages, no privileges, to distinguish one personality from another, Jean-Jacques substituted subjection to popular sovereignty, in which the sacrifice of man's individuality forces him to guide himself by his kind and to merge himself in them.

To return to our narrative—he fled. As he drove on in his cramped and uncomfortable post-chaise, he scribbled in pencil a sort of prose poem called *Le Lévite d'Ephraïm*, inspired by the Bible. Thus occupied, he reached the Berne

THE REFUGEE OF MÔTIERS-TRAVERS 229

frontier. He immediately leapt out of the carriage, and to the utter amazement of the postilion, who thought he had lost his senses, he prostrated himself and kissed the ground, exclaiming rapturously:

"I praise thee, O Heaven, protector of virtue! Here I attain the soil of freedom!"

He immediately took his place in the chaise once more, and a few hours later, on June 14, 1762, he reached Yverdun. There he was received with open arms by his "dear Papa," Daniel Roguin, by Roguin's niece, Madame Boy de la Tour, whom he also called "Mamma," and by her daughters. His "native air, the friendly welcome, the beauty of the region and of the season," as he wrote Madame de Luxembourg, quickly dispelled the fatigue of the journey, and he sent word to Thérèse that he was merely waiting to learn her decision before picking out a permanent refuge. He felt no anxiety on her account, for Rey the publisher had settled on her a yearly income of 300 francs. But he hoped that she would join him, because he had grown to depend on her companionship. Obviously quite sure that he was shortly to see her again, he gave her directions for the trip into Switzerland in case she decided to make it, requested her particularly to have a bandage made for him like one which Monsieur Alamanni had shown him, and also asked her to bring his candlesticks but to be very careful about wrapping and packing them.

He had already drawn advance royalties on his *Héloïse*, his *Contrat social*, and his *Émile*, for which he was to be paid 4,860, 2,200, and 7,000 francs, respectively. So he was not short of money. This was fortunate, for he was fated to be the victim of such harassing difficulties, if not of persecution, that he could hardly have surmounted them if he had had to contend with financial troubles also. Things began almost immediately after he had settled at Yverdun. He learned that the *Émile* had been banned by the Council of Geneva, as it had been by the Parlement of Paris nine days earlier. "All the gazettes, all the newspapers, all the pamphlets" were sounding "the most terrible alarms." He was considered an enemy of religion, a dangerous lunatic, a wolf-man. Anticipating the decree of the Senate of Berne, which expelled him from Yverdun, he crossed the mountains and took refuge in the County of Neuchâtel, where Madame Boy de la Tour had offered to lease him a furnished house which belonged to her son, in the village of Môtiers, in the Vale of Travers, for the sum of thirty livres a year.

The County of Neuchâtel belonged at the time to the King of Prussia, a circumstance which considerably complicated the situation of the unhappy refugee, hitherto the outspoken opponent of that monarch. Through the governor of the district, a Scotchman named George Keith, who bore the title of Hereditary Court-Marshal of Scotland and who was popularly called "Milord Marshal," he sent Frederick II the following letter, arrogant in tone but remarkably clever in its very impudence:

"I have come to seek refuge in your dominions. Possibly my mistake was in not starting there; that is the kind of eulogy you deserve. Sire, I have earned no favor at your hands, and I ask for none; I thought it my duty to announce to your Majesty that I am in your power and that of my own accord I put myself there. You may do with me as you please."

Jean-Jacques must have felt a thrill of satisfaction as he signed his letter, intended to show the world how the author of a work like the *Contrat social* expresses himself in writing to the representative of one of those monarchies of which he has foretold the impending fall. As a matter of fact, he knew so well the nature of the sovereign in whose black books he affected to be, that he could not have been seriously afraid of his resentment. He knew he

THE REFUGEE OF MÔTIERS-TRAVERS

ran little risk in throwing himself on the King's mercy, as he later had the frankness to admit. The Victor of Rossbach returned a kind answer. He not only granted permission for Jean-Jacques to remain at Môtiers, but he also called on "Milord Marshal" to give him assistance. Out of deference to his feelings, however, the prince commanded that this assistance take the form of gifts in kind rather than of money. Jean-Jacques expressed his thanks, and would have done well to stop at that. But not at all. He rejected the tactful proffer of aid in an arrogant tone, addressing the King familiarly, with utter miscomprehension of the considerations behind the motives, not of the motives themselves, which actuate well-bred men in conferring benefits, and he bombarded Frederick with a crushing barrage of exhortations and advice. One wonders how he could have imagined—for he doubtless did—that his counsels would have any effect, and that the King, who was at war with France, might sheathe his sword. But Frederick made no answer, nor, significantly enough, did he ever address a word to Jean-Jacques in person. This conduct at least forced Jean-Jacques to shift the object of his stream of communications and direct them to the King's representative at Neuchâtel. For he was not content to feel grateful to the monarch he had previously anathematized. He became "so tenderly attached to him" that he, "the enemy of kings," felt inspired to "go and die at the foot of his throne." The pleasure having been denied him, he developed "as keen an eagerness for his glory" as he had before felt "indignation at the injustice of his successes." He wrote "Milord Marshal": "I must confess that heretofore I never liked the King, or, to put it better, I was misled; I hated another man under the name of the King. You have given me a change of heart, a heart, this time, proof against any test, whose feelings toward both you and him will never alter."

So we find him at Môtiers, and again with Thérèse, whom the Prince of Conti had loaded down with kindness, and who came to meet him at the end of July. Knowing perfectly that in herself she was nobody, and would at once disappear, if she left him, into the obscurity from which he had lifted her, she did not take advantage of his offer to set her free. To him she was as indispensable as ever, though he had felt for some time that his affection for her was "cooling off," and he was more than ever pleased with her readiness to humor—when she did not aggravate—the suspicions by which he was obsessed. Grasping as she was, moreover, she had learned to make a show of approving his rabid scorn of wealth, for she had come to see that his refusals of gifts worked to her profit. At Môtiers it was Thérèse who got not only, as in former times, the offerings of game, poultry, fruit, spices, and even tobacco, for Jean-Jacques now smoked a pipe, but even the money which he could not be induced to accept. "Milord Marshal," who grew fond of Jean-Jacques, and called him "my son the savage," or "my child," asked leave to give "a hundred pounds to Mademoiselle Levasseur," either outright or as a legacy, a sum sufficient to assure her "a small annuity which would help her to get along." Jean-Jacques consented, and thus one more generous action swelled the capital which Rey had already founded for his "governess."

And so we find Jean-Jacques settling down peacefully in the country, surrounded by friendly souls—"Milord Marshal" in the first rank, then Colonel de Pury, Peyrou the American, Monsieur and Mademoiselle d'Ivernois, and the Count d'Escherney, all of whom liked him and pitied his misfortunes. He was the central figure of a choice group of acquaintances, and enjoyed life as he was fitted to enjoy it, but as he had too often been prevented from doing, even more by his own pride and fancies than by circumstances. His interest in botany revived—partly, no doubt, because he learned, in October, 1762, through Monsieur de Conzié, of the death of Madame de Warens, which had taken place on July 29th of that year, and the event, by saddening him and reawakening melancholy memories, drove him again to seek solitude. He spent much time taking long walks and collecting plants, or retiring to dream on a bed of moss in some wild-wood retreat. At other times he entertained himself by making shoe-laces. He sat before his door chatting with the passers-by like the village women, or took his pillow with him when he went to see the neighbors. The products of his industry were presented to the young girls, on condition that when they married and became mothers, they would nurse their children themselves. Sometimes he wandered along the banks of the Areuse in the moonlight, singing serenades or ballads to which the simple folk of the neighborhood listened in speechless amazement.

He was certainly a peculiar figure, and he made himself appear still more peculiar by adopting the Armenian costume. His infirmities justified him in wearing comfortable garments, cut loose and long. But it was mere fantasy and the desire to be odd that dictated the embroidered coat, the caftan, the fur cap, and the belt of the Kurds or Turkomans in which he rigged himself out. Nor was he content with a simple if exotic wardrobe, but fussed over the details of his get-up with the utmost particularity and the bizarre taste of a child. He had to have gold lace and a gold tassel on his cap, and thus bedizened he went to Communion, having asked the pastor, Monsieur de Montmollin, for permission to partake in the divine service, and having obtained it.

The first time "Milord Marshal," with characteristic British imperturbability, came upon Rousseau in his outlandish attire, he accorded him only a phlegmatic "Salameki" by way of compliment. It is not surprising, however, that the country folk, excited by the townsmen of Neuchâtel, who were themselves stirred up by the municipal magistrates and ministers, began to persuade themselves that there was some truth in the legend that he was possessed by a devil. The fact that he lived with a mistress in a Puritan community was enough to expose him to hostile criticism. When he went about in Oriental garb picking flowers, it was natural that he should be accused of witchcraft, even of being Antichrist.

One day, not long after he had taken Communion, the news came that he had been condemned by the Sorbonne and that an edict, signed by Christopher de Beaumont, Archbishop of Paris, had been issued against him. His controversial fury was immediately rekindled, and he replied in a denunciatory epistle which is nothing less than a masterpiece. At the same time the authorities of Geneva, who had been appealed to in vain by the Rousseau family and a certain number of other citizens to nullify their condemnation interdicting from fire and water the author of the *Émile* and the *Contrat social*, answered with a confirmation of the sentence. Tronchin, the procurator-general, felt in duty bound to support the decision of the Council of Two Hundred, approved by the Lesser Council, by publishing his *Lettres écrites de la campagne*. In them he explained, with considerable moderation on the whole, the danger to religion lurking in the *Émile*, and that to the aristocratic constitution of Geneva in the *Contrat social*. Jean-Jacques had already made a public renunciation of his citizenship; he now took up his pen and produced the *Lettres écrites de la montagne*, in refutation of his adversary's able arguments. Undoubtedly Jean-Jacques was taking a correct stand when he asserted, in these letters, that his actions were in accordance with the true basic principle of the Reformation—namely, freedom of inquiry—and when he ridiculed the infallibility of Calvin as the creation of "an insolent and tyrannical orthodoxy." His argument unfolded with irrefutable logic, an astounding performance when one thinks that its author was in such acute suffering, both physical and mental, that he was actually contemplating suicide. For so he wrote to Duclos. He was in agony, more than ever before, on account of the failure of his bladder to function, having been driven to chop wood in the midst of winter in order to force out of his body by his perspiration the poisons which he could not otherwise eliminate.

In spite of his condition, his combative spirit kept him up to his own standard, or even inspired him to surpass himself. He swept down before him the venerable body of pastors of Neuchâtel, who endeavored to protest against the collected edition of his works edited by Fauche, and he challenged Monsieur de Montmollin to have him haled before the consistory of Môtiers to be excommunicated. Unhappily "Milord Marshal" had just been recalled to Scotland, and Voltaire published anonymously *Le sentiment des citoyens,* of which it was said that it seemed rather to be written "in the water of Phlegethon than in ink." It is indeed a venomous attack, but Jean-Jacques did not at first dream of attributing it to his arch-enemy, perhaps because he did not suppose Voltaire capable of descending to such abject depths. One wonders whether the former master of Les Délices, now become the Patriarch of Ferney, where he was both receiving the sacraments and instituting proceedings against them, had connived against Jean-Jacques at Geneva to the extent of helping the Calvinist city to decide in favor of defending "the cause of God." Perhaps he had, in devious ways. Anyhow, the only thing certain is that he had not forgiven Jean-Jacques, and that after accusing him, in *Le sentiment des citoyens,* of "having abandoned his children in the street, of trailing a common whore about in his wake, of being rotten from debauchery, and other little pleasantries of the sort," he let Jean-Jacques in his frenzy attribute all the insults he had heaped upon him to a certain pastor named Vernes, smiling up his sleeve in derision at the mistake.

He struck his blow with a master hand, and it proved effective. Voltaire hit exactly the proper note, best calculated to inflame the hatred of all bigoted Protestants, when he professed to see in Jean-Jacques "an infamous inciter to sedition" and called for the death penalty. He had seen to it that copies of his work were scattered all about Môtiers-Travers, thus arming with invincible weapons the irreconcilable enemies of the wretched refugee in their campaign against him. All to no purpose, Jean-Jacques endeavored to refute with quibbles the accusation, in *Le sentiment des citoyens,* that he had *abandoned* his children at the portals of the home instead of *delivering* them into the public charge; in vain he protested that he had no shameful disease, and that Mother Levasseur had died a natural death. Voltaire bespattered him so thoroughly that he could not possibly clear his skirts of all the mud that stuck to him. Every last man about him, down to Monsieur de Montmollin, who had hitherto stood up for him, finally turned from him in disgust. This dignitary, egged on by his colleagues at Geneva, shortly went so far as to deliver a sermon from his pulpit against the ungodly reprobate, and to forbid him to partake of the Communion—in the face of the authorities of Neuchâtel and of stern letters from Frederick II himself.

Popular imagination was further kindled against Jean-Jacques by the broadcasting of a quotation from one of his books, claiming that women have no souls. The persecuted wretch, still further depressed by news of the death of the Marshal de Luxembourg, which caused him deep sorrow, fell into despair and into the depths of melancholy.

"Oh, for peace!" he sighed. "What else matters in this short life?"

It is not known who gave to the author of the libelous attack on Jean-Jacques the information concerning his desertion of his children. He attributed the deed to Madame d'Épinay and her satellites, Diderot and Grimm. Thérèse, wild with impatience to get out of the Vale of Travers, so assured him, and saw a way to accomplish her desire by taking advantage of the hue and cry raised about him. Struggling, as he fancied, in the midst of a net, watching the slackening and tightening of the meshes in a fever of anxiety, he was urged on by Thérèse, who fanned all his fears, to ask "Milord Marshal" for naturalization papers, in order to be prepared for any event. From then on he viewed with suspicion all who came to call on him, whether they came in sincere admiration or from simple curiosity. Their courtesies and expressions of sympathy, however kind, seemed to him inspired by ulterior motives or tinged with spite and ill will. The very children whom he had been accustomed to encourage in their races, giving cakes as prizes to the fastest runners, joined with the street urchins in following him on his walks and shouting after him, and the village people screamed insults and threats at him in the streets. Thérèse saw her wish fulfilled. Her natural bad temper was as effective as were her deliberate efforts in making Jean-Jacques still more unpopular. Pastor Sarrazin wrote some time later: "The humble folk were less ill-disposed toward Rousseau himself than toward his governess. No one ever had cause to like her—quite the contrary." Vixen that she was, she reported to Jean-Jacques with exaggeration whatever was said about him in Môtiers, and her "violent outbreaks and her evil tongue" continually aggravated a situation which she had already managed to make bad enough. Finally, during the night of September 6th–7th, 1765, the house which Jean-Jacques occupied was riddled with pebbles, and one window was broken by a "stone as big as a man's head," which struck near his bed.

In the letter which he wrote to Monsieur Guy on the morning after the occurrence, Jean-Jacques certainly exaggerated his danger. He spoke of nothing less than a band of murderers who had forced his door, and he declared that he was expecting to have to withstand a siege that night. He had made his preparations, acquired weapons, secured a guard—his bluster would provoke our laughter if we did not know how terribly he was upset. He claimed that the pastor himself led the gang of cutthroats who fell upon him. Was it Thérèse, as one witness testified, who bribed the assailants? Was the affair a sudden outbreak of mob violence? No one can say. But it is probable that the aggressors were innocent of any such criminal intentions as Jean-Jacques imputed to them in his unbalanced state of mind, further stimulated by his "governess," whose natural inclination to give the most lurid interpretation to ordinary events was as marked as her ingenuity in doing so.

In spite of Jean-Jacques's fears, no second attack materialized. Twenty-four hours later he was able to depart unmolested for the island of La Motte, or Saint-Pierre, in the middle of the Lake of Bienne, leaving Thérèse behind. She had expected to leave Switzerland, and must have been disappointed by his decision. After waiting three weeks, she joined him, and found him delighted with his new mode of life. At last he could be happy in a quiet haven. He had retreated into the only house on Saint-Pierre, that of the tax-collector, and was living with the members of the official's family, his assistants, and his servants, all people "of an honest sort, very merry, and easy to get on with."

Saint-Pierre is a cheery little island rising like a bower of greenery out of the waters of the lake, with aged oak-trees, vineyards, and orchards. Jean-Jacques, like a child, was

THE REFUGEE OF MÔTIERS-TRAVERS 239

climbing the trees to pick apples, or, when not so occupied, was indulging, in carefree fashion, without any of the usual restrictions imposed by civilization, in his passion for botanizing. He had arranged with Peyrou for the publication of a complete edition of his works, setting his mind at rest by assuring him a regular yearly income, reverting after his death to Mademoiselle Levasseur, which meant he could live respectably. All he had to do before definitely abandoning his literary labors was to collect at his leisure the necessary materials for his *Confessions*. But his enemies were on the alert. Saint-Pierre was ruled from Berne, by the same lot of authorities who, as we know, had forbidden him to settle in their territory three years before. On October 17, 1765, he received from the bailiff of Nidau, Monsieur de Graffenried, a notice that he must leave the island within two weeks. In vain he begged Monsieur de Graffenried for a few weeks' respite in which to make his plans. He pleaded in terms which might have softened the hearts of sterner judges if they had been less prejudiced, but was refused it by their Excellencies of Berne.

As winter was coming on, he found himself once more obliged to move on, with no notion of where he could go.

CHAPTER V

ENGLAND

BEFORE Jean-Jacques left Saint-Pierre, he went through a period of perplexed indecision in the effort to choose a place of refuge among several which were open to him. The Prince of Württemberg invited him to Vienna, being of a mind, strange as it may seem, to entrust him with his daughter's education; while Paoli wished him to come to Corsica, there to frame a constitution for his fellow-countrymen. He might accept the hospitality of the Marquise de Frestoudam in Switzerland, or he could flee to Monsieur de Conzié at Les Charmettes. He could ask Frederick II for leave to settle at Potsdam or in Silesia. Lord Keith was inviting him to come to Scotland, Madame d'Houdetot was offering him shelter in Normandy, and Saint-Lambert suggesting that he hide in Lorraine. Lastly, though he had refused to heed Madame de Boufflers in 1762 when she advised him to go to her friend David Hume in England, he was now receiving urgent invitations from the historian himself, who promised to "seek him out a pleasant and tranquil haven in his own country."

In spite of advice to the contrary, or more likely because of it, he first decided in favor of Berlin. The fact that the sovereign who had welcomed and made much of "that clown Voltaire" showed no desire to include him also among his subjects was enough to inspire in Jean-Jacques a wish to become his guest. To his friends he sulkily returned no answer or pooh-poohed their suggestions, but Frederick's continued silence put him on his mettle. So he finally left

Bienne for Basle, where he arrived October 30th, ill, and already half regretting his decision. By the time he reached Strasbourg, on November 4th, his outlook had entirely changed. Though the enthusiastic welcome of the populace and the courtesy of Marshal de Contades, military governor of Alsace, consoled him for the brutality of the "ferocious wolves, wild beasts," of Berne, he was so utterly exhausted by his trip, "the most detestable in every way" that he had ever made in his life, that he declared he could no more continue his route to Potsdam than he could get to China.

So he was obliged to alter his plans. Sentiment had no weight with him in this crisis. He indulged in no dream of returning to Les Charmettes, whither he might have felt drawn by the desire to feel, with the coming of spring, stirrings of the sweet memories of his youth, nor yet did he dream of Madame d'Houdetot, whose idealized image had faded forever from his heart. He yearned to confront the unknown in a strange country.

In Basle a surprise performance of his *Devin* was arranged in his honor; his *Narcisse* was acted in the salons; he was so "sought after," to use his own term, that he was continually invited to receptions which tired him, and to bountiful dinners which upset his digestion. All these things piqued his curiosity to see how he would be received by the British, a nation that he had always detested. His extraordinary mentality impelled him, in spite of the persecution mania from which he suffered, to succumb to the temptation to take a chance, and to the morbid fascination of acting perversely. Though he had reached the point where he could no longer "even see a city street without a shudder," and would die of despair if he could not "see meadows, shrubs, and trees" from his window—still he came to the decision to go to London to live!

Turning to his *Dialogues,* we may read there what he wrote of himself: "He bore without flinching the yoke of physical necessity, but could not endure that of human compulsion. . . . With business to attend to, a call to make, a journey to go, he would set out promptly if there was no need to hurry; he would hang back if he had to act immediately." Such was this timid soul's brand of courage, an indication of his childish spirit of contradiction. Of two evils he chose the greater, discarded the prospect of many advantages in favor of trouble, if the advantages were urged upon him and if he felt that he chose the trouble of his own free will. Moreover, his anxious heart inclined him to distrust whatever appeared so simple or so easy that it might conceal a trap. In England, where the world least expected him to go, he had the best chance of avoiding the machinations of his enemies. He felt easier in his mind because Madame de Boufflers, Lord Keith, and Madame de Verdelin, three separate individuals among whom there was no point of contact, had corresponded with Hume independently, without the knowledge of anyone else. Hume himself had also written to him, and this guarantee of good faith on the part of a man known to be so honorable in his dealings that he was above all suspicion, finally put an end to Jean-Jacques's indecision. No account of the incident would be complete, however, without mention of his joyous anticipation of passing through Paris. His friends had procured a safe-conduct for him which assured his immunity, and he took delight in imagining the sensation his presence in the capital would create if he spent two or three weeks there before going on to London.

He wrote to Hume, on December 4th: "Your acts of kindness, Sir, touch me as deeply as they honor me; the most worthy answer to your proffers which it is in my power to make is to accept them; and I accept them."

He left by post-chaise on December 9th, and entered Paris by the Porte Saint-Antoine on December 16th, stopping at the house of the widow Duchesne, a bookseller in the Rue Saint-Jacques. His trip had been a difficult one, and at Épernay he had spent a night of agony. Hume had been living for three years in Paris as a secretary of the embassy, and was, in the words of Madame de Verdelin, "the household pet" of the aristocracy. He received Jean-Jacques as an author whose work he admired, and also as one whom he knew to be the object of interest among people of high position. He was a squat, heavy man, with an impassive face, round, bright eyes, and a soft, sensuous mouth, the antithesis of Jean-Jacques in every respect. Even though he had been forewarned, he could not help being amazed by the latter's feverish intensity, his capricious changes of mood, his exaggeration of every circumstance. He welcomed him warmly, however, showered him with attentions and expressions of admiration, and Jean-Jacques, greatly flattered, returned him every compliment and courtesy in kind. It was a veritable honeymoon, but a honeymoon unscreened from general view by the customary decorous conventions, heartily applauded at every step by all the best circles of sympathetic and intelligent people. Jean-Jacques was removed by the Prince of Conti for greater safety to the Hôtel de Saint-Simon, in the Temple enclosure, but he displayed himself in the gardens of the Luxembourg dressed in his Armenian costume, and was enraptured by the enthusiastic acclaim of society and of the populace. He was the object of the most gratifying curiosity, and people "of every rank and condition" flocked to see him in such numbers that, "like Sancho on his island of Barataria, he was on the stage all day long."

The Duke de Choiseul, alarmed by his popularity, notified Monsieur de Conti and the British embassy that he had better hasten his departure. The Parlement's decree had not been rescinded, and the police, less circumspect than the King's own minister, might take umbrage at his defiance of their authority. So he was prevailed on to leave

Paris on January 4, 1766, in company with Hume and Monsieur de Luze, a Genevan who was going to England on business.

The party was delayed at Calais for several days by bad weather, quite usual on the North Sea at that time of year. They set sail at last on Saturday, January 11th. Jean-Jacques had cared little for the sea the first time he saw it, and nothing in his writing indicates that he felt any more admiration for it when he crossed from France to England than when he contemplated it from the lagoons of Venice. He was a country-lover, through and through, and in spite of having been bred in the mountains, he always loved nature for her peaceful, smiling moods rather than for her grandeur and the magnificence of her convulsions. Though he speaks of having loved rocks, waterfalls, and rushing streams, the descriptive passages in his works are chiefly of meadows and woods. Imaginative, supersensitive, and emotional as he was, indolent and timid, his taste ran to nooks suggestive of security and repose, without too wide a sweep of horizon. The sea appeals to virile natures, those in whom the infinity of the ocean, revealed in its stormy aspect rather than in its celestial calms, stirs the love of action, an emotion unknown to the romanticist, and those who feel the exhilaration of struggle and the ardent desire to conquer. Rousseau was enraptured by a flower, moved to ecstasy by the sight of a swallow; they are excited by the tumultuous forest of waves, and their hearts go out to no birds save those which haunt the tempest.

The crossing lasted twelve hours, and Jean-Jacques landed at Dover in a distressing state of nervousness. In spite of a choppy sea and bitter cold, he had insisted on staying up on deck, in impenetrable darkness. No sooner had he left the ship than he suddenly broke through his self-imposed restraint, gave vent to a burst of enthusiasm at the thought of setting foot on free soil—no longer all alone, as in Switzerland, but in the illustrious company of Hume—flung his arms about the neck of his companion, who was still in a condition of seasick apathy, embraced him fervently in silence, and plastered kisses mixed with tears all over his face.

As soon as the news of the arrival of "the celebrated Mr. Rousseau" spread through London, on the ill-omened 13th of the month, a general stampede took place for his abode. Everyone turned out to get a sight of this personage, who, as the *London Magazine* announced, "had got himself into so much trouble by his eccentricities," and amazing demonstrations took place around him. General Conway, Lady Aylesbury, the Duke of York, and a host of other notables came to call on him or asked to be introduced to him. Even the Prince of Wales came to see him. To cap the climax, Garrick gave a dinner at the Adelphi in his honor, and then invited him to see his performance of the part of Lusignan in Aaron Hill's *Zaïre*, and his acting of the triple rôle of poet, Frenchman, and drunkard in *Lethe*. For this occasion Garrick took a seat for Jean-Jacques in the box opposite that which the sovereigns were to occupy. But as the hour approached, Jean-Jacques announced that he had changed his mind and would stay at home. He had brought along his dog, no longer the Turk of yore, but an animal by the more impressive appellation of Sultan, whom he had not the heart to leave alone lest it escape if someone happened to open the door in his absence.

"Well, then, lock the door and take the key with you in your pocket," said Hume.

Jean-Jacques agreed, but had hardly started down toward the street when the dog began to whine so piteously that his master could not bear it, and sped again up the stairs to pat him. Hume exerted all his powers of persuasion in his effort to induce Sultan's overindulgent owner not to create a scandal by staying at home from the theater.

He would have failed, we may suppose, had he gone no further than to invoke the respect due to royalty. But he argued that Mrs. Garrick had canceled other invitations in order to make a place for him in her own box, and Jean-Jacques, for the sake of French courtesy, which he flattered himself he represented in spite of being a Genevan, finally yielded—partly, too, because he had managed to quiet Sultan to some extent and to persuade him that he was not being abandoned forever.

When he entered the crowded theater at the precise moment with their Majesties, he was attired in the fantastic garb which he habitually wore, a long fur-lined robe belted in at the waist, and a fur bonnet trimmed with gold braid. He gave the King and Queen scant attention, gazing at them abstractedly at intervals; they, on the other hand, had no eyes save for him. All through the play he laughed, wept, shrieked, and stamped his feet like a child. Garrick's playing stirred him to such a pitch that he lost all control of himself, and leaned so far out over the edge of the box that he frequently had to be caught and held by his robe to keep him from tumbling into the orchestra. The English are not people to take offense at personal peculiarities, and the gentry united with the aristocracy in agreeing that the reputation of the author of the *Contrat social* was not overdone. Everyone who came into contact with him was charmed by him. Hume, however, who at first had praised the sympathetic manners of his guest and had spoken in highly laudatory terms of his emotional sensibility, soon began to feel that he had a little too much of him. "The extreme impatience" of Jean-Jacques and his "tendency to entertain unjust suspicions of his best friends" struck him first of all. Feeling inclined to pity him and to pass over his obsessions with indulgence, he labored, in spite of countless and ever-recurring objections on the part of Jean-Jacques himself, to find a place where he would like to live.

Jean-Jacques very soon left London, but objected to the first boarding place offered him in the home of a nurseryman at Fulham, and settled temporarily on a farm at Chiswick. There Thérèse promptly joined him, and his irritability and suspiciousness were increased by her chatter. He felt that Chiswick was too near London to suit his purposes, putting him at the mercy of curious visitors. He was advised to try the Isle of Wight, but declared that it was swept by constant winds and bristled with barren mountain peaks. He played with the idea of settling in an ancient monastery in Wales of which he had heard, but this plan proved impracticable and had to be abandoned. A certain Mr. Townshend, one of his admirers, then invited him to live with him, and, in order to make Jean-Jacques feel comfortable about the arrangement, offered to accept whatever he chose to pay for his board and keep. Unfortunately Mr. Townshend was married, and as Jean-Jacques insisted that, in spite of all hypocritical cant, Thérèse must be treated with the same consideration as if she were his wife, the negotiations came to nothing.

Another proposal from a Colonel Webb was discussed but fell through. The lodging which this officer offered to provide was not remote enough to please Jean-Jacques. Finally, by dint of endless searches, Hume discovered a refuge which met the approval of the wretched exile and put an end to his vacillation. This was at Wootton in Derbyshire, near Ashbourne, where a well-to-do landowner named Davenport owned a country house, prettily situated on the slope of a high hill, overlooking a landscape of "meadows, trees, and scattered farms." He agreed to lease it to Jean-Jacques for thirty pounds a year. Jean-Jacques professed himself delighted with the description he received of the place, and he settled there on March 22nd.

By this time he was in great haste to leave Chiswick, and

by the same token to separate himself from Hume. Not only had he ceased to like or admire the historian: he suspected him of evil motives and even believed that he was dabbling in the plots of his enemies, if he was not their actual accomplice. He dwelt in his mind on something that had happened—no doubt an hallucination—during the journey from Paris to Calais. Sharing a room with Hume in a hotel, he had heard him shouting in his sleep "with extreme violence" (but note that it was in French): "I have got Jean-Jacques Rousseau! I have got Jean-Jacques Rousseau!" He had made an effort to forget the incident, but was reminded of it after he reached London by the change in tone of the English papers, which at first eulogized him but then proceeded to make epigrams at his expense; and he held Hume responsible for having spread information about the peculiarities attributed to him.

To his mind other indications followed that Hume at least knew of the schemes of his persecutors. Hume had made a pretense of economizing for Jean-Jacques and had treated him like a pauper. Hume had ordered his portrait painted and had got the artist to represent him "with the face of a Cyclops." Hume had opened his letters. But there was worse to come: A letter purporting to have been written to Rousseau by the King of Prussia was handed about Paris, poking sly fun at Jean-Jacques, who was annoyed, indeed deeply hurt by it. Though the letter was not intended to harm him, it hit at his worst faults, and when he learned that it had been written in the salon of Madame Geoffrin by Horace Walpole, who was one of Hume's intimates, he no longer doubted that Hume had collaborated in its composition.

The evening before he left for Wootton, he was dining in Lisle street with Hume, whom he had so recently been addressing as his "beloved protector." He was suddenly struck by a strange glance directed at him by his host, and the "diabolical expression" of that look gave him such a turn that he feared for a time he was going to faint away. He then felt ashamed of his suspicions, suppressed his fear and horror, and threw his arms about Hume's neck, crying in a voice which shook with sobs: "No, David Hume is no traitor! It is not possible! If he were not the best of men, he would indeed be the very worst!"

It is easy to imagine the placid Scotchman's embarrassment at this inexplicable and tempestuous demonstration of emotion.

"Why, my dear sir! Indeed, dear sir! Now, now, my dear sir!" he repeated, for lack of anything better to say, patting Jean-Jacques's shoulder in an effort to calm him. But his amiability could not altogether cover his annoyance. Possibly he regretted, at the bottom of his heart, having chosen to treat Rousseau's malady lightly, instead of regarding it as seriously as it warranted. In taking Jean-Jacques under his wing, Hume had certainly acted on an unconsidered impulse, like any man on whom the position of society favorite imposes obligations, sometimes unpleasant ones. Afterwards, he had attempted to display his wit by joining to some extent in the laughter of the scoffers who predicted he would reap nothing but trouble from the companion he had taken up. Perhaps he did know something about the composition of the letter attributed to Frederick. In any case, he was on friendly terms with the band of philosophers who were Jean-Jacques's enemies, particularly with d'Alembert and Baron d'Holbach. Dr. Tronchin's son came to his house occasionally. He had a perfect right, the reader may say. Certainly! But, courtly and polished though he was, he either lacked tact or was a trifle dense, as the event was to prove.

At Wootton, Jean-Jacques calmed down, as he always did when he got out into the open country. He strolled in the fields and woods, botanized, or worked on his *Confes-*

sions, in the one of the two rooms he occupied which looked out over the valley. But Thérèse, furious for a second time at having to live like a savage, thinking of nothing but getting out of England, began again to practise the tactics which she had found so successful at Môtiers. She encouraged the illusions of poor Jean-Jacques, and intercepted his letters to make him believe that Hume was continuing to agitate against him from a distance. Whenever they conversed together, she turned the talk onto the plots of which he believed he was the victim. Consequently, in early April, when the spurious letter from the King was published in *Saint James' Chronicle,* Jean-Jacques was easily persuaded that his suspicions of Hume had been justified.

At this very time his patron informed him that through General Conway he had obtained for him the grant of a pension from the King. Jean-Jacques was aroused at the idea that the grant had been made only on condition that he should keep it a secret, and he saw in this another proof that he was the victim of a web of plots. He wrote to Hume, in high dudgeon, that he wished to have no further communication with him personally and that he would accept nothing that had been obtained through his agency.

Hume was indignant and demanded an explanation. Jean-Jacques replied in a long letter enumerating all his grievances, most of which were entirely imaginary. His letter alone should have shown any man in his senses that he was dealing with a lunatic. But Jean-Jacques, while he was writing to Hume, was also writing to all his friends and acquaintances. He wrote to Madame de Boufflers to complain of the traitor into whose hands she had "delivered him," to Madame Verdelin, to Malesherbes, and to Peyrou, to tell them that the man who had offered himself as his preserver had in reality schemed only to ruin him by dishonoring him. Frightened at the thought of what people might say, Hume felt obliged to write an *Explanation of the Controversy* which had arisen between him and his protégé. He might at least have handled Jean-Jacques with gloves, but unfortunately he denounced him with passionate resentment, almost ridiculous in a man who prided himself on his command of his temper. "He wound his trumpet" like a herald, in the words of one of Jean-Jacques's correspondents, to proclaim the truth, and when his work appeared not only in English, but also in French, translated by Alembert—who, it must be acknowledged, softened it down in certain passages—he regretted too late having given way to violence. Walpole, on his part, seized with remorse at having composed the wretched letter which started all the trouble, wrote to Madame de Choiseul at Chanteloup to ask her to intercede in favor of the wretched exile.

That witty lady, who called Jean-Jacques "a charlatan of truth," doubtless shared the opinion, by this time almost universal, that Jean-Jacques was ripe for the insane asylum. She answered Walpole that she was willing to exert her influence to have him confined there.

"His exorbitant conceit has always turned his head," she declared to Madame du Deffand. "He wants to be famous at any price; he would have burned the temple at Ephesus. I would not be surprised to have him end by proclaiming himself a prophet, wandering through the villages, calling the people together, working miracles, and finally being hanged."

Hanged! That was the very fate which Jean-Jacques feared might overtake him if he remained in England. Thérèse had given him the suggestion that he might again be stoned as he was at Môtiers-Travers, and he lived in a state of constant alarm. The foggy English atmosphere was certainly somewhat to blame for the attack of acute hypochondria to which he fell victim, but the fact that he had confided his suspicions to Hume had given them definite shape in his mind. He was no longer obsessed merely by figments of his brain, but was surrounded by fearful realities which he felt closing in upon him with dire menace. I cannot say whether the portrait which he complained that Hume had had painted of him is the one by Ramsay now in the Museum of Edinburgh. There is nothing grotesque or terrible in this representation of him. But how tragic is the expression of those eyes, feverishly intense, glowing below his Armenian cap! One can see nothing else in that wan face but their burning glance, like that of an animal at bay. His uneasiness was increased by the complete ignorance of French among the servants who waited on him. He communicated with them only by signs, and Thérèse, who abused them incessantly, complained that they were jeering both at him and at her, were gossiping about them and plotting against them in their jargon. It must be noted here that Voltaire and Jean-Jacques's other detractors abroad were still active in their attacks. He sent off letters which never reached those to whom they were addressed, failed to receive letters which had been dispatched to him, or received them only after they had been opened and resealed.

He was somewhat reassured, in June, 1766, when Mr. Davenport came to spend three weeks at Wootton with his family and treated him with great friendliness. But in April of the following year, the most violent scene that had yet broken out took place between Thérèse and the servants of that gentleman, and Jean-Jacques, having first sent word to du Peyrou that he was resolved to burn all his papers rather than let them fall into the rapacious hands of his enemies, wrote a note to his host to inform him of his determination to leave Derbyshire and England.

"The master of a house, Sir," he said, "is obliged to know what goes on in it, particularly what concerns foreigners whom he entertains there. If you are ignorant of what has been happening to me in your house since Christmas, you are at fault; if you know of it and countenance it, you are still more at fault. . . . I am leaving," he added, "my few belongings and those of Mademoiselle Levasseur, and I am leaving also the proceeds from the sale of my engravings and books, as a guarantee for the payment of whatever expenses I have incurred since Christmas. I am not ignorant of the pitfalls which await me nor of my helplessness to avoid them; but, Sir, I have lived my life; all I can do is to complete with honor a career which has been honorably spent. It is easy to oppress me but difficult to demean me."

On May 1st, having hastily packed up his manuscripts and a few indispensable books, he fled from Wootton, leaving his trunks with the keys in the locks. In his mad haste he mistook the road, and instead of reaching Dover, as he intended, he arrived at Spalding, about twelve miles from the Wash in Lincolnshire, paying his way at the inns as he went with pieces of flat silver. Mr. Davenport, with whom he had left property worth between twenty and thirty pounds, overlooked the irregularity of his behavior, and was entirely consumed with anxiety for his fate. He wrote him on the chance of reaching him at an address he had once given in London. But no trace of the fugitive was found in the city, and not until May 17th did Mr. Davenport hear from him, in a letter dated from Spalding nearly a week before. In it the poor wretch expressed the most acute remorse. He spoke of his piteous plight and declared he had decided to return to Wootton if Mr. Davenport was willing to have him there and would help him to get back. Mr. Davenport immediately dispatched a servant to assure Jean-Jacques he was ready to welcome him back as if nothing had occurred and to continue to guarantee him his protection. But at Spalding the messenger learned that Jean-Jacques, thinking, no doubt, that he would thus throw his enemies off the scent, had left for Dover four days earlier. The fact was that he had already been two days in Dover, having traveled the two hundred miles between that port and Spalding by forced marches.

The first thing he did on his arrival was to send General Conway a long missive, really a memoir, of incredible violence, in which he explained that he had been decoyed to England for no reason that he could fathom unless it were to dishonor him. He was convinced at this time that the object of his enemies was to prevent him at all costs from divulging what he knew of their treacherous maneuvers and from publishing his *Confessions*. He appealed to the general to allow him to set sail, being resolved "to leave England or die." So rife all about him were "dread signs warning him of his destiny," that he was quite aware he had only to appear to set foot on board a boat to be assassinated. But in order that General Conway might put no obstacle in the way of his desperate attempt, he pledged his solemn word not to say or write anything concerning Mr. Hume and the misfortunes which had befallen him in England.

As the reader can guess, no attempt was made to prevent his departure. But the fact that the wind was unfavorable and the boat could not sail on time was enough to throw him into an agony of fear. He was in such a state that he even suspected Thérèse—saint though she was!—and attributed to the intervention of a "higher authority" the poor atmospheric conditions. In his excitement he endeavored to win over the assembled multitude to his side, in case of a murderous attack on him, by climbing a hillock and haranguing the amazed spectators—in French, needless to state, for he knew not a word of English.

He got off to sea at last, and landed safe and sound at Calais on May 22nd, giving his name as Monsieur Jacques.

He wrote at once to du Peyrou to announce his providential arrival and to let him know that he might send news of himself to Amiens "addressed to Monsieur Barthélemy Midy, Merchant." He breathed more freely but was still only half assured. His continued anxiety is revealed in the letter he sent to the Marquis de Mirabeau, "the friend of men," father of the famous orator of the Revolution. In it he expressed the desire to go and end his days at the château of Trie, near Gisors, which belonged to the Prince of Conti. For several months he had been carrying on a fairly regular correspondence with the Marquis, who, because he was fond of Jean-Jacques and realized that he needed tranquillity, offered him, for lack of anything better, a temporary refuge at Fleury-sous-Meudon.

Jean-Jacques accepted the offer but did not reach Fleury until June 5th, having tarried at Amiens with Grasset, the author of *Vert—vert*, whose amiability had delighted him. He left Amiens just in the nick of time, for a town delegation had offered him a bottle of highly superior wine, called in local parlance "the wine of the city," leading him to imagine that they planned to make sport of him.

CHAPTER VI

APOLOGY FOR THE *CONFESSIONS*

JEAN-JACQUES stayed about two weeks with the Marquis de Mirabeau. Not for nothing was this disciple of Quesnay a southerner. He was outspoken to a fault, his truculent manner expressing an uncouth frankness which at times verged on brutality. Simple and honest all through, he made no effort to conceal from Jean-Jacques the fact that he did not share the latter's opinions. He even went so far as to take him to task for his own good.

"The best of minds," said he one day, "if it gives itself up entirely and unrestrainedly to its own imaginings, loses in the end the rudder of its thoughts, the thread of its simplest ideas, and in time falls into absolute dotage."

He dared defend Hume against the charges of his guest, whom he finally sickened by demanding that he read Hume's works on political economy and give him his opinion of them. Jean-Jacques craved peace. He declared he would have no more to do with literature in any form. Having come to an understanding with the Prince de Conti, who flattered his "fancies" and advised him to continue to conceal his identity for greater safety, Jean-Jacques took courteous leave of Monsieur de Mirabeau, set off once more, bag and baggage, and arrived at Trie under the name of Renou, the maiden name of Mother Levasseur.

He had been less than two months at the château when he was again upset, as he had been at Wootton, by the hostile relations between Thérèse and the household staff. When he was refused fruit and vegetables from the garden, he laid no blame, needless to state, on the shoulders of his "governess." He attributed his situation, "like that of Tantalus, who was surrounded by water but was unable to obtain a single drop for love or money," entirely to his enemies, who had ferreted out his latest retreat or obtained the secret of it from someone who had betrayed him. He dared not complain of his grievances to the august Prince in person who had given him "this asylum," so he addressed his reproaches to the Prince's mistress, Madame de Boufflers. He also informed the Marquis de Mirabeau that he was experiencing the worst possible treatment at the hands of all the residents of the region. Not only Monsieur de Conti's household, but even the priests and the rustics, were in collusion to destroy him.

"Ah," he sighed, "if only I had a thatched roof to shelter me, instead of a castle!" But if a peasant's hut had been his abode, he could hardly have invited as many as seven guests at one time to a meal, as he did at Trie—an imprudent gesture, one might think, on the part of a man in hiding. The reader would be justified in supposing that he acted with meet discretion at these little festivals. Not at all; on the contrary, he ran amuck. One can guess at the kind of answer returned to the inquiries of the curious country folk, puzzled at his strange appearance and demeanor, by the servants, who hated Thérèse.

It was Thérèse, to be sure, who "received the most insults and the worst." But the sly fox, while she kept reminding him of his tragic experiences at Môtiers, yet counseled patience, and advised him not to cast off his disguise and thus lay himself open to arrest for violating the decree of the Parlement, lest by so doing he fall into the trap set for him. Her desire was not that he should move on once more, only to lurk in hiding in some forgotten corner of France, but that he should arouse enough sympathy for his martyred state to obtain eventually the annulment of the accursed ban which prevented him from appearing in his true colors and openly returning to Paris.

I doubt whether there is any truth in the statement that he lived practically as a prisoner at Trie and that the castle was "closed, barred, and barricaded" at every door to prevent his going out on botanizing expeditions. I doubt it particularly in view of his remark that after so many real misfortunes he was beginning to fear lest he "perceive some which may be imaginary." He wrote to Coindet: "I shall expect you, but not in the evening. There is a gang of thieves hidden in the wood who kill everyone." He was convinced that one of the methods which would be employed to dislodge him would be to instigate an attack on him among the inhabitants of the neighboring villages. A servant died. "The household accuse me," he cried, "of having murdered the man with a concoction of poisonous herbs," and he demanded that an inquest be held. Peyrou came to see him and fell ill. As he lay delirious, Jean-Jacques heard him utter suspicious phrases, as he had heard Hume do the same in a nightmare. But then, he thought, this is impossible! Peyrou is loyal! It is a mistake—this unfortunate man is another who believes that Jean-Jacques seeks to poison him. It is all clear: the crew of philosophers have got their hands on him and have affected his brain. Indeed, what man can boast that he has got beyond the reach of those indefatigable conspirators and of their "servile, rascally satellites"? Think of the howl of triumph they would raise if once they laid their diabolical claws on Jean-Jacques's memoirs! The destruction of these, and the annihilation of their author, is all they think about. They seek his ruin. They seek his life. By stifling him, they hope to stifle the truth. What can he do to elude them and escape from their toils? His mind was full of the question. So entirely absorbed was he in this one problem, to the exclusion of every other thought, that he let pass almost unheeded a poem by Voltaire, *La guerre de Genève*, accusing him of having set fire to the theater of the Calvinist city.

He wrote a humble letter to the Duke de Choiseul, soliciting his protection or at least the grant of a passport. He also planned with the Prince of Conti how he might get to Paris to the sanctuary of the Temple. But just when everything was ready to receive him, after La Roche, the former personal servant of the Marshal de Luxembourg, whom he trusted implicitly, had set out to fetch him, he wrote a brief letter saying good-bye to the Prince, and literally fled from Trie, on June 12, 1768. He left Thérèse behind and hastened straight to Lyons without a rest, then later to Grenoble and on to Bourgoin. One wonders whether his sudden decision was made to foil his enemies in case they had stationed assassins in ambush along the road he would take to Paris, or indeed whether he feared to trust even the Prince, and suspected him of the wish to draw him into a trap.

He made the journey from Normandy to the neighborhood of Lyons in six days, and was utterly worn out when he arrived. But he was pleased, almost wild with joy, at the thought that he had extricated himself from the worst danger that had ever threatened him. He had taken nothing with him besides his precious manuscript of the *Confessions*, except his portfolio of pressed plants, and at Lyons he made "some botanical pilgrimages" with Monsieur de Tourette and the Abbé Rosier to take his mind off his obsessions, which, as he said, "made his head turn round."

At Lyons he saw his aged friend Madame Boy de la Tour. At Grenoble, after he had said a prayer and meditated on the tomb of Madame de Warens, he was given his invariable welcome and an enthusiastic reception. In a wine-shop at Bourgoin he became involved in a quarrel with a leather-worker named Thévenin who demanded compensation for a sum of money which he claimed he had lent Rousseau some years before. The Count de Clermont-Tonnerre, the King's lieutenant in Dauphiny, went on his bond and took over the case for him. However, he soon alienated his powerful friend by his violent recriminations, and when a lawyer named Bovier took up the case for him with ardent zeal, Jean-Jacques attributed the darkest designs to him for that very reason. Thévenin he described as not only a common crook, but a "rascal gangster suborned to murder him." He saw enemies everywhere, and at Bourgoin he scribbled on the door of the room he occupied after coming from Grenoble the following manifesto:

"*Sentiments of the Public, in its various factions, concerning me.*

"Kings and nobles do not say what they think, but they always treat me honorably.

"The true aristocracy, which loves glory and knows that I have attained it, honors me, and keeps silent.

"Magistrates hate me because of the harm they have done me.

"Philosophers, whom I have exposed, are out to destroy me at all costs; they will succeed.

"Bishops, proud of their rank and their state, esteem me without fearing me, and do themselves honor in treating me with courtesy.

"Priests, bound over to the philosophers, bark at my heels by way of paying court to me.

"Wits avenge themselves by insulting me for my superiority, of which they are aware.

"The People, whom I have worshiped, see in me only my unkempt wig and my decrepitude.

"There are women whom a brace of scornful nincompoops have played false, who betray the man most deserving of good treatment at their hands.

"Magistrates [again] will never forgive me the harm they have done me.

"The magistrates of Geneva know they did wrong, know that I forgave them, and would make me amends if they dared.

"Popular leaders, whom I have raised aloft upon my shoulders[?], would like to conceal me in order that they alone may be seen.

"Authors steal from me and accuse me [no such are recorded]; rogues hate me, and the common mob hoot at me.

"Respected and worthy men, if any still exist, lament my fate in secret. As for me, I give them my blessing, and hope that some day it will prove instructive to mankind.

"Voltaire, whose slumbers are troubled by me [he returned it in kind, forsooth!], will write a parody of these lines. His gross insults to me are a tribute which he is forced to pay me in spite of himself."

Possibly one need pay no heed to this composition except to excuse it by attributing it to insanity. But I never read anything which pained me more, especially in view of the fact that Jean-Jacques, jesting in a fashion one is tempted to call silly, declared that he wrote it "to amuse himself."

At this time he suddenly decided to summon Thérèse back to his side and to marry her. When he fled from Trie, he was no longer so sure of his "governess" as he had been in the past, and even in England he had entertained no small suspicion that her lack of brains had induced her to play him false. He gave her to understand, if not that he desired to leave her, at least that he foresaw he would soon die, and he advised her to think of her future.

During their stay at Môtiers, probably from a wish to persuade him to leave the hateful spot, she had expressed the intention of retiring to the depths of some remote province where living would be cheap and quiet enough, there to live out her life, "either in a home for women or in a little establishment of her own in or near some village." He wrote her from Grenoble, on July 27, 1768, that if she received no more news of him during the ensuing week, she was not to wait for him any longer but was to make her own plans for herself with the help of the patrons she knew about, in whom he had complete confidence. "Consult Madame l'Abbesse," he said, "Madame de Nadillac, abbess of Gomerfontaine. She is kind and charitable and intelligent. She will give you good advice." But he had hardly settled at Bourgoin when he sent for Thérèse and, on August 28th, was legally joined to her in marriage, with no religious ceremony or even much civil ceremony, in the presence of the Mayor and two witnesses. The latter were "men of worth and honor" who were moved to shed floods of tears by the fair and holy promises which consecrated "a tender and pure relationship." He felt he had accomplished a master stroke in attaching Thérèse to himself by indissoluble ties. Kind, devoted, and faithful as his angel was, according to his own expression, she was human and a woman. She would be all the more true to him if, in betraying him, she should betray herself as well. At least, so he reasoned. Even though Voltaire, the well-to-do seigneur of Ferney, Baron d'Holbach, Alembert, Diderot, Madame d'Épinay, Doctor Tronchin, Hume, and all their kind might come to make him honorable amends, begging his humble pardon and groveling at his feet, he would still fear the Parlement, Geneva, France, and the universe in general.

After staying a few months at Bourgoin, he became utterly disgusted with the "nest of plots" of which he was the object, and began to entertain hopes of fleeing to the remotest parts of the earth, to the islands of the Archipelago —Cyprus, for instance—or to some other part of Greece or Turkey. He had obtained a passport from Monsieur de Choiseul. So unstable was his mind that he even thought of returning to Wootton, imagining perhaps that he had less to fear in a place with which he was already acquainted than where he would be a stranger.

Moulton offered him the château de Lavagnac, near Pézenas, for a refuge, and the Prince of Conti an estate in the Cévennes. But he dreaded lest these offers be made with some secret motive.

"I am a little afraid of any remote abode," he declared, "since I have perceived in those who have my fate in their hands so strong a desire to shut me up in one. I do not know what they plan to do with me in a wilderness, but they are of a mind to get me there, by force if necessary, and I have no doubt that was one of their reasons for driving me away from Trie, where I was not sufficiently isolated for their purpose."

He was in such a state of anxiety, and was also so impatient to plead his cause against his innumerable enemies, that from Monquin—where he had been living since February, 1769, while he looked about for some better place, because the marshy air of Bourgoin made him short of breath and gave him fever—he sent a long letter full of confidences to an officer in the Dragoons, Monsieur de Saint-Germain, with whom he had become acquainted. This letter and those previously written to Monsieur de Malesherbes are the strangest products of his pen known to us. On the strength of Monsieur de Saint-Germain's reputation for justice and steadiness of character, he had picked this gentleman to be the recipient of his most private thoughts and to hear his self-justification, before the publication of his memoirs, which were to be his real vindication of himself. He had written to him first from Bourgoin to request an interview, saying: "I have not the honor of your acquaintance. But Monsieur de Saint-Germain is not deceived by appearances, still less is he a man to be intimidated. Forgive me the informality of the expression,

Monsieur: you are exactly the man I need. I shall have to confide, Monsieur, in a good and true man, whom my confidence will not dishonor, and it will give me relief. If you are willing to be the magnanimous recipient of it, be good enough to appoint me a day and hour for an undisturbed hearing, and I will be there."

Monsieur de Saint-Germain had heard him out, and the letter of which I spoke above, about twenty-five pages long, was written in order to deposit with him a record for posterity of the things Rousseau had told him orally. In it he enumerated his grievances against Diderot, who continued to hate him for having wronged him; against Grimm, who tore up the eulogies he addressed to other men; against Madame de Boufflers, who had not forgiven him, first, for having written, in *La nouvelle Héloïse,* that a charcoal-burner's wife was more worthy of respect than a prince's mistress, second, for having thought nothing of a tragedy she had written, third, for having scorned her in person, that is, for having declined her offer of her favors; against Madame de Luxembourg, who had been pained by his blunders; against Doctor Tronchin, whom he had made basely envious of his glory; against Baron d'Holbach, whom he had made brutally jealous; and so on. But Choiseul, who had taken a criticism in the *Contrat social* to be directed against himself, was most guilty of all. It is certain that Jean-Jacques at this time regarded Choiseul's attitude as the cause of his miserable fate. Because he had not been able to persuade Choiseul to rescind or nullify the decree of the Parlement, so that he could return to Paris to confound his enemies, the minister was responsible for nearly all his trials and tribulations. He perceived his hand everywhere, even in the annexation of Corsica to France (1769). For there seemed no doubt that Corsica had been taken into the royal domain in order to prevent Jean-Jacques from conferring on the island the

APOLOGY FOR THE CONFESSIONS

constitution which its people had requested him to frame.

Fate had been utterly unfair to Jean-Jacques. His loyalty to his friends was unimpeachable, nor did anything else in his conduct make him a deserving victim of fortune's slings. He was no gamester, nor did he live a dissolute life. He was neither ambitious nor greedy for wealth. Far from being miserly, he was charitable to prodigality. He loved glory, to be sure, but can that be called a crime? Of sins, only one can be attributed to him, that of abandoning his children. And Heaven is his witness that he expiated that sin in full! With that one exception, his faults and weaknesses harmed no one but himself, "and his whole life could be revealed to all the world, even to his most secret thought, without fear of reproach."

This is the whole tone of the *Confessions*. "I am aware that I am a just man, kind, and right-minded," he concluded, "as much as any man on earth. On this conviction rest my hope and my sense of safety. Though Providence may appear to have entirely forgotten me, I never despair. How splendid a recompense must be in store for good men, since they are so neglected here below!" But it is worth noting that though he cannot point out a single act of open violence directed against him, he claims that man has exerted all his ingenuity to invent base methods of tormenting him, methods worse than any torture, and will continue in future to invent still other devices to make his life intolerable.

"I shall never be out of their sight," he said. "I shall never take a step without being followed. I shall be deprived of all means of finding out anything either of what concerns me or of what does not concern me. The gazettes will be kept out of my hands; letters and packages will never reach anyone to whom they are addressed except those who seek to betray me; all correspondence will be cut off between me and anyone else; every question I ask will invariably be answered: 'We do not know.' Amid the most garrulous people on earth, I shall live as among deaf-mutes. If I travel, everything will be arranged in advance to supervise me wherever I go; I shall be entrusted to the care of passengers, coachmen, waiters; I shall hardly be able to eat with other guests in the inns; and I shall hardly be able to find a place to live which is not removed from all society; in short, care will be taken to spread all along my way so strong a feeling against me that my heart will be torn with grief by everything I see."

Morbid, indeed, are these imaginings! They show the final complete collapse of his reason, which had at first been affected only slightly. If the reader desires further proof that he was demented, it will be found in the verses he began, while at Monquin, to write at the beginning of his letters, which he dated in the following peculiar manner: He divided the four figures indicating the year into two equal groups and set down between them a fraction of which the numerator stood for the day of the month, the denominator for the month itself, numerically indicated. For instance, he wrote to the Abbé M——:

"Monquin par Bourgoin, $17\frac{9}{2}70$.
"Blind, wretched fools are we!
O Heaven, unmask all evil arts,
Force those with barbarous hearts
To disclose all for men to see!"

Whether he wrote the miserable quatrain himself or borrowed it from someone else, we do not know. His invariable habit of repeating it on everything he wrote proves the extent to which he was obsessed by his fixed idea. That fixed idea determined him, after he had bestowed his name on Thérèse in order to strengthen her fidelity to him when he suspected it of wavering, to offer her her freedom from him if she wished it, during the summer of 1769. I feel fairly certain that at this time he perceived something suspicious in her behavior. Her secretiveness and underhandedness aroused his anxiety—also her intimacy with a certain priest of whose identity we are ignorant. Possibly he had caught her intercepting his letters. The one sure thing is that he quarreled for some serious cause with "his governess, his friend, his sister, in fact his all, who had become his wife." In the passage of the *Confessions* on which he was at work about the time the quarrel took place, he said: "The strength of my affection [for Thérèse] will be realized when I tell of the wounds, the hurts, she dealt me at the very height of my unhappiness." He repeats the statement in the same words in a letter he wrote to his companion at Monquin the day before his departure on a trip which was to take him a couple of weeks. Thérèse loved him no more. Thérèse had threatened to leave him on short notice without his even knowing where she intended to go. If his company no longer entertained her, if she again wanted, as she had already said she did, to go and board in some home, why did she not talk the matter over with him? He believed that they must separate, if only to teach them a lesson by showing them how absolutely they were suited to each other. The separation could not last forever. Later, after they had forgotten their grievances, they would again live together and wend their way in peace towards the grave.

Such considerations as these were not vital to the subject which preoccupied him. But Jean-Jacques would not have been Jean-Jacques if he had not woven a web of mystery about that subject. What was the journey he had to make, concerning which he wrote that "nature works her will with us at the moment when we least expect it"? Why did he feel called upon to assure Thérèse of his Christian sentiments by telling her that whatever happened to him, it would not be because he despaired, and that consequently he would never commit suicide? These are unanswerable questions. He reminded his wife solemnly that "we have sins to weep for and to expiate."

The unhappy wretch believed that the memory of having left their children at the foundlings' home would be enough to keep her from ever leaving him permanently, if she was seriously considering the step. But she was not considering it. I am sure that her threat to separate from him was only one of the moves in the game she was playing with him. She was going to let him rest only after he ceased his everlasting and disastrous wandering, and settled down again in Paris. In any case, she never left Monquin during his absence, and welcomed him back there as if nothing had happened. She was waiting for the approach of winter to disgust him with the discomforts of the house he was occupying, which he had already experienced. It was swept by every wind that blew, and from November on was completely buried in snow and almost inaccessible; his confinement was rendered even more burdensome by quarrels between Thérèse and a farm girl whom he called "a bandit in petticoats."

But Thérèse had another card to play. Possibly she had private information from the very people with whom he accused her of being more intimate than with him, in the letter I have mentioned. In any case, she assured Jean-Jacques that he would be perfectly safe in Paris. Eight years had passed since the *Émile* had been banned, and there were reasons to think the ban might be lifted. The Parlement which had driven Jean-Jacques out of the country was weakening, and Monsieur de Choiseul, who had kept him an exile, was on the eve of falling from power. On the other hand, the Prince of Conti, of whose good faith Jean-Jacques had been for some time suspicious, advised him not to go to Paris. That in itself would be enough to make him go. In addition, he had put the last touches

APOLOGY FOR THE *CONFESSIONS* 269

on his *Confessions*, using, to be sure, China ink for the final chapters because somebody had adulterated his ordinary ink with water. As they were not to be published during his lifetime, as he repeatedly stated, he was burning with the desire to read them to a picked audience.

He left Monquin at the end of May, 1770, and on June 2nd he stopped at Lyons to spend several days with his loyal friend Madame Boy de la Tour. He then went on through Montbard, kneeling, as at the threshold of a temple, at the door of Monsieur de Buffon's writing room, and paid his respects to the Prince of Conti at Nevers. He reached Paris on June 30th, and went to stay at the Hôtel du Saint-Esprit in the Rue Platière.

As the reader has seen, Jean-Jacques wrote the *Confessions* during the most troubled years of his entire existence, between 1765 and 1770. He began them at Môtiers, finished the first five books at Wootton, the sixth at Trie, the last six at Monquin. Fate brought him back to repicture the romantic episodes of his adolescence and youth amid surroundings similar to those in which he had lived at the time they took place. But unless he had been the victim of persecution and had believed himself in greater danger than he actually was, he could hardly have revived with the essential note of wistful delight the memories of so many happy, carefree hours, nor have revived them so exactly in their characteristic settings and the beauty of their landscapes, the rocky, forested banks of the Lake of Bienne, the mountain crests that broke the Wootton horizon, the woods of Trie, the vales of Monquin.

And note that by a curious coincidence he began to compose his memoirs on the very date with which he ended his recital, so that his writing seems designed as much to bring back the past for his own pleasure as to call it to witness in his justification. Hence the dual character of this unique work. I consider it the most original thing he wrote, or at least most characteristic of his genius; that is, in it he best expressed himself, and it was, of all his works, the one he was best fitted to undertake.

My readers are all familiar with the rhetorical statement which opens the *Confessions,* the statement with which Rousseau sums up his sins, to begin with, and, so to speak, forces God to accord him the absolution he accords himself: "Eternal Being! Gather together about me the innumerable multitude of my fellow-men, that they may hear my confession, lament my wrongs, blush for my misfortunes. May each one of them in his turn lay bare his heart at the foot of Thy throne with like sincerity, and then may any one of them who dares, declare to Thee: 'I was a better man than that one.' "

We know his theme. He repeated many times in his letters that he wished "to make his soul transparent to the eyes of his reader," to reveal himself *intus et in cute;* that is, to write "not his external life, as other men do, but his real life," the narrative of his most intimate feelings, to do what no man before him had done and what no one else would do later; to leave far behind "the rhetoric" of Saint Augustine and the "false appearance of sincerity" of Montaigne. He had been traduced, disparaged, wrongly represented, besmirched; he meant to rehabilitate himself and, by his own efforts, to regain his rightful place in the full light of the sun. But when he came to the labor of exposition and attempted to enumerate and explain the crimes of his enemies in order to give foundation to his charges, the effort so clarified the situation in his mind that the crimes became perfectly intangible. He had no facts whatever to cite as proof of the accusations he made in attempting to demonstrate that he was the victim of a conspiracy. The light of reason, playing on the mountain of infamy which he had erected in his demented dreams,

APOLOGY FOR THE *CONFESSIONS*

shrank it to a molehill. No doubt the diabolical perfidy of the Voltaires, Diderots, Grimms, and Holbachs was all the more undeniable since their plots were so subtle as to vanish into thin air at any attempt to analyze and expose them, but he had to be content with denouncing them, with revealing the causes of them, and showing up the underhand methods in which the whole band connived, keeping in mind that he could foil them by exhibiting to the world the true Jean-Jacques in place of the one they had fabricated to foist upon it.

Pride drove him to undertake the task, and he lingered over its completion with delight, or rather with rapture, hampered by no sense of modesty. The vices of the society in which he mixed inspired him, too, to compare his life with the lives of other men, and he dilated on his own experiences in a spirit of ignoble competition. He had nothing to fear from a complete revelation of himself, and could not delve too far into the truth, his object being to confound his detractors. In his own words: "The worst that could happen to me would be that I should be only half understood." For nothing about him could be attributed to real wickedness. By describing his passions, he gave a complete picture of the man he was as his Maker had created him, and he swept out of his path, as he went on, the innumerable base deeds which littered it. He worked without compulsion and without restraint. Following the road to the end, one comes upon a virtuous man, for the ethical sense is the result of an immoral life. Listen: "Experiences are to be gained from our mistakes which are better worth having than if we had committed no mistakes."

It matters little that these mistakes may have harmed other people. The impression they have made on our own selves, the influence they will bear on our own future actions, are the essentials. Jean-Jacques, it must be remembered, was a poet, and his work is that of an artist, not of a historian. As Joubert has so admirably said: "He was his own Pygmalion." What he produced was a romance, the first of what are nowadays called novelized biographies. Though he put away the temptation ever to tamper with the truth as he knew it, he admits that he frequently expressed himself in fables. The essential point was that he should be true to himself, that he should in no way distort the image of Jean-Jacques as he conceived him. Now Jean-Jacques modifying the facts of the case, putting a false interpretation on events, is Jean-Jacques to the life. As I have said, when he accepted his emotions as the essence of his being, when he gave a dream-shape to actual things, misrepresenting them to himself or making them over to suit his preferences, when he told untruths, not from deliberate intention, but "affected by a fever of the imagination," he was his truest and deepest self. At those times he was the Jean-Jacques of pulsating inner life, not the Jean-Jacques of reason, who was the most capricious of logicians; then he was the authentic Jean-Jacques, devotee of pleasure, not the man of duty, who was the worst of all falsifiers. Reason—duty—the reader has already seen how he subordinated these abstractions to his impulses or twisted them about to serve and justify his instincts. It was he who called the ethical sense "the sixth sense."

"I wrote my *Confessions* after I was old," he declared. "I wrote them from memory, from a memory which frequently failed me or served me with inaccurate recollections; and I filled the gaps with details which I imagined to complete the recollections, but were never incompatible with them. I loved the act of dwelling on the happy interludes in my existence, and occasionally I embellished these with adornments suggested to me by fond regrets. I told of the things I had forgotten as it seemed to me they must have been, perhaps as they had been; never in

APOLOGY FOR THE CONFESSIONS

any different way from that in which I remembered they had been."

Therein lies the charm of this fallacious work, so strangely fascinating even when it jars on the reader, a book for which one reaches with the left hand after one has pushed it away with the right. Discontented and unsatisfied creatures that we are, we are astounded by the spectacle of a man who revels in himself and never has enough of himself. In the beginning, one hardly perceives the plaint of the hurt plebeian. The dominant note is wistful enjoyment, the enjoyment of an aging man who reminisces of his happy time and still thinks of himself with affection for having been an incorrigible lover. In his memory he continued his wanderings from the strait and narrow path and led himself still further afield. He reviewed his life with infinite detail and infinite care, starting it anew with the keenest pleasure. Perhaps, his temperament being what it was, he actually enjoyed the remembering more than he had enjoyed the living. His book, like a mirror, reflected to his own gaze every minute characteristic of himself, down to his physical infirmities, and he contemplated them all with rapture as a certain type of lover feasts his eyes on the defects of his mistress. Such an exhibition of cynicism, or call it frankness, is almost upsetting to our balance, tempting us to question whether life could be better spent by any of us than as this happy-go-lucky fellow spent it, enriching his store of experiences up to the time he was nearly forty years of age, drifting irresponsibly, gathering the hours and reaping their sweets, prolonging his youth to the point of effeminacy. To be sure, his youth had never been remarkable for vitality, but languorous with the sensuous rhapsodies which filled it, rhapsodies which he never definitely sought but accepted whenever they presented themselves. The *Confessions* are a revelation of a species of hermaphrodite; hence, even while we succumb to their enchantment, we necessarily scorn them somewhat and are repelled by them at the same time. "Happiness is an ideal of our youth attained in our maturity," said Vigny: Jean-Jacques, in the early stages of his existence, had no ideal. He was without determination, without ambition—that is, without any guiding ambition, for it cannot be said that in a man the desire to be liked and to be loved constitutes an ambition.

He had no needs beyond the physical. He let himself be sheltered and coddled like a girl until he was past the age at which the most backward of us are beginning to realize the results of our struggles and our sufferings. Reflecting a moment, we see the futility of the happiness we might have felt inclined to envy him. "We are not happy because of accumulated delights," he wrote in one of his letters, "but because of a settled state of mind, independent of definite actions." His attitude was passive; he took no hold of life, but was swept up and carried on by it. Moreover, his heart ruled his head; his intellectual qualities were subordinated to his emotions.

Once the narrative of his early wanderings is over, his book shows evidences, as did his life, of the bitterness born in him by the passage of the years and the annoyances inflicted by his enmities. The same Jean-Jacques who whined and broke out into paroxysms of childish rage, ever incapable of comprehending why all the world did not join in petting him and indulging his every whim, was he who wrote the last six books of the *Confessions*. These books, together with the *Dialogues* of which I shall speak later, have for us little more value than the ravings and railings of a gossipy old maid, mere chatter much of the time, rank slander occasionally. The work is relieved by no humor; for though it contains amusing passages, the author was never amused. It was not in his nature to laugh, still less to smile. When he left off being chatty, or picturesque, or sentimental, he was grave and solemn. Irony, particularly that brand of irony which the wise man directs at himself, was not in him.

He remained loyal to his motto, *Vitam impendere vero*, and in 1770 he finished the image of himself which he had set out to fashion, and to erect in the market-place for the admiration and reverence of all time. The image resembles him. Like Janus, it was two-faced, the one face sensuous, the other sinister; but there was no viciousness in either. In the first face, there is something womanish, in the second, something crazy. But in both, it seems to me, there is altruism, if not true kindliness. The setting of the effigy is important, is not to be disassociated from it; it is such a setting as makes of Priapus himself, shaded amid leafy boughs with moss or ivy wreathed about his obscene parts, a harmless deity. The *Confessions* are steeped in nature; nature is in and about them all, and purifies them.

The spectacle of Jean-Jacques in the act of purifying himself remains to be shown.

CHAPTER VII

THE COPYIST OF MUSIC

AS might have been predicted, Jean-Jacques was entirely unmolested in Paris, where he settled in the Rue Platière, now called the Rue Jean-Jacques Rousseau. He had first stopped at the Hôtel du Saint-Esprit, then moved to a near-by dwelling, owned by a retired grocer named Venant, who let him one fifth-floor room which he used for cooking, sleeping, and living. The approach was through a tiny entrance-hall, "where cooking utensils were arranged in excellent order." Two small beds "of coarse cotton cloth, striped blue and white" like his hangings, a spinet, "a bureau, one table, and a few chairs composed all his furniture." On the walls hung "a map of the forest and park of Montmorency, and a print representing the King of England." "A canary sang in a cage suspended from the ceiling; birds flew to peck at the bread" laid in the windows which opened on the street; "and on the sills in the hall stood pots and boxes filled with such plants as nature loves to sow."

I have borrowed the description, so like a Chardin interior, from Bernardin de Saint-Pierre, who adds that in the philosopher's modest home was "an atmosphere of neatness, tranquillity, and simplicity which was delightful." I do not doubt it. Madame Rousseau had orderly ways and was industrious. She was also a good cook, as we know, and so far as material things were concerned, she gave Jean-Jacques perfect satisfaction.

Dressed in a robe of Indian print, wearing a cotton cap to protect his bald head, he spent his days chiefly copying music. He resumed the calling he had previously practised in Paris, not so much to support himself, since he had an income of 1,800 francs on which he could live, as to play his part and appear as a free man working with his hands. When he had earned approximately his two francs a day at the rate of ten sous a page—he must have written out between six and eight thousand pages in six years—he gave himself time to sit at his spinet and play his own accompaniment while he sang "in his weak voice, already cracked and quavering," a ballad of his own composition—"*Que le jour me dure,*" or "*Que j'aime à voir les hirondelles.*" From time to time he took up the *Philosophia Botanica* of Linnæus or opened the Bible, Plutarch, Tasso, or *L'Astrée,* interrupting his reading occasionally to replenish the fire or skim the soup-pot entrusted to him by Thérèse when she went out on her errands.

He had left off wearing Armenian costume, and when he went out to play chess at the Régence or to take his walk in the garden of the Palais-Royal, he wore a coat and trousers of nankeen or gray cloth, a round wig, and a plain three-cornered hat, and carried a long cane to replace the sword which once swung at his side. Among the curious spectators who crowded along his way, there must have been numbers of children who, grown to manhood, thought of him during those scorching July days of 1789, and roused their own enthusiasm by invoking his name when they tore the leaves from the chestnut-trees, at the bidding of Camille Desmoulins, as the emblem of their rising.

But after dreaming with rapture for so long of the popular ovation he craved, Jean-Jacques was, as usual, annoyed and exhausted by actual evidence of curiosity concerning himself. He wrote to Monsieur de la Tourette: "I have been so burdened by calls and invitations to dine, ever since my arrival, that if this state of things continues,

I cannot possibly hold out, and unhappily I have not the strength to defend myself." It seemed as if all the world were consumed with ambition to entertain him and everyone competed for the privilege of showing off the strange creature to a tableful of guests. When Sophie Arnould, the actress, was unable to prevail on him to sup with her, she invited a tailor who looked exactly like him to take his place, stipulating that he should under no circumstances open his mouth except to put in food. Unfortunately the rascal interpreted the provision too freely when it came to drinking, and, when the meal was over, was in no condition to remember the instructions he had received. He burst out with incoherent maunderings, which the party, however, was pleased to accept as sublime utterances, and not a guest, as he took his leave, omitted to congratulate Mademoiselle Arnould on the genius of her lion of the evening.

In spite of everything, Jean-Jacques became little more tranquil or assured. He had reached a point where peace of mind could be at best only relative and temporary. No doubt he felt pleased that he had found in Paris a refuge from his enemies, by simply and openly coming there to settle under the very eyes of the authorities, and, in so doing, placing himself under their protection. He sent word to Monsieur de Sartines, who at the time was lieutenant of police: "I assure you that the advantage of living under the eyes of an honest and vigilant magistrate, a man who is not easily deceived, was one of the motives which decided me to leave the country, where I was thrown helpless upon the mercies of those who provided for me, and was the victim of their hangers-on." But while he was convinced that the opposition of his enemies was as unbroken as ever, he could not live in perfect peace.

Thinking to break their ranks and to do himself justice, he arranged first for one meeting and then for a second, almost immediately after he went to Paris, in order that he might give readings of his *Confessions*. In the audiences he summoned, not a single one of his friends was included. For both occasions, one at the house of Dorat and the other at the house of the Marquis de Pezai, he sought not sponsors, but impartial witnesses. But, alas! the crowd he assembled—the Marquis de Juigné, Prince Pignatelli, the Marquise de Mesme, the Count and the Countess d'Egmont—who listened to Jean-Jacques for seventeen mortal hours, with two brief interruptions for refreshments, had no ears except for the scandals he could divulge. They recollected nothing in the memoirs except the most ribald stories, which grew more spicy in the retelling as they were whispered about to the accompaniment of stifled laughter. Nothing else was talked of in the salons of Paris. The sensation grew as it spread, and excerpts from his narrative which Jean-Jacques gave out in other quarters produced as great an effect—indeed, a greater. For whatever he suppressed, malicious imaginations filled in, as always, with innumerable supplementary details. Everyone who had heard anything at all handed it on from memory, copied it out to give around to his acquaintances, and embroidered it to suit his fancy. Using Ruhlières as an intermediary, the King of Sweden succeeded in getting the manuscript, whereat Jean-Jacques was incensed at the "duplicity of Duclos," who had used the sacred trust confided in all friendship to him "as a means of deception and treachery."

High society flew into a panic, and though Grimm and the philosophers kept calm, and even Madame d'Houdetot and Madame de Luxembourg faced the situation cheerfully, Madame d'Épinay took alarm and shortly raised a hue and cry. She sent a complaint to Monsieur de Sartines, and prevailed on him to order Jean-Jacques to be silent. Jean-Jacques was silent. However, he continued to date his letters in the manner he had adopted at Monquin, and to head them with the same quatrain, adding to their embellishments the motto of Geneva, *Post tenebras lux*. Truth must triumph; though it be smothered here and now, it will raise its head elsewhere. And if perchance it vanish from the world, open the heart of Jean-Jacques, for there shall truth live on. He suffered the pangs of a woman who cannot deliver her child, and again fear began to gnaw his vitals. "I can face calmly the troubles which are upon me," he wrote, "but not those which I dread for the future. My frenzied imagination weaves them together, turns and returns them, lengthens them out and increases them."

For some time he braved the assaults of the court ladies and the "little amber-powdered dandies who whistled when they talked." Then he shut his door against them by contriving a grated window which he could open, when his door-bell rang, to see who was there. When he judged the visitor to be some inquisitive stranger, or perhaps a spy, he shut his peek-hole with the brusque announcement: "Monsieur Rousseau is not at home." He broke with all his former circle, and except for his clients, who rarely got into his private apartment, accepted calls from very few people—Dusaulx, Rulhières, Grétry, Corancez, Eymar, and Bernardin de Saint-Pierre. Those on whom he called were still fewer—he went to no houses except those of Madame Dupin, Chenonceaux, Genlis, and perhaps Créqui.

He was quicker to pick quarrels than to make friends, and one must acknowledge that in some cases he had right on his side. Certainly he was justified when he took offense with Ruhlières for attaching himself to him only in order to observe him with a view to writing a comedy entitled *Le défiant*. But Dusaulx, seeking to distract him, took him to see Piron, and Piron, though he was old and blind, confused Jean-Jacques with his exuberance and deafened him with his noisy talk. He laid the blame for his fatigue on Dusaulx, who made the mistake of attempting to advise him. The dense fellow could not sympathize with his obsessions. For instance, Jean-Jacques once said to him: "From here, by my fireside, where we sit, I see and hear everything that is said, everything that is being plotted against me, for a hundred leagues around. For ten years, ever since I have been hunted down like a wild animal, I have never chatted freely until nightfall, when my enemies are dropping off to sleep. But I am talking nonsense! Even then they have their spies watching me." "You are ill," replied Dusaulx. Jean-Jacques was furious, and from that time on took every occasion to offend him. Eventually he wore out the patience of his friend, who regretfully took leave of him, hoping but hardly expecting that he would recover. And yet Dusaulx had seen him "gracious, cheerful, sublime," and had listened to his talk with the same pleasure he had taken in his books. For when Jean-Jacques was not in the throes of terror or of rage, he overflowed with sweetness and kindliness, was courteous, simple, childlike, "merry" even, and tolerant toward all his enemies, those who existed as well as those who did not, down to Voltaire, of whom he was never heard to speak harshly in his latter years. He had crises of repentance and apologized for having been unjust to Alembert. His piety was inspiring. Thérèse, when she told of his death, could say: "If my husband is not a saint, I do not know who is." Bernardin de Saint-Pierre compared him to Socrates, to Epictetus, and to Marcus Aurelius.

In resignation he doubtless found a way to rise above his troubles, or perhaps a release for one part of himself while the rest of him kept up the struggle with his phantasmal enemies. His serene manner covered a lurid inner life. For he had never been so demented as at this period when he appeared a sage to his admirers and indeed became a sage by the exercise of his highest genius. His natural disinterestedness and his contemplative mind took him out of the world, but his pride in his works dragged him back into it and delivered him over to the torture of his persecution mania. To make his escape from the enemies whom he accused of dishonoring him and of ruining him in the esteem of the coming generation, he would have had to forget that he had written the *Discours,* the *Émile,* and the *Contrat social.* This he could not do, and he went through alternate periods of rebellion and of submission, forgetting other men when he was out in the open country, suddenly brought back to consciousness of them when he returned from his excursions.

During the four years 1772–1776, he wrote the three sinister dialogues entitled *Rousseau, juge de Rousseau,* in which shrewd criticisms of himself mingle with extravagant absurdities. Eventually he found out where he stood, but wandered far from his path in the process, and his masochistic tendency forced him to inflict agony on himself and to experience a savage joy in inflicting it. He imagines himself in discussion with a Frenchman who accuses him of crimes, slanders him shamefully, considers him a monster of vice. He extenuates himself by explaining his character in all good faith and with extraordinary acumen, but he passes through inconceivable anguish in detailing the miseries from which he believed he was suffering. All the while he wrote—and the *Dialogues* cover no fewer than five hundred and forty pages, overloaded with repetitions because he had not the courage to reread what he had written—he continued to suffer terrible "depression of spirit" which certainly hastened his end.

He felt bound by mysterious chains and weighted with invisible fetters. Spies, disguised as street women or as ragamuffins, were all about him. His letters were being opened, and the books he wanted were being filched from the publishers. Whenever he entered a place of public resort, everyone in it approached him and fixed him with a stare, never speaking a single word. If he took a seat at the play or at the opera, an usher or policeman was always stationed beside him. Wherever he went, there were men at his heels whose looks were suspicious. He was pointed out to porters, clerks, peddlers, and all the riffraff. Bootblacks and ferrymen refused to serve him. To humiliate him, tradesmen were prompted to sell their wares to him at lower prices than to others. Beggars were set along his way to throw back at him the alms he gave them. Any apparent attempt to approach him on business meant that he was being spied upon. His walls, his floor, his locks, were all false. His persecutors were working to drive him to despair and to make him commit suicide.

Occasionally he had times of relative tranquillity, in which he went through his daily routine automatically, living a nightmare from which nothing could distract him. When, in 1775, his *Pygmalion* met with great success, he was grieved instead of being delighted, because he believed that it had been produced only to stir up "a ridiculous scandal." He laid this crime, too, to the account of his enemies. One day Ducis called on him, and, when dinner time drew near, got up to go. "I will not detain you," said Jean-Jacques. "If any little mishap should occur to you at my table, I should be accused of having poisoned you." At times he suddenly lost consciousness, and began to mutter incoherently, his face wan, his arm wound over the back of his chair, clinging to it. The best that could be done at such times was to keep perfectly still and wait for the first pretext to leave him quietly. Bernardin de Saint-Pierre, the kindest and least touchy among the friends of his latter years, often saw him incensed at nothing. He realized he had made a mistake when he included Jean-Jacques among the friends to whom he had distributed a consignment of choice coffee—Jean-Jacques accepted charity from no one. But he could not understand why his friend should give him an angry look when he brought back a book he had borrowed. "If I speak to him," said our author, "he answers only in monosyllables, and goes on copying music; he constantly rubs or scratches out his notes. To give myself something to do, I open a book which lies on his table. He says, in a worried tone: 'You like to read, sir?' I get up to leave; he gets up at the same time, and escorts me to the top of the staircase, saying, when I beg him not to take the trouble: 'One must do so with people one does not know pretty intimately.'"

He could never see children nor speak of them without sadness. When Bernardin de Saint-Pierre pointed out a group of children playing in the walks of the Tuileries and said, "This is what you have done: it was the *Émile* which set those captives free," Jean-Jacques showed symptoms of irritation. Yet on one occasion he was heard to sigh: "Oh, if only I might still have sincere demonstrations of affection from someone, even a tot in short dresses!"

As I said, he escaped from "his train of evil-doers" and found deliverance from his melancholy only when he was away from Paris. On such occasions, Bernardin de Saint-Pierre, who accompanied him on his excursions and botanized with him, heard him express noble and serene thoughts while they walked among the "lovely young woods and mauve heath" on the heights about Sèvres, over the "lonely moors" of Saint-Cloud, or on the gentle slopes of Ménilmontant or Romainville. Nature gave him inspiration; he talked of natural things with a feeling which delighted his disciple, and unaffectedly interpreted for him the poetry of every landscape. He proved himself a good companion, cheery and sympathetic, always ready with his reminiscences and comments. Walking enlivened him and, as he himself said, "awakened" his ideas. In order to think, he had to bestir his body. Out of doors, in forest or meadow, nothing reminded him of his own tragic situation. He beamed with his whole soul; the mists which shrouded it were dispelled. He noticed young girls in the Bois de Boulogne prinking in the open air—or they took a ferry to the foot of Mont-Valérien and together climbed the height to the hermit's retreat on the summit. There they were offered a light repast, but Jean-Jacques preferred to sit down at a table in a cabaret and to cook his own omelet and bacon while Bernardin de Saint-Pierre made the coffee for which he had brought along the ingredients.

But instantly when they crossed the city line into Passy or Belleville, the spell broke, the glamour fled. Jean-Jacques's brow clouded over at first sight of the houses of the suburbs. He frowned, hastened his pace, sank into silence. Once more his torment began. Unknown dangers awaited him around the curve of an alley and lurked in dark corners or rose from the very pavement. It is an actual fact that one evening, when he was knocked down on the Ménilmontant Hill by a large dog, the Great Dane of Monsieur de Saint-Fargeau, rushing at top speed between his legs to greet its master, he recognized in the incident a plot against his life and trembled because the wretches who were conspiring against his peace of mind had contrived a new method of hurting him. One day, when he was out on the streets with Bernardin de Saint-Pierre, he said: "I would rather be set out amid the Parthian arrows than exposed to the gaze of men."

One wonders why, when he so dreaded Paris, he did not move somewhere else to live. It is sad to realize that he not only could be at peace nowhere, but also no doubt enjoyed with a dreadful kind of pleasure being at the very center of the web of conspiracies against him, in the same way that he enjoyed the writing of the *Dialogues*. He was actuated by the same morbid fear which makes a murderer return to the scene of his crime, and he clung to whatever tortured him; possibly he was dominated by the same feeling which, as it is stated in a manuscript which Grimm gave to Naigeon and which was later owned by Edmond de Goncourt, took him sometimes to an obscure house in the Rue Maubée where he could have himself whipped for a few pennies.

He copied out his lengthy manuscript of *Rousseau, juge de Rousseau,* in his precise, fluent, neat hand—but note that he filled out the blank ends of all the lines with dashes extending to the margin, in the manner characteristic of him—wrapped it with great care, inscribed on the cover "Left in Care of Providence," descended his four flights of stairs with it in his hand, and walked straight to Notre Dame. This was at two o'clock in the afternoon, on February 24, 1776, in the dead of winter, one of the coldest winters ever recorded. He entered the cathedral, intending to set his manuscript on the high altar. For Louis XV, hated as cordially by the common people as he himself, had died; consequently, he reasoned, he was now the sole object of the hatred of the French, and he hoped that news of his action would reach the ears of the new king, who was said to be a good man. Louis XVI would then wish to read the book and would realize the truth. But he found the grilled gate of the choir closed—a proof that God was against him, or had refused to intercede for him. In a desperate state of mind, he left Notre Dame, firmly resolved never again to enter it as long as he lived, and, seized with dizziness, wandered through the streets in a trance until fatigue, cold, and darkness drove him home.

Such emotional crises were little calculated to improve his already feeble health. Thérèse was at a critical age and was herself ailing. He composed three documents in the form of circulars, and handed out copies, which he made himself in longhand, to "every Frenchman who still loved justice and truth." The first was a protest against the alterations made by the publishers in his books; the second asserted his independence and the wickedness of his enemies; the third implored assistance for himself and his companion. "No matter what treatment I myself receive," he wrote, "whether I be definitely shut up or left at nominal liberty in some asylum or in a desert, whether I be with kind men or with harsh, with liars or truth-tellers (if there are still any such), I consent to anything, provided that my wife be given the care her health demands and that I be given shelter, the simplest of clothing, and the most frugal of food until the end of my days without being forced to do anything at all. We will pay what we can, in money, goods, and securities, and I have reason to hope that it may be enough in the provinces, where living is inexpensive, and in houses established for this purpose, where economy is understood and practised, especially as I will cheerfully submit to any routine adapted to our necessities."

His plea was denied, the more courteous answering that he could not mean it for them, others jeering or treating him with scorn more humiliating than the jeers. His perverted pride had reduced him to the extremity of feigning to beg—masochism again. But in spite of the failure of the populace to respond to his appeal, the aristocracy, who never ceased to take an interest in him, stepped to the fore. The Count d'O had been offering for a year to take him in. Monsieur de Flamenville and Monsieur Menon and Lieutenant-Colonel Count Duprat followed suit. Monsieur de Duprat, however, made his offer with two conditions attached—that Jean-Jacques must go to mass, and that he must keep his identity a secret. Jean-Jacques answered him, on February 3, 1778, that he "had no feeling whatever against taking such precautions as seem proper to avoid making too great a sensation." Elsewhere he wrote: "I have no objection to going to mass—quite the contrary. Whatever be the religion, I shall always feel I am among my brothers when I am with those who are gathered together for the service of God." But he wished to bind himself to the performance of no duty, and still less was he willing to have it supposed, in the region where Monsieur Duprat had offered to lodge him, that he was a Catholic. As to assuming a false name, he had learned by experience the uselessness, and even the danger, of this precaution, "because of the mystery attached to it." In short, he raised objections: the proposed place of refuge was remote, and he doubted whether, crippled as he was by rheumatism, he could bear the long journey. The prospect of having to make any effort or endure any fatigue made him unutterably indolent, and Thérèse had at that time little more energy than he.

While he was allowing Corancez to fit up a dwelling for him at Sceaux, he was playing with an invitation from the Prince de Ligne to come to Flanders. But in the end he accepted an offer from the Marquis de Girardin. He was enchanted with the idea of returning to the region with which his happiest memories were associated, and determined to end his days in a lodge at Ermenonville attached to the château of the Marquis, Field-Marshal, and man of letters.

CHAPTER VIII

ERMENONVILLE

A CHASTENED Jean-Jacques was he who, on May 26, 1778, took possession of his new haven in company with Le Bègue de Presle, the private physician of the Marquis de Girardin—a Jean-Jacques of burned-out passions, half his soul already weaned from this earth. The last work in which he had testified his interest in the concerns of the world is his treatise on the *Gouvernement de la Pologne*. He had left Voltaire on his deathbed in Paris, and had been among those to acclaim and applaud him. He was shortly to hear of the patriarch's death and to remark: "I feel that my existence was bound up with his. He has died; I shall not be long in following him."

He took with him the manuscript of the *Rêveries d'un promeneur solitaire*, an admirable monologue which, unfinished as it is, takes rank with his *Confessions* as the most individual and fresh of his works. Here we have no more of the torturing inquisition of the *Dialogues*, but a reposeful interrogation of Jean-Jacques's own conscience, recollections of his happiest memories, communion again with nature in his reminiscences. "For me, all is over," he declared. "I can no longer be harmed." To be sure, he adds, "I am as immutable as God Himself," for his pride was to him as a shirt of Nessus, of which he could divest himself only by tearing it off in shreds and flaying himself in the process. He recognized, however, that he had deluded himself in counting on a repetition of his successes with the public, and that he did wrong to combat fate. His inability to abjure his own writings, concerning which he was as sensitive as in his pride, was all that held him back from the admission that his life had been a failure.

"Cast adrift in my earliest years on the storm-swept world, I soon learned by experience that I was not fitted to live in it." He judged himself impartially, from an exalted plane. "My excitability and my fits of indignation threw me into a fever which ten years were not too long to cure, and during this time, by committing mistake after mistake, error after error, blunder after blunder, I by my own rashness gave to those who controlled my fate plenty of means, which they were quick to use, to turn it into channels from which it could not change its course." Doubtless he was as unbalanced as ever—the accents of insanity can be detected even in these words. But the dominant notes of his utterance were no longer those of insanity. His spirit was like a tossing sea subsiding, heaving its last swells after the tempest. He looked with some degree of detachment on everything, even on the criminal attempts which he believed were on foot against him, and acted almost as if someone else were involved. From the torment of "anxiety and terror" he was at last free. "It would be in vain for men to return to me now," he declared grandly. "They would no longer find me."

His daily strolls were filled with delightful observations, and the leisure of his body quickened his mind to greater activity. He rose almost to serene heights in his feelings, his thoughts, his "ethical inner life." He no longer drank deep of the ecstasies of dreaming, and of the raptures of feeling himself hover "over the universe on the wings of imagination." He tasted with delight the joys of peaceful meditation in place of the reflection which had exhausted him. By degrees "the spirit of living" died down in him. He cared little to know how he ought to have lived; he was concerned rather with learning how to die. "I have not Solon's happiness," said he, "of being able to learn something every day as I grow old; I must even avoid falling into the danger to which pride lures me, wishing to learn what I can no longer master. But though I can hope for few acquisitions in the way of useful knowledge, I still have highly important ones to make in the way of the virtues I need; on that score it is time to enrich and adorn my soul with such acquirements as it can carry away with it. Freed from this body which befogs and blinds it, perceiving the naked truth, my soul will finally see the pettiness of all this knowledge, the pride of our false scholars, and will lament the time wasted in attempting to amass it during this life."

He reviewed his own faults, and dwelt with remorse on two in particular—the abandonment of his children, and the lie which he had told when he accused Marion, Madame de Vercelli's maid, of having stolen a ribbon. He was especially pained that he had been false to the truth, when the motto which he had adopted laid him under heavier obligation than other men to be loyal, and he realized that in daring to wear his proud device, he had been presumptuous. Whole-hearted was the reparation he made—he descended to humility. "Never," he said, "did deceitfulness prompt me to lie. All my falsehoods came from weakness, but that is a poor excuse for me. With a weak spirit, a man can at best keep himself from vice; but it is arrogant and boastful to dare to profess great virtues."

Gazing on the spectacle of the works of God, growing with long practice familiar with them, he finally achieved an attitude of resignation. He chanted a hymn in their honor: "Bright flowers, enameling the plain, streams, groves, and greenery. . . ." There was an element of "childishness"—he used the word himself—in his methods of amusing himself as he wandered in search of plants through woods or fields, but they did not lack dignity, nor were they out of keeping with his tenets. No matter if they did: his unrestrained enjoyment not only lightened his melancholy, but restored the innocence of his first youth. He experienced none of the devout, rapturous exaltation of, say, Saint Francis, but he participated in Lenten observances, and as he left his house less and less frequently, he worked at home on pretty portfolios of pressed plants and dried flowers, or carefully stretched sprigs onto bits of paper, which he framed in red, as serious-minded children collect postage stamps. No plant was too humble for his taste—not pimpernel, sorrel, groundsel, nor sage, and, as he put it, he pursued his botanical studies as far as the bird-cage. Perhaps he carried off no victory over the phantoms which had beset him earlier, when he aspired to wisdom or had it almost within his reach, but at least he thrust off to a distance the things which terrified him. The thought of his work, though it was still heavy within him, no longer obsessed him, and he felt almost as if he were living alone with his own soul. On April 22, 1778, when he was sixty-six years old, he began the tenth of his *Rêveries,* which he was destined never to finish. He wrote: "To-day, Flowery Easter, it is exactly fifty years since I first met Madame de Warens." Singularly enough, the chimes of the bells of Easter, with which life opened before him, rang again as his life closed, and one may say that all his existence was bounded by those resonant peals, and was played out to the accompaniment of their ominous undertone.

Monsieur de Girardin, who had heard of Jean-Jacques's distress through one of his ardent admirers, a young Knight of Malta named Filamainville, welcomed him kindly. He installed the philosopher in a furnished dwelling, since, on leaving Paris, Jean-Jacques had instructed Thérèse, who was to join him a little later, to sell all his household goods. Monsieur de Girardin left him free to come and go as he pleased, but gave him every care and attention. When he first settled down, the change of scene and the happiness of being in the country at the height of the spring season seemed to restore some of his declining spirits. He threw himself with his whole soul into botanizing, and went to work collecting plants with enthusiasm. Occasionally his expeditions were shared by his host's son, Louis Stanislas, a lad of sixteen whose education he had consented to supervise, but more frequently he departed alone at sunrise and returned about seven o'clock for his morning coffee. From time to time he accepted an invitation to dinner from Monsieur de Girardin, who had written a book on the art of landscape gardening and could talk with him of the things which interested him. He liked the Ermenonville country, which was not more than five or six leagues from Montmorency and resembled it, though there was something wilder and more mysterious about it as soon as one had left the valley, the little stream with its waterfall, and the lake on which floated a tiny island shaded by tall Italian poplars. His own cottage was on the edge of a pond, twenty minutes' walk from the spot in the forest of Ermenonville known as "the desert." This was a vast expanse of sandy plain, tufted here and there with pines and birches, and hemmed in on all sides with heather, a scene admirably adapted to his melancholy mood. But he also loved the romantic beauty of the landscaping which Monsieur Girardin had done, transforming the confines of the lake into a perfect stage-setting. The island delighted him especially, and there the Marquis had to arrange a concert for him, one beautiful summer evening, a week before he died. The plaintive notes of the violins, dying away in languor over the water, brought tears to his eyes, and he could not forbear expressing to his host the wish that he might be buried on that spot where he had been so deeply moved.

The charm of an island scene has always worked its spell on idealistic natures. No Utopian but has dreamed of a bit of land all surrounded by water, a universe in miniature, where he might found his ideal community as one cultivates some gigantic tropical tree in a pot. Jean-Jacques's own happiest days had been spent among the islands of the Lake of Bienne, if we are to believe the account of his life there, so convincingly and poetically given in one of the *Rêveries*. The feeling which led him to people one of those islands with rabbits may well betray a twinge of regret that he had not himself been able to try out there the idyllic existence he believed practicable with companions of his liking.

He had not so completely sloughed off his old skin, however, as to accept his lot as Monsieur de Girardin's guest without complaints. Unalloyed as was his happiness at Ermenonville, he was nevertheless troubled by the thought that he was not standing on his own feet. Over a door he wrote: "No man is truly free who needs the help of another's arm to reach beyond his own grasp for what he wants." Perhaps he actually contemplated flight, as he states, without knowing where he could go. But his strength was ebbing fast. He again fell victim to attacks of nervousness and of vomiting bile, like an epileptic, as in the summer of 1777; and his old friend Moulton, who went to see him, heard him tell of a fit of vertigo which had seized him the preceding day. Shortly afterwards he had a recurrence of the vertigo, so violent this time that he thought he was going to die. Mental anguish accompanied his physical pain, and those who hold that he committed suicide advance the hypothesis that he suffered at perceiving the confidential relations between his wife and John, one of Monsieur de Girardin's grooms. This, however, is very doubtful. Thérèse, quick as she was to embark on affairs of the heart, had not yet been at Ermenonville

ERMENONVILLE

long enough to become involved with the drunken Irishman, nor was it until a year after the death of Jean-Jacques that her scandalous behavior obliged the Marquis to turn her away, and she went to live with her lover at Plessis-Belleville. In any case, Jean-Jacques could not at that time have been so deeply affected by a shocking discovery of the sort as to wish to put an end to his life. He knew too much already about Thérèse—incidentally, that she drank heavily; and he had found a way to meet the situation, if the story is to be relied on that he himself went down to the cellar for the wine to forestall her from going after it and remaining there. The fact is doubtless that his old ailment, which had attacked him forty years earlier with such severity, had developed, and that his death was due to its final onslaught.

On the morning of July 2nd he left home about five o'clock in search of botanical specimens, as was his custom. Only a short time before, Maximilien Robespierre, then a young law-student, had come from Arras for the sole purpose of seeking an interview with him, and had been received. At seven o'clock he came in and took his cup of *café au lait*. The scene is vividly pictured for us in a contemporary engraving, helping us to reconstruct it in our minds—the fireplace with the pier-glass above, the embers of the wood fire, over which Thérèse had boiled the water for his coffee, Jean-Jacques, who had complained of feeling ill, sitting at his window beside his unmade bed with its chintz hangings. Suddenly he fainted and fell to the tiled floor, where he lay at full length, groaning. It was Thérèse who lifted him once more to his chair, opened the window, which looked out over the pond and the woods, and returned to his side to care for him. Overcome with dizziness, he stretched out his hands to the light, flooding his room with golden rays. As he made the gesture which seemed an attempt to grasp, hold, and press to his heart all nature, which he had so deeply loved, he fell again, cutting his forehead. When his wife turned him over in her effort to lift him, she saw that he was dead. Jean-Jacques, with his lifelong horror of the surgeon's knife, a horror which would surely have made him mourn the sanguinary crimes committed in his name, went to his death with his face all smeared with blood.

CHAPTER IX

LE BANC DES MÈRES

JEAN-JACQUES'S body was taken to the Panthéon on October 11, 1794, but for me his spirit still abides on the Island of Poplars, where the Marquis de Girardin had him buried and erected his mausoleum. The wretched author of the *Confessions,* after his turbulent life, was not to find peace even in death. He was hardly cold before his corpse was carved open, for in order to put all suspicions at rest, his host insisted on an immediate autopsy. This revealed a slight scar on the forehead, and two negligible hernias of the groin; in his stomach was nothing but the coffee he had drunk. No trace was discovered in his bladder of the disease from which he had suffered. On the other hand, the watery discharge on his brain proved that he had died of an apoplectic shock.

The body was embalmed and enclosed in a leaden coffin. On December 18, 1897, the government of the French Republic, in response to expressions of doubt as to the remains interred in it, ordered the coffin to be opened. The historian Georges Caïn, who was present on the gruesome occasion, had just time to catch a glimpse of the features of the "Man of Nature and of Truth" before the evanescent tissues fell to dust at contact with the air.

Seeking to conjure from the shadows of the past that face as Houdon has perpetuated it in his death-mask, I wandered one autumn day as far as Ermenonville. Following the footsteps of Robespierre, who many a time sought repose and inspiration in that spot, of Saint-Just, Necker, Franklin, Jefferson, Bonaparte himself, and Louis

Blanc, I seated myself on the Banc des Mères, which stands in the shade of a grove beside the lake, facing the Island of Poplars opposite the tomb of Jean-Jacques. Poets and authors as numerous as Rousseau's own disciples, philosophical or sociological, have made their pilgrimage to that rustic seat—Chénier, Bernardin de Saint-Pierre, Chateaubriand, Madame de Staël, Lamartine, Lamennais, Georges Sand—and have listened there in the silence of the valley for echoes of the grandest lyric strains of France's eighteenth century. Women, among whom have been a queen in shepherdess costume and a Creole decked out as an empress, have come there to confide their own hearts' secrets to the lover of Héloïse. I put the question to myself whether I had interpreted his heart aright and understood his widespread influence, an influence as dominating, certainly, as that of Calvin, of which it was the complement. No other man personified as did Rousseau the new spirit of revolt against the established order—not Voltaire, whose destructive criticism concealed a conservative spirit; not Montesquieu, who struggled to set up a liberal form of government for the purpose of safeguarding the absolutism he thought essential; not Diderot, by nature more of the middle class than of the people, who was bound by his labors within the narrow limits of Encyclopædic ideas. Was Jean-Jacques a great and good man, as his followers would have him, or was he merely gentle, kind through weakness, like those egotists who have so much compassion for themselves that they tend finally to feel compassion for mankind too? I have said that he was of this temper, and I continue to believe so, nor do I think I slander him in stating that his one point of superiority over others of his sort was that he was not ill-natured, that he bore no malice even in envy. Because he was easily touched and supersensitive, he believed himself that he was magnanimous and charitable. "I love men too much," he wrote, "to need to choose among them. I love them all." Such words as these are the excuse for any injustice, and for accepting any sacrifice, including the sacrifice of one's brother men.

Because he had no moral sense, he could boast of having an infallible "moral instinct." Because he had no common sense and no training, his pride was hurt by his inability to adapt himself to the ways of the society whose doors his genius opened to him. He vacillated between the two extremes of weakness and pride, the effeminacy of his nature inciting him to take Plutarch's heroes as his models, his presumption making him bow in his own cult and set himself, in spite of his Christian faith, on the same level with his God. Longing to be a superman, lacking power to realize his desire, he was unhappy, maladjusted, unable to adapt himself to existing conditions. He could not possibly have been content except in such a community as he dreamed of, where a set of values might prevail different from those in the world of men which hurt him. Hence his disdain of civilization and the vulgar egalitarianism with which he proclaimed that the king should accept the hangman's daughter into his family if she suited his son.

Imagination he had, of course—nothing, in his eyes, had beauty except "that which did not exist." But he was of that subjective class of imaginative beings who view everything in relation to themselves and whose judgments are consequently tainted with falsehood and bias. He acknowledged in the *Rêveries*, the most serene and impartial of his writings, that he had never taken an objective view of the world and of life. He assimilated his experience in terms of his own ego and his own aims, then used his knowledge to read lessons to the rest of men, professing only scorn for all ascetic theories which seek to advance spiritual life, and for those organizations which assume the duty of regulating and encouraging that life, the only life worth while. As he was intelligent, he might have adjusted himself to reality and corrected his utopian tendencies if he had been thrown into contact with men at an earlier age. But his lot was to live apart and not to study his kind until his character had matured and had been irrevocably molded. Hence he remained, until just before he died, a voluptuous child, credulous though sly, indolent and unambitious in spite of his sudden bursts of courage which drove him to exhaust himself in work, work which absorbed every fiber of his being. A child he was and remained, in his untrammeled but petty and vague passions, in the weak spirit with which he craved love from all the world, and in his very madness, the persecution mania which pursued him to his grave, comparable only to the child's fear of phantoms.

I should like to be able not to pity him, for pity, together with idle curiosity, led the nobles of his days to welcome him with open arms, to their own cost. It is best to forget the man, to remember only the harm he did, and to reflect that everything that was most sympathetic in him—his best qualities as well as his faults—was responsible for the harm. The fact that he declaimed against the institutions of the Old Régime with as much feeling as if he personally had suffered on account of them, explains the effect his denunciations produced. He had a poet's soul, but the assassins of the September massacres wore on their hearts the image of the poet as Perseus wore the Gorgon's head upon his shield. For his own misfortunes, he had no one but himself to blame. But in his wild idealism and in his cry of revolt were the germ and the herald of other misfortunes brought on mankind by men.

I hold it up against Jean-Jacques that with all his love for nature, he opposed to nature the only civilization which has worshiped her and endowed her with a soul. I hold it up against him, too, that he should have revealed truth to the individual man, leading him back to an understanding of the harmony of nature, only to blind him again by his social compact, and that he constructed his jointly governed city, a city of slaves to abstract ideas. In this connection, Napoleon made a significant remark: "It would be better for France if I and that man had never existed." In associating his own accomplishment with that of Jean-Jacques, Napoleon interpreted the one by the other and demonstrated what they had in common of primitive traits, or of brutality and artificiality. Napoleon made another profound reflection: "I have removed the smirch from the Revolution." The hero carried on the work of the poet, but the dream of both was shattered amid the snows of Russia, on the soil of Mongols who, from the time of Tolstoi to that of Lenin, continued to pick up the litter of what they left behind.

Jean-Jacques was the first French writer to break with French tradition. "He was not French," it has been answered. True, but he was Swiss, and, moreover, a Genevan —his origin does not explain him. In spirit he was Oriental, from the land of plagues and devastating pestilences. Though he was no Byzantine by birth, and no Asiatic blood, to the best of our knowledge, ran in his veins, yet the sensuous mystery of the East was in his soul and was reflected in his troubled dreams. Something of this is suggested when it is said: "He changed the moral atmosphere of France." His father was for a time official clockmaker to a harem in Constantinople, he considered going to end his days in Turkey or on the island of Cyprus, he wore Armenian costume, and over the face of the dead Héloïse he drew a shroud of "cloth of gold embroidered with pearls" from the Indies. His phraseology is like none other so much as that of the prophets of Jehovah. To me it appears that he had a real affinity with Eastern races, fascinated by the supernatural, the races by whose conquest Napoleon would have won glory. Over their dark powers he cast a veil of Christian sweetness, making them all the more destructive and insidious.

His features, not glossed over by French interpretation as they have been perpetuated by the painters and engravers of his time, but the features of Houdon's death-mask, floated before my eyes that autumn evening as I sat in reflective mood amid associations which may reveal more of a man than months of study. The smooth countenance, the bald forehead, might have been lifted off the shoulders of some Buddhist priest to be reflected in the sparkling waters of that French lake. The quenched fire of those eyes, the one opened more widely than the other, held me with their look, which seemed to seek the past, in quest of an idea far removed from any actual observation. The forehead is fine, the chin willful or obstinate, the mouth wide, with slightly drooping corners; the most striking feature is the preternatural development of the central part of the face, pushed out to the sides by the protruding cheekbones. It is exactly the face of an emotionalist, a creature of unbridled impulse, gourmand, a devotee of mystical orgies—and a face of kindliness, tolerance, passion, and natural religion.

As evening falls, the wisps of floating mist take spectral shapes. There is the "Incorruptible," holding a bunch of wild flowers to lay on the high altar of the Supreme Being, as on a tomb; the "Friend of the People," borne above the turbulent mob in his armchair, like a pirate in his cockleshell; the "Child of the Century," a stray dog howling at the moon among the rocks of Franchard; the "Little Corporal," with his nation in arms, performing fortuitous feats of heroism, within the reach of all; the "Shakespeare Child" of the Ardennes, torturing his intellect to become a primitive man; Karl Marx the Jew and his band of strikers cut down by gun-fire. The Western nations, when they raised their great cathedrals to the sky, were animated by different impulses from those which moved them when they burrowed in the mud to dig their network of trenches, irrigation-ditches running gore. The result of a hundred and fifty years of thought along the lines of Jean-Jacques's teaching has been a work of death, not a work of life. The reign of aristocratic civilization is at an end. The interests of wealth are not in my mind—those interests Jean-Jacques advanced when he essayed to combat them. Whenever an appeal is made to man's instincts, he who profits by them is the savage with the strongest appetites, and the way is opened for the triumph of mob selfishness over the altruism of the few. Only the pick of society ever accomplished anything truly magnanimous or great.

No need to talk of the new order of things. The old has not yet been superseded, and the reforms accredited to the influence of Jean-Jacques would have been made if he had never been born. Before the time of the author of the *Émile* and the *Contrat social*, there existed a tradition subordinating material things to the laws of the spirit, and this he destroyed.

For Product Safety Concerns and Information please contact our EU
representative GPSR@taylorandfrancis.com
Taylor & Francis Verlag GmbH, Kaufingerstraße 24, 80331 München, Germany

www.ingramcontent.com/pod-product-compliance
Lightning Source LLC
Chambersburg PA
CBHW071804300426
44116CB00009B/1198